Barbarians
at the Plate

Barbarians at the Plate

Taming and Feeding the Modern American Family

◆ **Marialisa Calta** ◆

PERIGEE BOOKS
NEW YORK

The Berkley Publishing Group
Published by the Penguin Group
Penguin Group (USA) Inc.
375 Hudson Street, New York, New York 10014, USA
Penguin Group (Canada), 10 Alcorn Avenue, Toronto, Ontario M4V 3B2, Canada
    (a division of Pearson Penguin Canada Inc.)
Penguin Books Ltd., 80 Strand, London WC2R 0RL, England
Penguin Group Ireland, 25 St. Stephen's Green, Dublin 2, Ireland (a division of Penguin Books Ltd.)
Penguin Group (Australila) 250 Camberwell Road, Camberwell, Victoria 3124, Australia (a division
    of Pearson Australia Group Pty. Ltd.)
Penguin Books India Pvt. Ltd., 11 Community Centre, Panchsheel Park, New Delhi—110 017, India
Penguin Group (NZ) cnr. Airborne and Rosedale Roads, Albany, Auckland 1310, New Zealand
    (a division of Pearson New Zealand Ltd.)
Penguin Books (South Africa) (Pty.) Ltd., 24 Sturdee Avenue, Rosebank, Johannesburg 2196,
    South Africa
Penguin Books Ltd., Registered Offices: 80 Strand, London WC2R 0RL, England

Copyright © 2005 Marialisa Calta
Text design by Pauline Neuwirth
Cover design by Charles Björklund
Cover art by Ed Koren
Interior art by Mimi Harrison

PRINTING HISTORY
Perigee trade paperback edition / June 2005

PERIGEE is a registered trademark of Penguin Group (USA) Inc.
The "P" design is a trademark belonging to Penguin Group (USA) Inc.

Library of Congress Cataloging-in-Publication Information
Calta, Marialisa.
      Barbarians at the plate : taming and feeding the modern
American family / by Marialisa Calta.—1st ed.
        p.cm.
      Includes bibliographic references and index.
      ISBN 0-399-53152-1
      1. Dinners and dining. 2. Make-ahead cookery.
3. Quick and easy cookery. I. Title.
TX737.C25 2005
641.5'55—dc22

                                    2004043157

PRINTED IN THE UNITED STATES OF AMERICA

10 9 8 7 6 5 4 3 2 1

✦ Acknowledgments ✦

A SPECIAL THANKS TO . . .

. . . all the families involved in this book, especially my own; Dirk, Hannah, and Emma, you make dinner time my favorite time of day.

. . . my mother, Diana Calta, taught by example the importance of family meals; my aunt, Antoinette Calta, reinforced the message.

. . . those who fed me and shared their mealtime sagas, especially the Gallagher family of Calais, Vermont, the guinea pigs for this project. Also, the Durhams and the Grays of Iowa City, Iowa; the Neals of Cromwell, Oklahoma; the Knoxes of Sturbridge, Massachusetts; the Millers of Lawrenceville, New Jersey; the Brancos of Bellevue, Ohio; the Hills and Masons of San Diego, California; the Ortiz-Haneys of Jersey City, New Jersey; the Brodsky-Rybecks, Lisa Lovett, and Julie Ruben, all of Cambridge, Massachusetts; and the Jackowskis of Brighton, Michigan.

. . . others who shared their stories and recipes; Chris Vineis, Columbus, Ohio; Nancy Wolf, Glide, Oregon; Terri Brandmueller, Brooklyn, New York; Jacquie Wayans, Bronx, New York; Linda Lipsett, Washington, DC; Kathy Schulz, Escondido, California; and Tony and Irene Allen, Barrington, Rhode Island.

. . . Liv and Will Blumer of the Blumer Literary Agency, for hard work, good humor, and a totally civilized approach to life.

. . . the folks at Perigee Books, for putting it all together: John Duff, publisher and Marian Lizzi, editor par excellence; as well as Charles Bjorklund, Pauline Neuwirth, Tiffany Estreicher, Laurie Cedilnik, Cathy Dubowski, and Julia Fleischaker.

. . . Marianne Goldstein and Neil Gladstone at United Media, for encouragement and support; and to the readers of the "Food" column who responded to my plea for help.

. . . Ed Koren, for his wonderful drawing on the cover. And to Mimi Harrison, for between-the-covers art.

. . . Ellen Galinsky, president and cofounder of the Families and Work Institute, New York, New York; Dr. Robert L. Del Campo, director of the Marriage and Family Therapy Graduate Training Program, New Mexico State University at Las Cruces; and Dr. Cindy Post Senning, codirector of the Emily Post Institute, Burlington, Vermont, for sharing their expertise.

. . . Susan Stuck, for her astounding wealth of culinary knowledge, as well as for friendship and great meals.

. . . fellow writers Lorraine Bodger, Pat Holtz, Kathy Gunst, Sara Eckel, and Molly Stevens, for straight talk, always.

. . . friends who acted as "family finders:" Pam Mendels, Judy Polumbaum, Nina Simonds, Curtis Koren, Ruth Seligman, Lisa Foderaro, Tom Mulligan, Allison Cleary, Amy Trubek, Pam Knights, Jane Hadley, Ann Blackman, and my sister, Lauraine Brekke-Esparaza.

. . . Vermont neighbors and friends for sage advice and recipes: Debbie Clark, Linda Gray, Elaine Fitch, Carol Beatty, Jamie Cherington, Carole Naquin, and Jimmy and Maya Kennedy. And to Carolyn Casner, Lynne Woodard, and Maureen Garber, who never got properly thanked in print the last time.

And a special nod to all of the children in these families who are now a year or more older, and may feel that their new maturity is not reflected in the snapshot of their lives presented here.

◆ Contents ◆

GRACE NOTES

APPENDICES

Barbarians at the Plate

The Quest
for Civilization

THE FAMILY DINNER has fallen upon hard times. Among its enemies: jobs, school sports, music lessons, *any* kind of lessons, the telephone, after-school clubs, homework, exercise schedules, television, special diets, computer games, night classes, community meetings, and instant-messaging. Given the intricately plotted timeline of the average family's day, I was not surprised to find, in a friend's home, "The Serenity Prayer" affixed to the refrigerator—*upside down*.

I COME FROM an Italian family with a long tradition of great family meals. My mother, who left her job as a registered dietician when my older sister was born, devoted an enormous amount of time and energy to making delicious, healthy meals. My two grandmothers were also wonderful cooks, as is my aunt; even my dad could whip up a mean *pasta aglio e olio*. When I had my own two daughters—now teenagers—I knew I wanted to maintain the tradition. What I didn't realize was how hard it would be; exhausting, demanding, and sometimes not terribly gratifying. But since my husband and I like to eat even more than we like to cook, and since we like to spend time with our kids most of all, we persisted. As the girls grew older, it got easier, and I can truly say that we've had some of our best family times around the table.

I wanted to encourage other parents to hang in there, but I didn't feel I had the authority to speak: After all, I work at home—writing about food, no less—and am usually available when it's time to get dinner under way. That's why I felt it was important to ask other families—families headed by parents who work full-time outside of the home—how they do it, and to gather their insights, strategies, tips, cookbook recommendations, and recipes to inspire others to follow suit.

My travels took me from the East Coast to the West, with lots of stops in between. I shared suppers, snooped in pantries, poked into fridges and recipe files. I ate lots of good meals, met wonderful people, and learned a lot. The results of my quest are in these pages.

I found it especially inspiring to talk to women who say they hate to cook, or who think they are terrible cooks, and who do it anyway, because they think it's their job and they think it's important. They feel about cooking the way I feel about gardening, which I do even though I dislike it, because I like the results. This is admirable behavior.

People tend to like what they are good at, so if you make the effort to get good at cooking, you are bound to start liking it. Or, at least, not hating it.

WHEN I STARTED this project, I kept hearing about men who cook weeknight dinners on a regular basis, and fully expected to find them. I didn't.

I did find plenty of men in the kitchen, however: doing dishes. Some, like Jeff Jackowski of Brighton, MI, also act as sous chef to their "executive chef" wives. Jeff and others, like John Haney, of Jersey City, New Jersey, also do most of the shopping. At Karen Branco's house in Bellevue, Ohio, I found two young men cooking—her sons, Ben, fifteen and Dustin, thirteen. They had stepped up to help their mom when their father died in 1996. They cook and eat together with their mom and younger sister, ten-year-old Courtney, almost every night.

Kitchen Connection

"... cooking and caring for one another—this is our bright side. In cooking, we find our creativity, ingenuity. And I believe women want to embrace this connection because of our special history with food. If men want to join us in the kitchen, I think that's great. We need all the hospitality and caring we can get."

LAURA SCHENONE in A Thousand Years Over a Hot Stove:
A History of American Women Told Through Food, Recipes and Remembrances.
W.W. Norton & Co., 2003.

Barbarians at the Plate

HOW TO USE THIS BOOK

THIS BOOK IS organized by strategy, and the strategies can be generally defined as 1) preparing food ahead of time (see Cooking Ahead, 15–74), and 2) cooking quick meals at the last minute (Food, Fast, pp. 75–154). All of the families I spoke with used a combination of the two. Some relied heavily on leftovers recycled from weekend meals; some like to freeze homemade entrées and nuke them as needed, and some rely on the slow cooker. Others leaned more heavily to the seat-of-the-pants approach—grilling meats and fish, tossing together salads and pastas—as their solution.

Some strategies may not suit you. If you don't have a large freezer, for example, the freeze-ahead method might be a nonoption. If you are not a "morning person," and can't get it together to throw ingredients into a slow cooker, rule out that idea. Generally, different strategies work for different days of the week . . . or phases of the moon.

A NOTE ON THE RECIPES

SOME OF THE recipes in this book come from families I interviewed; most are from my own recipe files. They are plain and simple, meant for week-night cooking, not for leisurely entertaining. They generally rely on mini-mally processed foods. You don't need any special equipment or know-how to make them, and the ingredients can be found in any decent-sized super-market; in the few cases that something "exotic" is called for, I have given substitutes. Recipes that can be made to be vegetarian-friendly—or, con-versely, adapted for the carnivores at your table—are marked, as are do-ahead and storage suggestions.

I tried to write the recipes as comprehensively as possible, but there is nothing sacred about them. Feel free to add, subtract, and substitute ingre-dients according to your family's palate and what's handy in your kitchen. This applies to all the recipes except the few baked goods included in the final chapter. Baking is a science, and when you start messing with pro-portions, you can run into trouble.

. . . AND ON COOKING TERMS

BEFORE I STARTED writing about food, I had no idea what a "chiffonade of basil" was, and was daunted every time that phrase, or some other "chef-y" term (mandoline, chinois, coulis) appeared in a recipe. Thus, I've

The Quest for Civilization

tried to keep the cooking terms simple. I'm all in favor of expanding one's culinary vocabulary, but not on Tuesday night when you've got to get to a basketball game, for crying out loud. (FYI: *chiffonade* means "made of rags" in French—that is, thin strips or shreds; a *mandoline* is a slicing device, a *chinois* is a kind of sieve, and a *coulis* a sauce.) Here are the terms I use:

- *Chopping:* No need to get all technical about whether you are dicing, mincing, chopping, or whatever. I use the terms *chopped, coarsely chopped,* and *finely chopped.* Generally, you will want to chop most vegetables for one recipe about the same size, so they cook at the same time; the smaller you chop them, the quicker they cook. You probably want garlic chopped more finely than, say, green peppers, unless you like chunks of garlic.
- *Small, medium, large:* What's a "large" onion and what's a "small"? I've taken a one-size-fits-all approach here whenever possible. Use your judgment: If you have an onion the size of a beach ball, you may want to use only a piece of it (or submit it to *Guinness World Records*). Since potatoes and tomatoes come in so many different sizes, I have listed them by weight (or cups, chopped), not number.
- *Reactive and nonreactive pans:* Reactive pans are made from a material that reacts chemically with acidic foods such as tomatoes, vinegars, and citrus fruits. Aluminum pans are reactive and will impart a metallic taste and/or discolor the food. When a recipe calls for a nonreactive pan, use glass, plastic, stainless steel, or enamel ware. Cast iron is considered reactive, but for short-term exposure it seems to work fine for tomato sauces and other acidic foods.
- *Zest:* Zest is the outer, colored part of the rind of a citrus fruit. The white pith just underneath the zest is bitter, so remove zest carefully, using a vegetable peeler, a grater, or a little gadget known, quite accurately, as a zester.

WHAT'S FOR DESSERT?

ONLY ONE OR two families I interviewed regularly serve dessert. Some, like Lois and Karen Gray of Iowa City, will allow their children a piece of candy after dinner. Others, like Kathy Schulz of San Diego, California, keep ice cream on hand for those gotta-have-it evenings. (I hate to blow Kathy's cover, but she even admitted to having a "secret stash" of Ben & Jerry's in the back of the freezer.) Since there do not appear to be a lot of desserts

Barbarians at the Plate

out there on the American weeknight dinner table, there are few dessert recipes in this book.

The recipes I have included are for desserts that you might make if, on some demented impulse, you have invited weeknight guests and feel that dessert is essential. Generally, fresh fruit fits the bill; top it with yogurt if you want to get fancy.

Likewise, there are no appetizers, hors d'oeuvres, or first-courses recipes in this book. Soups and salads included here are all main-course meals. Again, if the worst happens, and you wind up "entertaining" on a weeknight, put out a bowl of baby carrots, some nuts, and some olives or chips and salsa. That should tide everyone over until dinner is served.

HEADS UP

SOME PEOPLE ALREADY know about the evils of trans-fats, the usefulness of kitchen shears, and how to use coupons most efficiently. Some people don't. For those in the latter category, I have crammed what I consider essential-for-all, but redundant-for-some information into the Appendices. You'll find a section on making meals more healthful (page 199), shopping strategies (page 204), stocking the pantry (page 208—it includes a section on convenience foods that I and others have found very useful), equipping the kitchen (page 216), and food safety (page 222) near the end of the book.

Titles of useful, weeknight-friendly cookbooks appear scattered throughout the book and at the end of each recipe section. There is also a list of general, family-friendly cookbooks in Appendix 5. Some of the books may be out of print, but are so useful they are worth hunting for: Check your local used-book dealer, the online bookstores, or www. alibris.com, a Web site that specializes in used books.

COMING CLEAN:
CONFESSIONS OF A CULINARY KIND

LIKE ANY OTHER recipe collection, this one is colored by the collector's likes and dislikes. And there are certainly a few foods I dislike. Cream-of-anything soup is one of them. Also: most canned vegetables (I make an exception for canned corn and peas, although I prefer frozen), "nondairy whipped topping," processed cheese food, anything that comes with sprinkles, blue food (except blueberries), canned pasta, hot dogs (except when eaten, out-of-doors, at a ball game or fair), "instant" stuff (oatmeal, rice, grits, pudding, powdered drinks), artificial sweeteners, and boxed "meal helpers." You will not find these foods in this book, although many women I talked to swear by some or all of these products.

On the other hand, I have fed my family boxed mac-and-cheese, cakes from mixes, prepared pie crusts, frozen ravioli and tortellini (what? like I'm going to *make* them?), store-bought spaghetti sauce, canned stuff (soup, tomatoes, beans, fruit), and frozen pizza. This is by way of saying: We all have our prejudices. Now you know mine.

Family Meals:
Why Bother?

A CASE FOR THE FAMILY MEAL

"The appearance of food sharing marks the very turning point toward humanity by primates."

MACKENZIE, MARGARET, Ph.D., RN, "Is the Family Meal Disappearing?"
Journal of Gastronomy, vol. 7 no 1, winter/spring 1993.

MY NEIGHBOR SARAH Gallagher was putting the finishing touches on a weeknight dinner when her son Isaac, then ten years old, wandered into the kitchen to claim his usual place at the well-worn table.

"Tyler," he said of a friend, "has lice."

There in a nutshell is one great reason for the family meal: the exchange of vital information.

There are many other great reasons: forming family traditions and passing down values; making an end run around the fast-food corporations and their invasive marketing; providing better nutrition in an age of burgeoning health problems related to obesity; saving money. But the exchange of information is just as important. A friend of mine, the mother of teenagers, puts it this way:

"When else during the day," she asks, "do you get to look your kids in the eye and see if their pupils are dilated?" Vital information indeed.

It sounds like a simple thing, family dinner. Legions of cookbooks are devoted to making it simple: meals made in fifteen minutes; meals made with four ingredients; meals thrown into the slow cooker in the morning and ready for your delectation at night. So how come Americans, who in 1950 spent nearly five times as much money on meals *at* home as on meals *away* from home, in 2001 virtually split their food budget between eating at home and eating out? How come articles keep appearing about families eating separate meals, in the car, in front of the tube, in shifts? Why is it that this simple act of cooking and eating together is such a challenge?

The ugly truth is that cooking is work.

Many people seem surprised by this. It's as if the last few generations have grown up believing that modern life should by rights include a "Rosie the Robot," the electronic maid in the old *Jetsons* cartoons: Push a button on her torso and an entire turkey dinner appears. No one I know has a robotic Rosie, although I have read about people with personal chefs (and I hope they pay them well). The reality is that, no matter how you slice it, putting anything even vaguely homemade on the table requires shopping, prepping, cooking, setting the table, and cleaning up. And then, the next day, it starts all over.

The other ugly truth is this: Dining *en famille* can be a trying experience. There's the whining, the fighting, the sulking, the picky eating . . . and that's just the adults. Add small children and teenagers to the mix and, well, it can get pretty grim.

Then, if you *do* manage to cook, it's not like everyone is sitting around the table saying "Thanks, Mom. Great meal!" Half the time the response is more like "*eewwww*" and "*gross*." The milk is spilled, your youngest refuses to use utensils, your partner is berating your oldest for a failure to focus on the soccer field, and your born-again vegan is lecturing you on the exploitation of animals, epitomized by tonight's beef tacos.

Since it's human nature to avoid what can be difficult and unpleasant, it's no wonder that families are running to the fast-food counter and the freezer section, and putting Domino's on speed-dial. So why should we bother making and sharing family meals?

First, we should bother because, no matter what our schedules, incomes, or geographical location, we still have to eat. By one measure—quantity— Americans seem to be excelling at this: We eat 300-plus more calories a day than we did twenty years ago, and experts tell us our waistlines are expanding proportionally. It's clear that *someone* has to decide what to feed our families; if we don't step up to the plate, we are in essence leaving the decisions to processed-food corporations with multibillion-dollar advertising campaigns. I would argue that the folks who put chocolate in frozen French fries, and who make squeezable margarine in shocking pink, may not have your family's well being in mind. But why should they? Their job is to make money. Yours is to teach your kids that potatoes come in one flavor.

We should bother because cooking and eating together can teach us— among other things—cooperation, respect, and patience. Because studies indicate that teenagers who eat dinner with their families at least five nights a week are less likely to take drugs or be depressed, and that they

Barbarians at the Plate

do better in school and in relationships. Because almost anything we cook ourselves is going to be more nutritious than something we buy in a frozen tray or at a drive-through window.

Some of us bother because we want to pass along our parents' and grandparents' culinary traditions so that our children will have a sense of their cultural identity. Others want to teach children a respect for the land and what it can produce, and a respect for the effort it takes to turn that produce into dinner. Some just want to make sure they hear about the lice.

The family meal gives parents the opportunity not only to learn how our kids are doing in school, but also to explore the politics of the playground and the study hall. Family meals give kids a chance to hear about their parents' lives. It gives them the opportunity to learn how to shape a story, or tell a joke. At the table kids learn—not always pleasantly or quickly, but they do learn—not to interrupt. They learn how to eat soup without slurping. They learn how to *sit*. They learn skills that will help them not just in school but in the rest of their lives. They learn, in short, how to be civilized.

Unless we make family dining a priority, we are in danger of becoming a nation of barbarians at the plate.

I DEFINE A "family meal" as one cooked entirely or partially by a member or members of a family (and friends) and shared communally away from a turned-on television and outside of a moving vehicle. It can be as simple as grilled-cheese sandwiches and carrot sticks. It can even be Domino's pizza and a salad. Sometimes.

If you are organized enough to get your tired self dressed and to work every morning, to perform a job, to keep track of the kids' vaccination records and soccer games, and to take the car in for an oil change, you have the tools to organize yourself to get food on the table. Like exercise and flossing, it's a matter of priorities.

You don't have to quit work and chain yourself to the stove, but you do have to figure out a way to create the time to cook and eat together. Give up something—an evening TV show or some Internet surfing—and use that time to prepare tomorrow night's dinner. Let another chore slide: Decide that dinner is more important than perfectly folded laundry or waxed floors. If you are a morning person, wake up a bit earlier and get the meal started.

Divide and conquer: Parcel out the jobs (shopping, cooking, setting the table, cleaning up), enlisting the aid of your partner and children. Set aside a block of time on the weekend to cook, and freeze food for the coming week.

It can be done. It *is* being done.

Words of Wisdom

"It doesn't matter when you eat, and it doesn't matter what you eat, the thing that matters is that you are all together, facing each other around a table. It's not a throwback, and it's not old-fashioned. It's part of what makes us human—the desire to share food together—and it's part of what brings us and keeps us together."

KATHY GUNST of Berwick, Maine, mother of two and author,
The Parenting Cookbook, in a telephone interview.

"There should be a rule that families have to eat together more times a week than not."

DR. ROBERT DEL CAMPO, director, Marriage and Family Therapy Graduate
Training Program, New Mexico State University in Las Cruces,
in a telephone interview.

". . . Dinner rituals have nothing to do with class, or working women's busy lives, or any particular family structure. I've had dinners of boiled potatoes with families in Siberia, suppers of deli cold cuts with single welfare mothers in Chicago, bowls of watery gruel in the Sahara—all made memorable by the grace with which they were offered and by the sight of youngsters learning through experience the art of human companionship. . . . Like the Passover Seder or the Communion bread, the ritual of nutrition helps to imbue families, and societies at large, with greater empathy and fellowship. However, all rituals involve, to some degree, a sacrifice, and the home meal requires genuine sacrifices of time and energy, large expenditures of those very traits it nurtures—patience, compassion, self-discipline."

From a review of the 1995 movie Kids, titled "Starving Children,"
Copyright © 1995 by FRANCINE DU PLESSIX GRAY, *The New Yorker*,
vol. 71, issue 32, October 9, 1995. Reprinted by permission
of Georges Borchardt, Inc., for the author.

TV OR NO TV? THERE IS NO QUESTION

The average adult American (age 18 and older) will have watched 1,669 hours of television in 2004. This is the equivalent of about 70 days.
US CENSUS BUREAU press release, "Facts for Features," March 2004.

If there is only one change you make during your family's mealtime, let it be this: turn off the tube. While you're at it, let the answering machine

Barbarians at the Plate

take the phone messages. That's what these "labor-saving" devices are all about.

If you need background noise, play some music on the CD or radio. If someone is unhappy about missing a "favorite show," tape it (that's what kids are for, to teach you how to do these things). Try—I know it may sound weird—talking. If this is all new to you, don't expect miracles. But eventually, you'll all get the hang of it.

Kathy Gunst, author of *The Parenting Cookbook* (Castle Books, 2001), writes about her mother trying to "civilize the family meal" with what she called "the Kennedy routine" after the country's then-First Family.

"According to a magazine she had read, the Kennedys had a nightly custom of going around the table and having each member of the family report on an incident that occurred that day," Gunst writes. But "the ritual failed in our family, because it felt forced and unnatural."

So, don't try to *force* conversation. But that doesn't mean you can't help it along. Asking kids "What'd you do in school today?" is almost guaranteed to elicit a grumpy "nothing." Linda Lipsett, a lawyer in Washington, D.C., says she decided to play to her children's strengths. "I ask them, 'What did you say today that was funny? Who did you make laugh?'" Ellen Brodsky of Cambridge, Massachusetts, says she has friends who play a 1-2-3 answer game (example: "Tell us one thing you learned in social studies," "Name two people you sat with at lunch," etc.). Ask their opinions; kids have lots of them. My dad used to like to teach us new words at the table, and some of them (*phlegmatic, loquacious, hyperbole,*) stuck. You might dedicate part of a meal each week to talk about upcoming menus. If you solicit ideas, use them, so your kids know you really are listening.

Don't forget to talk about *your* day, too. You've been away from your kids for six, eight, or ten hours; surely there's *something* of interest you can report.

DINING A LA CAR

IT'S HARD TO resist bashing fast-food franchises; they are such obvious targets. Eric Schlosser did it brilliantly with his heavily researched book *Fast Food Nation* (Houghton Mifflin, 2001), and Morgan Spurlock did it hilariously in the 2004 film *Supersize Me.* We all know that fast-food portions are too large, that cheap sugary drinks are too abundant, and that fresh fruits and vegetables are hard to come by. Even fast-food salads— once you take into account the fat-laden croutons, dressing, and, in some cases, fried chicken—are high in calories, fat, and sugar.

But let's face it, a fast-food franchise can be a lifesaver when you are traveling and need to find a clean rest room or a play space, or when your children are crazy with hunger and you need to get some calories into

Family Meals: Why Bother?

11

them, *stat*. Schlosser said he ate "an enormous amount of fast food" while researching his book. "Most of it tasted pretty good," he wrote.

Of course, no one is *making* you buy the large fries, the fried nuggets, and the shakes. In the ideal world, you could hold a reasoned discussion with your children about making wise food choices, and about moderation; they might choose, for example a small portion of fries and low-fat milk. In the real world, however, kids usually succumb instantly to those lurid, backlit pictures (giant cookies! milk shakes with candy!) and what starts as a "reasoned discussion" often precipitates a major meltdown. Plus, they want the toy.

It's bad enough that too often we wind up feeding our kids liquefied candy bars. What's worse, in my book, is that we often wind up feeding them liquefied candy bars *in the car*.

Eating in the car—even if you are together—does not count as having a family meal. First of all, it's got to be dangerous; I myself once narrowly avoided a collision when the grease from take-out lo mein caused my hands to slip on the steering wheel. What's more, it encourages the virtual inhaling of food, disturbs digestion, and gives you no time to savor or appreciate what you are eating. It is easier to overeat when there's a bag of something greasy and salty sitting on the seat next to you. It leaves your car smelling funny and littered with take-out trash. Conversation grinds to a halt when the serious scarfing gets going. Eating in the car is, in short, about as barbaric as it gets.

If you *must* feed children while you drive, take along some snacks that that you can pack quickly, can be left unrefrigerated for several hours, make a minimum of mess, and are relatively healthy: snacks like grapes, cherries, clementines, mini carrots, grape tomatoes, string cheese, mini bagels, rice cakes, dried fruits and nuts, granola or other favorite cereals, and water (it won't sour like milk or ferment like juice). But whatever you do, please don't call it "dinner."

JUST SAY NO

MARY KAY AND Stephen Knox, parents of nine-year-old Katie and six-year-old Sam, have limited their children's activities to two each. Katie is a Brownie Scout and takes art lessons. Sam plays soccer and T-Ball.

"It's enough," says Mary Kay. "Any more activities take away from family time. And the kids get overwhelmed."

"Besides," she says, "I don't want to spend my life behind the wheel."

Brave folks, those Knoxes. In the rush to keep our children busy, motivated, and "on track" (think of *that* image), to build self-esteem and résumés, and to send them hurtling toward college acceptance (a race that starts, in

Barbarians at the Plate

some communities, in preschool), the Knoxes are taking the less-traveled route. "We all 'know' that kids who are involved in extracurricular activities are 'winners' in school, right?" says Dr. Robert Del Campo, the director of the Marriage and Family Therapy Graduate Training Program at New Mexico State University in Las Cruces. "Well, some kids are way overloaded; they've got to pick and choose, and their parents have to help them." Perhaps your fourth grader doesn't need to be on the "travel team" for soccer *and* take gymnastics. Maybe your teenager could cut back on that after-school job and survive without a new sound system for her car.

Say "no" for yourself as well. With those twenty-two fewer hours a week (see below), think twice before accepting extra assignments at work or in the community.

It's hard to say no, until you consider the cost of "yes."

> "The traditional family—one breadwinner and one homemaker—has been replaced by the 'juggler family,' and American parents have twenty-two fewer hours a week to spend with their kids than they did in 1969."
>
> KORNBLUH, KAREN. "The Parent Trap,"
> Atlantic Monthly magazine, vol. 291, no. 1, Jan/Feb, 2003.

> "Others may think after-school sports are good for children. They should be home having dinner with the family. People are living a motel life."
>
> MARION CUNNINGHAM, cookbook author, quoted in
> The New York Times, December 15, 2003

HOMEMADE CAN MEAN HEALTHIER

LOW-FAT, LOW-CARB, trans-fat, high-protein, phytochemicals, antioxidants . . . nutrition is constantly in the news, and it's confusing. I'm not a nutritionist, so I'll borrow the words of Marion Nestle, who is. Dr. Nestle, who teaches at New York University, is the author of *Food Politics: How the Food Industry Influences Nutrition and Health* (University of California Press, 2002). Asked by *Eating Well* magazine what the "answer" is to people's dietary questions, she said:

"... It's really simple. Most of the diet should be plant foods: fruits, vegetables, and whole grains. Meat and dairy in much smaller amounts and those processed things that are in the center aisles of the supermarkets, even less."

Look, if you're going to make the effort to cook, it makes sense to pay attention to nutrition. For example, a serving of homemade Macaroni and Cheese (page 110), if made with reduced-fat cheese and low-fat (1%) milk, has about one-third of the fat and twice the protein of the stuff from a box, even when the boxed stuff is prepared with 1% milk. If you buy the cheese already shredded, it takes the exact same amount of time to make.

For more on this subject, see Appendix 1: Making Meals Healthier, page 199.

THE COOKBOOK SHELF:

Bissex, Janice Newell, M.S., R.D. and Weiss, Liz, M.S., R.D. *The Moms' Guide to Meal Makeovers: Improving the Way Your Family Eats, One Meal at a Time!* Broadway Books, 2004.

Ely, Leanne. *Healthy Foods: An Irreverent Guide to Understanding Nutrition and Feeding Your Family Well.* Champion Press Ltd., 2001.

Pivonka, Elizabeth and Berry, Barbara. *5 A Day: The Better Health Cookbook.* 2002. Out of print, but worth looking for.

One way to learn about the nutritional content of the foods you eat, and to calculate the nutrition facts for your own recipes, is to log on to www.nutritiondata.com.

HOMEMADE CAN MEAN CHEAPER

MY SIXTEEN-YEAR-OLD and I went out to dinner at the local outpost of a chain of "family" restaurants. We both had a chicken skillet costing $8.99 each—grilled chicken, sautéed summer squash and bell peppers, tomatoes and a side of flour tortillas served with a scoop of salsa—and she had a lemonade ($1.99) I had water (free). No apps, no dessert, no alcohol. The total, with tax and tip, was $25.50.

I then went to the grocery store. I was able to buy four boneless, skinless chicken breasts ($6.29), a pound of summer squash ($2.50), a large green pepper ($1.03) two large tomatoes ($2.99) an entire jar (12-ounces) of salsa ($2.50), and eight flour tortillas ($1.79). Using about two tablespoons of my own oil, salt and pepper, I was able to cook dinner for twice as many people, for nearly $8.50 less than the restaurant meal. And I had lots of salsa and tortillas left over.

Of course, for the restaurant meal, I didn't have to spend time shopping, cooking or cleaning up. But I was still amazed that had four of us gone out to eat, it would probably have cost us nearly $17 more than the home-made version of the same meal.

Barbarians at the Plate

Cooking Ahead

Strategies for Planners

The Slow Cooker Solution

❖

Once-a-Week Cooking:
Weekend Feasts to Weeknight Meals

❖

Freezer Feeds

The
Slow-Cooker Solution

The Return of the Slow Cooker:
Dinner in a Mere 8 to 10 Hours

YOU MAY HAVE relegated your slow cooker to the yard sale heap, but all over the country home cooks are putting it to good use. They gave me new respect for what I had thought of as a "retro" granny-ish, appliance.

Slow cookers (Crock-Pot is a brand name trademarked by the Rival Company) offer the busy parent several benefits.

First: You walk in the door, tired from a day of work. The kids are howling with hunger, as is the dog. There is a stack of mail to read, bills to consider, and several "urgent" phone calls to return. Even if you have a stash of fabulous fifteen-minute meal recipes up your sleeve, where do you find the fifteen minutes? If you've planned it right—and used the slow cooker—the house is redolent of a simmering soup or stew and dinner is ready to be served. Everyone can grab a plate, a fork, a placemat, and a napkin, and sit down together for a meal.

Second: Slow cookers are virtually burn-proof. So what effort you put into dinner won't be wasted by scorching it.

Third: Slow-cooker recipes usually require very little oil or fat, and work best on inexpensive cuts of meat. Savings all around.

A Note on the Slow Cooker Recipes in This Book

The entire point of using a slow cooker is to put stuff into the unit in the morning and have it done when you come home at night. I have included here only recipes that can be cooked on LOW for at least 8 to 10 hours (i.e., during an entire work day). If you want to cook them more quickly, put the slow cooker on high and cook for 4 to 6 hours. Most of the recipes can also be adapted to the stove top; add more liquid as needed and let them simmer for 45 minutes to one hour. Likewise, many of your favorite recipes can be adapted to the slow cooker—see page 19.

The idea is to make a one-dish meal in the slow cooker, but sometimes you need to cook a separate starch (see Simple Sides, pp. 157–175). Consider making large batches of rice or mashed potatoes (page 199) in advance and freezing them in family-size portions; then you just need to nuke them to serve. Egg noodles, couscous, and prepared polenta are quick to cook, and are recommended in several recipes.

Slow-Cooker Tips

- ❖ A 4- to 6-quart slow cooker will suit a family of four; if you really get into slow cooking, you may want to buy two, to make double batches and freeze them, or to cook a main dish and side dish simultaneously. Be advised that "multipurpose cookers," which can work for other types of cooking (such as deep-frying) require supervision and stirring and don't work for many 8- to 10-hour slow-cooker recipes.
- ❖ For easier cleanup, spray the interior of the slow cooker stoneware with cooking spray.
- ❖ Resist the temptation to peek. It takes about 20 minutes for the slow cooker to get back to cooking temperature every time you lift the lid.
- ❖ Remove leftovers from the slow cooker and cool, cover, and refrigerate or freeze as soon as possible.
- ❖ Do not reheat cooked food in the slow cooker. Leftovers can generally be microwaved or heated in a saucepan on the stove.
- ❖ You can prep many ingredients in advance:
  - ◆ Chop ingredients the night before. Separate vegetables from meat, and store, covered, in the refrigerator. (Do not cook or partially cook meat the night before. The exception is ground beef, which can be thoroughly cooked, cooled, wrapped, and refrigerated until using, or frozen in usable portions for up to 6 months.)

Barbarians at the Plate

◆ Assemble and combine spices or other ingredients, and lay out any necessary cooking utensils.

❖ When cooking meat or poultry that has been frozen, make sure it is fully thawed (partially frozen meat will slow cooking time).

❖ Consider taking the time to brown meats and poultry, and to sauté vegetables in a small amount of oil in a stove-top skillet before adding them to the slow cooker. This does take more time (and, worse, dirties another pot), but the sautéing process breaks down and releases natural sugars and enhances eye appeal.

❖ Frozen chopped onions and bell peppers are time-savers in the kitchen, but tend to disappear in slow cookers. These dishes will taste better if you use fresh.

❖ Raw root vegetables like potatoes and carrots should be cut no larger than 1-inch thick and placed in the bottom of the pot, since they take longer to cook.

Converting Traditional Recipes to the Slow Cooker

❖ Decrease the amount of liquid called for by half. When making soup, add only enough water to just cover the ingredients. You can thin the soup by adding more water or broth toward the end of the cooking time. If doing this at the last minute, just heat the water or broth first.

❖ If you want to use dried beans instead of canned, soak the beans overnight before cooking them. Drain, cover with water, and boil for 10 minutes on the stove. Then add to recipe.

❖ Milk, sour cream, and cream break down over long periods of cooking. Do not try to make cream-based recipes in the slow cooker, unless you will be around during the last hour of cooking and can add the dairy ingredients at that time. Cheese should also be added near the end of cooking.

❖ According to the Rival Company, makers of the Crock-Pot, a conventional recipe that cooks for 30 minutes on the stove will cook in 4 to 6 hours on LOW and about 2 hours on HIGH. A recipe that takes 45 minutes on the stove will cook 6 to 10 hours on LOW and 3 to 4 hours on HIGH. A recipe that takes 1 to 3 hours on the stove will take 8 to 18 hours on LOW and 4 to 6 hours on HIGH.

Dinner with the Durhams
Iowa City, Iowa

IT'S GETTING ON toward dinnertime at the Durham household in Iowa City. Three-year-old Maya, wearing a princess crown and a flowered party dress, is in the colorful, crowded kitchen diligently practicing hopping on one foot and singing a song about Snow White and the Seven "Dorfs." Her six-year-old sister, Sonali, sits at the dining room table, writing a "book" titled My Trip Around the World and working on the North Pole chapter.

"She means *dwarves*," Sonali explains solemnly, carefully inking a smile on one of the polar bears. "But she's too little to say it right." The hopping stops. "Dorfs!" crows Maya. "Dorfs! Dorfs! DORFS!"

In the kitchen Meenakshi ("Gigi") Durham, raised in Canada and in her parents' native India, is putting the finishing touches on this Monday-night dinner. She has had a chicken curry simmering in the slow cooker all day while she and her husband Frank were at work, teaching journalism to students at the University of Iowa. Sonali, now home from school, has helped set the table. Sonali and Maya's settings get colorful plastic plates; Maya has a sippy cup; Sonali has a "big girl" drinking glass. The grown-ups get china and wineglasses. There are pink cloth napkins for all, long-stemmed Gerber daisies in a vase, and candles on the polished pine table.

"I love our flowers, but they are kind of pokey," says Maya, gingerly touching a stem. "Prickly," Sonali says. Maya sticks out her tongue, quickly pulling it in. "Prickly," she says softly.

"It's been a very busy day," says Gigi, sighing as she sinks into her seat at the table.

Indeed it has. Gigi and Frank woke at 5:30 a.m. to get their day going—making coffee, doing laundry, reading the paper, showering, packing lunches, and breakfasting before rousing the girls up to get them washed, combed, dressed, fed, and out the door by 8:15. One of Gigi's morning chores is to get dinner planned, if not started. She finds that on days like this one—when she knows she will be running constantly at top speed—the slow cooker is a life-saver. For the curry, she sautéed the onions with spices the night before. Then she browned the chicken and threw the ingredients into the slow cooker early in the morning. When she walked in the door after work, dinner was done.

SATURDAY MORNING, AFTER an unhurried family breakfast—often fruit, muffins (baked that morning, extras frozen for use later in the week), eggs, or pancakes—Gigi sits at the family's dining table, writing her shopping list. Sonali hangs over her shoulder, suggesting menu items—she lobbies for the Thai noodle dish, pad Thai, which is one of her favorites. Gigi keeps a running list of needed items on the refrigerator door, and fills in missing items according to her planned menu before she shops. Her trip takes her to three stores: a newly opened Indian store, where she buys lentils, Indian breads, and other specialties; an upscale natural foods store for cheese and wine; and a large supermarket for the rest of the food. She shops carefully, comparing prices and buying only what she knows she will use, and manages to keep the total bill at about $125 for a week's worth of food, including breakfast and the lunches that Sonali and her parents will take with them when they head out the door each morning (Maya is fed at day care). Once a month Gigi visits a large box store for paper goods and cleaning supplies. While she is out, Frank stays home with the girls and cleans the house, the sound of the vacuum competing with the *Madeline* video ("I can hear the theme song in my sleep!" protests Frank) or the sound of piano as Sonali practices. Sometimes, on weekends, the family goes out for a meal—often to a potluck at the homes of friends who also have children. Frank still laughs about being invited out to dinner on a Wednesday night by a childless colleague.

"As any parent knows," he says, "going out on Wednesday night simply doesn't happen." For one thing, the disruption of routines—dinner, bath, reading—is hard on the kids. For another, "I haven't seen them all day, and I want to spend time with them," he says. "And the routine is kind of pleasant, if you dive right in."

Eating together has always been a priority, possibly because both husband

and wife grew up in families that gathered at the table. Gigi says her mother, a retired physicist and teacher, is a "fantastic" cook, who will often spend all day in the kitchen preparing elaborate Indian feasts from scratch. "I don't even try to compete," she says. Frank comes from a family of connoisseurs in New Orleans, arguably the most serious city in America when it comes to food. (He makes, he says modestly, a "killer" red beans and rice.) Eating out regularly during the school year is not an option.

"There are so many distractions in restaurants," says Gigi. "It's hard enough at home to get the kids to sit still long enough to eat." Restaurants are not only distracting but expensive. And she can cook healthier food at home.

DESPITE THE CANDLES and flowers, dinner with a six-year-old and a three-year-old has its less-than-elegant moments. Finishing her curry at lighting speed, Maya crawls under the table, meowing like a kitty. Sonali has to be persuaded to put aside her "book" to eat. But the curry is a hit. Sonali particularly likes the parathas, flat Indian bread that Gigi has heated in an ungreased skillet. After dinner the kids drift into the adjoining parlor/playroom, where a kid-sized table is overflowing with toys and crayons, and a well-loved couch makes a convenient "fort" when needed. They return in full dress-up regalia—tutus and veils—to announce the start of their "dance recital" in the living room. Frank turns on his favorite Los Lobos album, and Sonali begins to twirl and somersault about the room. Maya, mimicking her big sister, executes a lopsided twirl, then settles down to some earnest hopping. The song ends. The kids collapse, giggling, on the floor. They squirm away as Frank and Gigi try to corral them for a bath, trying to postpone the inevitable for as long as possible. Sonali finally demurs, noting with some relief that at least it's not a "hair night" (shampoos are administered every other night). After bath, books. After books for the girls, it's the adults' turn. Gigi and Frank will struggle to stay up reading until 10 p.m. The next morning, at 5:30, the alarm will ring.

Barbarians at the Plate

❖

Slow Cooking for Sleepwalkers:
Six Easy Pieces

YOU DON'T NEED to be a "morning person" to make these foods. You hardly even have to be *awake*.

◆ Turkey Legs ◆

YIELD: 4 servings.
Recipe from Gigi Durham, Iowa City, Iowa.

4 turkey legs
olive oil or vegetable oil
salt and pepper

SPRAY THE INSIDE of the slow-cooker stoneware with cooking spray to prevent sticking. Rub each turkey leg with oil and season with salt and pepper. Put them in the slow cooker, cover, and cook on LOW for 8 to 10 hours. The skin will be rather pale and unattractive; remove it before serving or run under the broiler to brown.

GIGI DURHAM'S MIDWEEK "THANKSGIVING DINNER"

Serve with steamed green beans, boxed stuffing, or Almost Instant Mashed Potatoes (page 163), and canned cranberry sauce.

◆ Pork Roast ◆

YIELD: 6 to 8 servings.
Recipe from Karen Branco, Bellevue, Ohio.

1 (2 to 3 pound) pork roast
salt and pepper
3 large tart apples (like Granny Smiths), peeled, cored, and sliced
¾ cup apple cider or apple juice

Spray the inside of the slow-cooker stoneware with cooking spray to prevent sticking. Season the roast with salt and pepper. Place the pork, apples, and cider (or juice) in the slow cooker, cover, and cook on LOW for 8 to 10 hours.

Transfer the pork roast to a cutting board and slice. If desired, stir a spoonful of brown sugar or maple syrup into the apples, and sprinkle with cinnamon. Serve the pork with the cooked apples on the side.

PORK LEFTOVERS

❖ Make a quick Hominy Stew (page 31), substituting cooked cubes of pork for the uncooked pork. This will need only about 20 minutes of cooking on the stovetop.

❖ A classic Cuban Sandwich consists of sliced cooked pork, sliced ham, lettuce, tomatoes, cheese, and dill pickles layered on a bullet-shaped roll of Cuban bread (or French or Italian bread). Lightly butter exterior of the sandwich and grill in a panini pan, sandwich maker, or countertop grill, or cook in an ungreased skillet set over medium heat, pressing firmly with a spatula and turning over when brown and crisp.

❖ Add cooked cubes of pork roast to Blackirican Beans and Rice.

❖ Substitute pork for the roast beef in the recipe for Hash (page 52).

◆ Brisket ◆

YIELD: 8 to 10 servings.

1 envelope onion soup mix
1 (4 to 5 pound) beef brisket
1 cup canned beef broth (or ½ cup beef broth and ½ cup red wine)
2 tablespoons all-purpose flour

Spray the inside of the slow-cooker stoneware with cooking spray to prevent sticking. Pat the soup mix on both sides of the meat. Place the meat in the slow-cooker and pour the broth (or broth and wine) over. Cover and cook on LOW for 10 to 14 hours. Transfer the meat to a cutting board and let it rest, covered with a tent of aluminum foil, while you make the gravy.

Spoon the flour into a small bowl and add 6 tablespoons of the cooking liquid, stirring to make a smooth paste. Scrape the paste into the slow cooker, stir, cover, and turn to HIGH. Cook for about 15 minutes, or until gravy thickens.

Barbarians at the Plate

Slice the brisket across the grain and serve with gravy on the side.

SERVING SUGGESTION: Serve with buttered egg noodles, Almost-Instant Mashed Potatoes (page 163), Parsley Potatoes (page 165), Classic Coleslaw (page 169) or other vegetables and pickles.

BRISKET LEFTOVERS

❖ Place sliced leftovers on toasted sourdough French bread and top with gravy for an open-faced sandwich.

❖ Shred leftovers and toss with barbecue sauce. Serve as is or on a bun, with Classic Coleslaw (page 169).

❖ Dice leftovers and use in the Leftover Stroganoff (page 51) or Hash (page 52).

◆ Whole Chicken ◆

YIELD: 4 to 6 servings.

Even a tough fryer turns out moist and delicious, and the liquid that winds up in the slow cooker makes a tasty, rich gravy.

1 (3 to 4 pound) whole chicken, giblets removed, rinsed and patted dry
salt and pepper
garlic powder, onion powder, Italian herb blend, or other seasonings of
    your choice
½ lemon or orange
½ onion
1 tablespoon olive oil or other vegetable oil
2 to 3 tablespoons all-purpose flour

SPRAY THE INSIDE of the slow-cooker stoneware with cooking spray to prevent sticking. Season the cavity of the chicken with salt and pepper and other seasonings of your choice, then add the lemon or orange half and the onion half.

Rub the exterior of the chicken with the oil. Season with salt and pepper and any other herbs or spices you like. Place in the slow-cooker, cover and cook on LOW for 8 to 10 hours.

Transfer the chicken to a cutting board and let it rest, covered with a tent of aluminum foil, while you make the gravy.

Spoon the flour into a small bowl and add 6 tablespoons of the cooking liquid, stirring to make a smooth paste. Scrape the paste into the slow cooker, stir, cover, and turn to HIGH. Cook for about 15 minutes, or until gravy thickens.

Slice the chicken, removing the skin as you slice and placing the slices on a serving platter. Pour the gravy over the slices and serve.

LEFTOVER CHICKEN

- ❖ Shred and freeze the chicken for future use.
- ❖ Used diced, leftover chicken in Chicken or Turkey Salad (page 49) or Chicken Pot Pie (page 48).
- ❖ Use in Chicken Enchilada Casserole (page 126).
- ❖ Add to pasta with Sesame/Peanut Sauce (page 114)

◆ Baked Potatoes ◆

YIELD: 2, 3 or 4 plain baked potatoes,
or 6 servings of twice-baked potatoes.

Put these in to bake in the morning to add a homemade touch to an evening meal of rotisserie chicken or deli meat loaf, or use as a base for twice-baked potatoes.

FOR PLAIN BAKED POTATOES:
2, 3, or 4 large baking potatoes, scrubbed
vegetable oil
salt and pepper

FOR TWICE-BAKED POTATOES
(VEGETARIAN-FRIENDLY WHEN MADE WITHOUT HAM OR BACON):
3 baked potatoes
½ cup regular or reduced-fat sour cream
1 and ½ cups shredded regular or reduced-fat Cheddar, Jack, Colby, or Swiss cheese
4 scallions, trimmed and chopped
½ cup chopped ham or cooked, crumbled bacon or ⅓ cup real bacon bits

SPRAY THE INSIDE of the slow-cooker stoneware with cooking spray to prevent sticking. Prick the potato several times with the tines of a fork, to allow steam to escape. Rub each potato with oil, then season with salt and pepper. Wrap in foil, place in the slow cooker, cover, and cook on LOW for 8 to 10 hours.

For twice-baked potatoes: Preheat oven to 400° F. Cut three baked potatoes in half lengthwise and carefully scoop out the insides, leaving

Barbarians at the Plate

enough of a shell to act as a bowl. Place the potato flesh in a bowl and mash with the sour cream and ¾ cup of the cheese. Season with salt and pepper and stir in the scallions and ham, bacon or bacon bits (if using).

Spoon the mixture into the potato shells, place the shells on a cookie sheet, and scatter the remaining ¾ cup cheese over the tops. Bake for 15 minutes or until the cheese has melted and is beginning to brown.

◆ Overnight Pulled Pork ◆

YIELD: At least 12 servings.

This is not a slow-cooker recipe, but it certainly is a slow-cooking one, which cooks itself while you sleep. It comes from my friend, Mississippi-born chef Jimmy Kennedy, who, with his wife, Maya, runs the fabulous River Run restaurant in Plainfield, Vermont. The three of us wrote a cookbook together, River Run: Southern Comfort From Vermont *(HarperCollins, 2001), and this recipe is from that book. This is an amazing dish. It feeds at least 12 people, and it is cheap. Plus, people go bonkers for it. At River Run they call it "meat candy."*

> 5 pounds fresh (NOT smoked) pork butt, bone-in (look for the cut sold
>   as "Boston Butt"), trimmed of any visible fat.
> ¼ cup store-bought or homemade barbecue rub (page 144)
> 3 cups barbecue sauce plus several cups more, for serving

PREHEAT YOUR OVEN to 250°F.

Line a baking pan large enough to hold the pork with heavy-duty aluminum foil (this makes cleaning up easier). Put the meat on the foil and sprinkle the barbecue rub evenly onto the pork. Cover the pan with a tent of heavy-duty aluminum foil; fold over the edges to seal it. Bake for 8 to 10 hours; you know it's done when you poke at the meat with a fork and it falls off the bone.

Allow the meat to cool enough so that you can handle it. Using your hands, shred the meat, discarding any fat. You can do this in the morning, and cover and refrigerate the pulled pork until evening.

Heat the 3 cups of barbecue sauce in a saucepan set over low heat. Mix the shredded meat with heated barbecue sauce and simmer until heated through. Serve warm on a dinner plate, or on a sandwich roll, with extra, warm barbecue sauce on the side.

SERVING SUGGESTION: Classic Coleslaw (page 169) is a traditional "side," as are cooked greens (page 172). Also biscuits (page 190) or corn bread (page 192).

PULLED-PORK LEFTOVERS

Wrap leftovers in a warm flour tortilla for a pulled-pork burrito.

❖ ❖ ❖

◆ Slow-Cooker Curry ◆

YIELD: 4 servings.
Recipe from Gigi Durham, Iowa City, Iowa.

Vegetarian-friendly (when made with tofu)

The spices in the dish are understated; the curry flavor—which comes from a combination of spices, not from curry powder—is not overwhelming.

2 tablespoons canola oil or other vegetable oil
2 pounds boneless, skinless chicken pieces, breasts or thighs, or a combination (see note)
1 onion, peeled and diced
1 clove garlic, peeled and chopped
1 tablespoon grated fresh ginger or 1½ teaspoons ground ginger
1 teaspoon ground cumin
1 teaspoon ground coriander
¼ teaspoon ground turmeric
¼ teaspoon cayenne pepper (optional)
4 tablespoons chopped fresh cilantro
1 (28-ounce) can diced tomatoes, with juices
1 (10-ounce) package frozen green beans or other vegetables
salt and pepper
½ cup canned, unsweetened coconut milk (found in the supermarket where they stock Asian, "gourmet," or "international" foods)

FOR SERVING:
3 cups cooked rice (from 1 cup uncooked)

Spray the inside of the slow-cooker stoneware with cooking spray to prevent sticking.

Heat the oil in a skillet set over medium heat. Brown the chicken on both sides, about 4 minutes per side, then transfer to the slow cooker. Add the onion and garlic to the skillet and cook, stirring, until they begin to soften, about 5 minutes. Add the ginger, cumin, coriander, turmeric, and cayenne (if using) one at a time, stirring well after each addition. Transfer

Barbarians at the Plate

to the slow cooker. Add 2 tablespoons of the fresh cilantro, the tomatoes, and the green beans (or other vegetables) and stir in salt and pepper to taste. Cover and cook on LOW for 8 to 10 hours.

Just before serving, stir in the coconut milk and allow to heat for a few minutes. Adjust the seasonings. Serve over rice, sprinkled with the remaining 2 tablespoons cilantro. The chicken will fall apart, but that's okay.

NOTE: Bone-in chicken pieces add more flavor, but the meat does fall off, leaving the bones floating unattractively around in the curry. You can remove them, or just avoid them when serving.

VARIATION (TOFU CURRY): Omit the chicken. Cook as directed, adding 1 pound of diced, extra-firm tofu about 20 minutes before serving. When tofu is heated through, serve.

PREP AHEAD: The night before, chop and cook the onions, garlic, and spices. Make the rice (reheat in the microwave or on the stovetop). Alternatively, make large batches of rice, freeze in family-size servings, and reheat in microwave.

FREEZE: Up to 2 months. Add the coconut milk and cilantro after reheating.

SERVING SUGGESTION: Indian breads such as pappadums (a flatbread made with lentil flour) are available in some supermarkets and are easy to prepare. Parathas (flakier breads made with wheat flour) are sold in specialty stores.

◆ Slow-Cooker Cacciatore ◆

YIELD: 6 to 8 servings.

When I had my second child, a neighbor, Linda Gray, who describes herself as "not a great cook," brought me a pot of this savory stew. She sure fooled me.

½ cup all-purpose flour
1 teaspoon garlic powder
1 teaspoon salt, plus more as needed
½ teaspoon pepper, plus more as needed
about 4 pounds boneless, skinless chicken thighs, or assorted pieces
2 tablespoons canola oil or other vegetable oil
½ cup dry white wine or white vermouth (page 211)
¼ cup tomato paste
⅓ cup canned chicken broth
2 teaspoons dried basil
2 teaspoons dried oregano
1 teaspoon thyme
1 onion, peeled and chopped
2 cups (6 ounces) sliced white button mushrooms
1 bay leaf
2 tablespoons brandy (optional)

FOR SERVING:
1 pound egg noodles, cooked, drained, and buttered or 1 (16-ounce) tube prepared polenta, heated according to package directions

SPRAY THE INSIDE of the slow-cooker stoneware with cooking spray to prevent sticking. Set aside.

Combine the flour, garlic powder, salt, and pepper in a heavy-duty plastic bag or a shallow bowl. Working in batches, shake the chicken pieces in the bag until coated, or dredge them on both sides. Discard excess flour.

Heat the oil in a skillet set over medium-high heat. Working in batches, brown the chicken on both sides, 4 to 5 minutes per side. Using a slotted spoon or tongs, transfer the chicken to the slow cooker.

Pour the wine into the skillet and cook for about 2 minutes, stirring to scrape up any browned bits. Pour into the slow cooker. Add the remaining ingredients, cover, and cook on LOW for 8 to 10 hours.

Serve with polenta or egg noodles. The chicken will fall apart, but that's okay.

NOTE: Bone-in pieces add more flavor, but the meat does fall off, leaving the bones floating unattractively around in the cacciatore. You can remove them, or just avoid them while serving.

PREP AHEAD: The night before, slice the onions, cover, and refrigerate. Skin but do not brown the chicken; cover and refrigerate. Combine the flour and seasonings as directed in the plastic bag or bowl (no need to refrigerate).

FREEZE: Up to 2 months.

◆ Mexican Pork and Hominy Stew ◆

YIELD: 4 to 6 servings.

Hominy is corn that has undergone a complex process called nixtamalization, which enhances its protein value. It is terrific in chili or any bean dish. Look for canned hominy in the vegetable, Hispanic, or "international" section of most supermarkets. Sometimes you can find canned hominy with chili spices and peppers already in it, which is also fine to use.

    1 pound pork (any inexpensive, boneless cut such as shoulder or butt),
        trimmed and cut into bite-sized pieces (you can also use boneless,
        skinless chicken)
    salt and pepper
    1 to 2 tablespoons vegetable oil
    1 onion, peeled and chopped
    1 bell pepper (red or green, or half of each, for color), stemmed, seeded,
        and chopped
    2 cloves garlic, peeled and chopped (optional)
    2 teaspoons chili powder
    1 teaspoon dried oregano
    1 teaspoon ground cumin
    ½ to 1 teaspoon hot red pepper flakes
    3 (15-ounce) cans yellow or white hominy, or hominy seasoned with
        chili peppers (do not drain)
    1 cup canned chicken broth, plus more, if needed
    ½ teaspoon sugar

    FOR SERVING:
    1 lime, cut into wedges
    hot sauce and chopped fresh cilantro (optional)

SPRAY THE INSIDE of the slow-cooker stoneware with cooking spray to prevent sticking.

Season the pork with salt and pepper. Heat the oil in a skillet set over medium-high heat, and, working in batches if necessary, cook the pork, turning frequently, until it begins to brown, about 7 minutes.

Using a slotted spoon, transfer the pork to the slow cooker. Add the onion, bell pepper, garlic (if using), chili powder, oregano, cumin, and pepper flakes to the skillet and cook, stirring, about 5 minutes, until the vegetables begin to soften. Spoon the vegetables and any liquid into the slow cooker.

Add the remaining ingredients, cover, and cook on LOW for 8 to 10 hours.

I like a thick stew. If you prefer a soupier version, add more chicken broth; if you are doing this toward the end of cooking, heat the broth almost to a boil before adding it to the slow cooker.

Serve in bowls with lime wedges. (Lime juice really brings out the flavor in this stew.) Pass the hot sauce and cilantro (if using).

PREP AHEAD: The night before, chop the meat. Cover and refrigerate. Chop the vegetables, cover, and refrigerate separately from the meat. Combine all the spices in a small bowl (no need to refrigerate).
FREEZE: Up to 2 months.
SERVING SUGGESTION: Serve with corn bread (page 192) or corn or flour tortillas, heated according to package directions and brushed with melted butter.

— ETHNIC FOODS AND FOOD TRADITIONS —

WHEN NANCY VERDE BARR wrote her Italian-American cookbook *We Called It Macaroni* (Alfred A. Knopf, 1996) she dedicated it to "all those first Italian-Americans who knew that food meant so much more than eating."

To many immigrants and their descendants—not just those from Italy—food is a way of taking hold of the past and making it present, of giving form and substance to one's heritage, and—no small thing—having a great meal while they're at it. But preserving those culinary roots is not always easy, especially for the working parent pressed for time.

Yvonne Ortiz says her seven-year-old son, Marcus, is often not interested in eating the foods of her native Puerto Rico.

"He goes through cycles, like any kid," she says, stuffing a chicken with annatto seeds into the oven of her small kitchen in a Jersey City, New Jersey, row house. "One week he'll eat only peanut butter. The next week it's mac and cheese." Her husband, John Haney, an African-American chef, is on a heart-healthy diet, but used to be more partial to the traditional

Barbarians at the Plate

foods of his upbringing: fried chicken, smothered pork chops, and the like.

And it's not like Yvonne isn't a good cook. One could even say she wrote the book on Puerto Rican cooking: It's titled *A Taste of Puerto Rico* (Dutton, 1994). She has worked tirelessly to keep her food traditions alive in her community, but sometimes she meets resistance on the home front.

Jacquie Wayans, a single, working mother of three in the Bronx, faces the same problem. She wants her children to grow up knowing the foods of the West Indies—Jacquie's mother is from British Tortola—but at least one of the three is guaranteed to refuse to eat the funji (a cornmeal and okra mush similar to Italian polenta), pepperpot soup, or Creole fish that she occasionally labors to make.

"It's very discouraging," she said. "You want them to have a sense of this rich ethnic tradition, and what they want is pizza."

Lack of enthusiasm, coupled with the time and effort it takes to produce many heirloom ethnic dishes, can wear any well-intentioned, culturally proud parent down. I rarely make my grandmother's gnocchi (Italian potato dumplings) anymore, because it's a half-day project, and when I finally get it to the table, my husband (who has Dutch, Irish, German, and who-knows-what in his blood) always seems less than thrilled.

But parents committed to cooking are nothing if not adaptable. Yvonne Ortiz has melded the African-American traditions of her husband's family with her Puerto Rican style of cooking to come up with what she calls "Blackirican" cuisine. Jacquie Wayans has developed a "five-minute funji" (page 165) that can be served with or without the Creole sauce on the fish, to please her kids' various tastes. Gigi Durham has adapted her parent's Indian cuisine for the slow cooker. I buy frozen gnocchi and make it for myself and my daughters, who like it, topped with my grandmother's special gnocchi sauce, on nights when my husband isn't home for supper.

"Immigrants bring with them food, religion, and language," a history professor once told me. Many of us don't have the language anymore. Some no longer practice the religion. But food can still serve as a touchstone, to remind us where we are from. The fact that we're making it in twenty-first century American kitchens reminds us where our ancestors who came here were going.

◆ Slow-Cooker Bourguignon ◆
(Beef Stew with Red Wine)

YIELD: About 6 servings.

The wine is essential to this deeply flavored stew; if you don't cook with wine, skip this recipe.

¼ cup all-purpose flour
1 teaspoon garlic powder
1 teaspoon salt
1 teaspoon pepper
2 pounds boneless beef, cut into bite-sized pieces
8 slices thick-cut bacon, chopped
1 cup dry red wine
4 shallots or 1 onion, peeled and chopped
3 cups (8 ounces) sliced white button mushrooms
1 teaspoon dried thyme
several tablespoons chopped fresh parsley

FOR SERVING:

1 recipe Almost-Instant Mashed Potatoes (page 163); 3 cups cooked rice (from 1 cup uncooked); or 1 pound egg noodles, cooked, drained, and buttered

SPRAY THE INSIDE of the slow-cooker stoneware with cooking spray to prevent sticking.

Combine the flour, garlic powder, salt, and pepper in a heavy-duty plastic bag or a shallow bowl. Working in batches, shake the beef pieces in the bag or dredge until coated. Discard excess flour.

In a large skillet set over medium heat, cook the bacon until much of the fat is rendered, but the bacon is not crisp, about 10 minutes. Using a slotted spoon, transfer the bacon to the slow cooker. Keep the skillet over medium heat.

Add the beef to the skillet and, working in batches if necessary, cook, turning, until well-browned on all sides, about 7 minutes. Using a slotted spoon, transfer to the slow cooker. Discard the pan drippings.

Add the wine, shallots (or onion), mushrooms, and thyme. Cover, and cook on LOW for 8 to 10 hours. Stir in parsley and serve.

PREP AHEAD: The night before, cut up the beef and the bacon (use scissors to quickly snip the bacon) and store them separately,

uncooked and covered, in the fridge. Chop the onions, cover, and refrigerate. Chop or snip the parsley, cover, and refrigerate. Combine the flour, garlic powder, salt, and pepper in the plastic bag or shallow dish (no need to refrigerate).

FREEZE: Up to 3 months.

PLAYING WITH FIRE

Just as candles can set a mood, flambéing a dish never fails to impress; it's a guaranteed attention-grabber, especially with kids at the table. Remove the inner ceramic pot from your slow cooker and place it on a trivet on the table. Heat ¼ cup (inexpensive) brandy, bourbon or rum in a small saucepan until just warm, but not hot, and set a match or candle to it as you pour it over the stew. This is especially effective if you turn the lights off first.

◆ Slow-Cooker Meat Loaf ◆

YIELD: 6 servings.

Holy Wonder Bread! With a slow cooker, meat loaf need not be a "retro" treat from the distant past, when Mom was at home darning socks while the meat loaf baked for an hour or more. Yes, like many other dishes, meat loaf can also be stuffed in the slow cooker and left alone for a full 8 to 10 hours while you work. Who knew? I certainly didn't, until I read The Best Family Slow Cooker Recipes *by Donna-Marie Pye (Robert Rose, Inc, 2003). I'm indebted to Ms. Pye's book for this method for hoisting the cooked meat loaf out of the slow cooker: Cut a 2-foot strip of heavy-duty aluminum foil, and cut the strip in half lengthwise. Fold each half into thirds to form two sturdy strips. Crisscross the strips in the bottom of the slow cooker, bringing the ends up and over the rim. Place the uncooked meat loaf directly on the foil strips and tuck the ends of the strips under the lid. Cover and cook. When done, remove the lid and grasp the ends of the foil strips to lift the meat loaf out. You can also line the stoneware with a large piece of cheesecloth, but the cheesecloth will get yucky and then you either have to wash it or throw it out.*

You can use your own recipe, or mine, below. It was given to me by a dear friend, the late Mary Ellen Cagle, of Mobile, Alabama. She called it "Mom's Meat Loaf." Of course. (Note: Do NOT brown the meat first.)

> 1½ pounds lean ground beef or ground turkey, or a mixture of ground meats (beef, turkey, pork, and/or veal)
> 1 onion, peeled and chopped
> 1 (8-ounce) can tomato sauce
> 3 tablespoons grated Parmesan cheese
> 1 teaspoon salt
> 1 teaspoon dried basil
> 1 teaspoon dried oregano
> ½ teaspoon hot red pepper flakes (optional)
> a few sprigs parsley, chopped, or a few teaspoons dried parsley leaves
> 1 egg, lightly beaten
> about ½ cup bread crumbs, plain or seasoned
> 2 strips bacon

IN A LARGE bowl, using your hands, mix together all of the ingredients except the bread crumbs and bacon until well combined. Add as many bread crumbs as you need to make the meat stick together without being too mushy.

Line the slow cooker with foil strips or cheesecloth (as above) and press the meat mixture into the slow cooker to form a round loaf. Chop the bacon

Barbarians at the Plate

or simply use scissors to snip it. Scatter it over the top of the meat loaf.

Cover and cook on LOW for 8 to 10 hours. Serve hot. Cool, cover, and refrigerate leftovers and slice for sandwiches.

SERVING SUGGESTION: Serve with Almost-Instant Mashed Potatoes (page 163), Oven Fries (page 164), and a salad (page 158) or cooked greens (page 172).

◆ Chinese-ish Beef with Broccoli ◆

YIELD: 4 to 6 servings.

The idea behind a slow cooker is to cook things over a long period of time. The idea behind a wok is to cook food as quickly as possible. Although the two methods seem totally contrary, the flavors in this slow-cooker dish are very close to the popular, wok-fried take-out entrée. All ingredients should be available in your supermarket; look in the Asian or the "international" aisle. Asian chili paste is sometimes sold as "chili paste with garlic."

1 tablespoon peanut oil or other vegetable oil
2 teaspoons Asian sesame oil (made with toasted sesame seeds)
1 to 1½ pounds steak (such as London broil, skirt steak, flank stake, or blade steak), sliced against the grain
1 onion, peeled and sliced
4 cloves garlic, peeled and chopped
2 tablespoons grated, peeled fresh ginger or 1 tablespoon ground ginger
1 (15-ounce) can straw mushrooms, drained
½ to 1 teaspoon Asian chili paste or hot red pepper flakes
1 cup canned beef broth
¼ cup regular or reduced-sodium soy sauce
1 tablespoon dry sherry, rice wine, or white vermouth (optional; page 211)
1 tablespoon cornstarch
2 cups chopped fresh or frozen broccoli or broccoli florets
1 (8-ounce) can sliced water chestnuts, drained

FOR SERVING:
at least 3 cups cooked rice (from 1 cup cooked)
4 scallions, trimmed and chopped

SPRAY THE INSIDE of the slow-cooker stoneware with cooking spray to prevent sticking.

In a skillet set over medium-high heat, heat the peanut (or vegetable) oil and sesame oil. Cook the steak until browned on all sides, about 7

minutes total. Transfer the meat and any accumulated pan juices to the slow-cooker.

Add the onion, garlic, ginger, mushrooms, and chili paste (or hot pepper flakes), the broth, soy sauce, and sherry (or rice wine or vermouth), if using, to the slow cooker. Cover and cook on LOW for 8 to 10 hours.

Spoon the cornstarch into a small bowl and add about 6 tablespoons of the cooking liquid, stirring to make a paste. Scrape the paste into the slow cooker, stir, and add the broccoli and water chestnuts. Cover and cook on HIGH for 15 minutes, or until the liquid has thickened slightly, broccoli is tender, and the water chestnuts are heated through. Serve over rice, with chopped scallions.

PREP AHEAD: The night before, combine the broth, soy sauce, and sherry (or other wine) in a jar and cover, and refrigerate. Slice the onions and chop the garlic and ginger, cover, and refrigerate. Make the rice (reheat in the microwave or on the stovetop). Alternatively, make large batches of rice, freeze in family-size servings, and reheat in microwave.

SERVING SUGGESTION: Serve with egg rolls (available in the freezer section of the supermarket) and with sliced oranges and/or fortune cookies (also in the supermarket) for dessert.

◆ Slow-Cooker Ratatouille ◆
(Vegetable Stew)

YIELD: 4 to 6 servings.
Vegetarian-friendly

Served with good bread, this makes a satisfying meal.

3 garlic cloves, peeled and chopped
1 onion, peeled and sliced
2 bell peppers, any color, stemmed, seeded and cut into large chunks
1 pound yellow squash or zucchini (or combination), cut into large chunks
1 pound eggplant, stemmed and cut into 1-inch chunks
1 teaspoon dried thyme
1 teaspoon dried basil
1 teaspoon dried oregano
1 (28-ounce) can crushed tomatoes
salt and pepper
1 cup grated Parmesan or Asiago cheese

FOR SERVING:

> 1 pound egg noodles, cooked, drained, and buttered, 1 (10-ounce) box
> couscous, cooked according to package directions, or 1 (16-ounce)
> tube prepared polenta, heated according to package directions

Spray the inside of the slow-cooker stoneware with cooking spray to prevent sticking.

Put all the ingredients except the cheese in the slow cooker. Cover and cook on LOW for 8 to 10 hours. Just before serving, stir in the cheese. Serve in bowls, over noodles, couscous, or polenta.

For the Carnivores: Slice a pound of hot or mild Italian sausage links into rounds and brown them well before adding them to the slow-cooker with the other ingredients, or cook sausage separately on the grill or in a skillet and serve on the side.

Prep Ahead: The night before, chop all the vegetables, cover, and refrigerate.

The Cookbook Shelf:

Slow Cooking

Betty Crocker's Easy Slow Cooker Dinners: Delicious Dinners the Whole Family Will Love. Hungry Minds, 2001.

Jager, Rebecca Field. *How to Make Love and Dinner at the Same Time: 200 Slow Cooker Recipes to Heat Up the Bedroom Instead of the Kitchen.* Adams Media, 2004.

Pye, Donna Marie. *The Best Family Slow Cooker Recipes.* Robert Rose, 2003.

Smothermon, et al. *Biggest Book of Slow Cooker Recipes.* Better Homes & Gardens, 2002.

Once-a-Week Cooking:
Weekend Feasts to Weeknight Meals

THE ONCE-A-WEEK KITCHEN

EVERYONE MAKES A big deal over those old-fashioned Sunday suppers, but the vaunted home cooks of yesteryear who weekly roasted big hunks of meat or poultry in the oven were in on a little culinary secret: Big hunks of meat and poultry *cook themselves*. So this strategy works for those weekends when you are going to be around for a chunk of time, but want to get the house cleaned or a novel read (don't you *wish*?) while dinner cooks. Here are a few points to consider:

❖ Even a family that loves turkey is going to get pretty sick of it by the third or fourth day. Alternate leftovers with other dishes.

❖ If you're going to be home anyway, why not roast up a hunk of meat even if you don't plan to serve it on the same day? There is no rule saying that a ham can't immediately make the transition from oven to leftovers, without a stop at the table in between. Slice some for the lunchbox, make your favorite leftovers, cool them, wrap them up well, and freeze them. On one of those nights when all hell is breaking loose, you'll be happy you did.

❖ While the oven is on, you can cook all manner of things that you

might not have time for on weekdays: baked potatoes, winter squash, desserts. Be aware that if you really stuff the oven, everything will take longer to cook.

❖ Most of the "Master Recipes" here produce a big carcass (chicken, turkey) or bone (ham, lamb) which can be made into delicious soups. It's helpful to deal with the carcass or bone immediately after cooking; toss it into the soup pot or, if you are just too tired, cool the carcass, wrap it, and freeze it for future use.

❖ If you want to cook the leftover recipes without making the "Master Recipe" first, you can easily do so in most cases. Rotisserie chickens, skinned and shredded (see page 47), or hunks of turkey from the deli will stand in for leftover chicken or turkey. Buy chunks of roast beef for the Stroganoff, or slices for the Roast Beef Salad. Buy hunks of ham at the deli for the Stuffed Peppers or the Ham-Balaya; the Lamb, Barley, and Carrot Soup can be made with lamb shanks and the Pea Soup can be made with a smoked ham hock.

Dinner with the Neals
CROMWELL, OKLAHOMA

DIANN NEAL REMEMBERS a day when her then-husband, who was working cattle near their home in Cromwell, Oklahoma, called her about an injured steer.

"He said they were just going to dispose of it," Diann says. "So I said 'Stick a knife in it and I'll be right over.' " She and her husband bled and butchered the steer on the spot. "Heck. That was a lot of Sunday dinners!" she said.

The story might seem a little, well . . . raw, to those accustomed to obtaining meat nicely wrapped at the grocery store. But Diann, a self-employed single mother of six, is used to working hard for everything—including food.

Diann and her kids live in "awl country," as they say in Oklahoma—that's oil country to those of us who don't—in the center of Cromwell, a town of 196. In late spring the meandering two-lane highway that serves as main street is lined with tall grasses and wildflowers: fescue, Indian paintbrush, honeysuckle, trumpet vine. The town itself comprises a few blocks of one-story houses (each, it seems, dwarfed by a huge truck in the driveway), a couple of convenience stores, four churches (two of them Baptist), and a K-12 school. Fences and clotheslines are fashioned out of cast-off oil pipe. Kids ride their bikes, helmet-less, on the side of the road. Fat armadillos try to outwaddle speeding pickups.

Diann has supported herself and her family over the years in such jobs as hauling rock, driving a truck, and working in the sheriff's department, a lawyer's office, as city clerk and treasurer, and as the director of economic development for the nearby city of Okemah; she has mastered the intricacies of butchering cattle and PowerPoint. She now works at home as a grant writer for nonprofits, is on the local school board, and is taking college classes online. In the meantime, she keeps an eye on the four children still at home—Emily, 16, Benjamin, 14, Aubree, 13, and Jedidiah, 11—and cares for an ailing neighbor who now lives in her spare bedroom (she calls him "the elderly gentleman" and says, "I just couldn't see letting him go to a nursing home"). And she cooks.

"Sometimes I feel like a Lone Ranger," she said, running her hand through her hair. "People look at me like I'm crazy when I'm canning vegetables or putting up jam. A lot of kids don't seem to know how to eat homemade cooking."

"I've had roast beef and mashed potatoes and green beans on the table and some visiting child will ask for a hot dog," she says.

The Neal house is an anomaly in Cromwell—the only two-story house in town, and a rambling one at that (it is rumored that it was once a brothel)—with a large, comfortable kitchen with a gas-burning "woodstove" on a stone hearth. On a Saturday kids wander in and out—some of them hers, some of them belonging to neighbors. Emily, her dark, just-washed hair wrapped in a towel, walks by with a laundry basket ("she does everybody's laundry," says her mom, sounding grateful) as a towheaded boy whom she is babysitting tries to play "Yankee Doodle" on the touch-tone phone. Aubree is putting the finishing touches on her hair for an evening at the local rodeo. The children all seem to eat endlessly—slices of tomatoes and apples disappear, all washed down with pop ("Too much pop!" Diann says, grimacing. "It's one thing I really wish I could get them to cut down on") until Diann puts supper on the table: Burgers simmered in cream of mushroom soup, canned asparagus and corn, strawberries and bananas for dessert. Diann is used to the constant munching. She is used to cooking breakfast for "a bunch." Sunday dinner, after church, usually involves anywhere from six to twenty people. On Thanksgiving she had thirty-eight.

She shops once a month, making the sixty-five-mile trek to Oklahoma City to the supermarket, where she loads up her van on sale items and tries to keep the family's monthly food budget to about $400.

"I tell my kids they'd better be hungry for what's on sale," she says.

She keeps most of her purchases in the freezer, an ancient, spray-painted silver hulk in her entranceway, along with a lot of the meat her sons or her neighbors have killed hunting: wild hog, venison, wild turkey, rabbit. ("If you kill it, you eat it," she has lectured her boys. Jed once killed a crow, and Diann insisted that he eat the bird—although she secretly substituted chicken drumettes in the dinner she cooked.) On Sunday she often roasts a big turkey and a ham, and will turn the leftovers into the week's dinners, sandwiches, stews, and something she calls "Refrigerator Soup," which, she says "pretty much has everything in it." For Christmas presents, she makes her own venison jerky and jams from the berries she and the kids pick each summer.

"Nothing is going to waste in this house," she says. "Who can afford waste?"

Barbarians at the Plate

◆ Master Recipe: ◆
Roast Chicken/Turkey

Roasting a chicken or a turkey (or a capon—see page 46) is easy, and there's no law that you have to make an elaborate stuffing (dressing, for you Southerners). The birds can be served with baked or mashed potatoes, boxed stuffing, rice, or noodles. If you cook one roasting chicken, consider cooking two: one for Sunday supper and one for weeknight dinners. (You can also shred the meat and freeze it for later use.)

Roasting chickens (as opposed to fryers) are usually 4 to 6 pounds. A 12- or 13-pound turkey is large enough for any day that isn't a holiday. A pound of uncooked, bone-in poultry will, when cooked, generously feed one person.

To Thaw:

A 6-to-8-pound fowl takes 18 to 24 hours in the fridge to defrost, a 10-to-12-pound bird takes 24 to 36 hours, and a 14-to-18-pound bird takes a year. (Just kidding). If you have to rush it, put the fully wrapped and frozen chicken or turkey in a plastic bag, and plunge the bag into a bucket full of *cold* water. Weight it so it stays submerged. Change the water periodically. A 12-pound turkey will still take at least 8 hours to defrost that way. You know it is fully thawed when the flesh feels pliable and you can easily wiggle the legs and wings at the joints. Whatever you do, do NOT try to thaw poultry at room temperature; scary things will happen.

To Cook:

❖ Remove the little packet of organs (liver, heart, etc.) from the bird, wash out the cavities and pat dry, season them with salt and pepper. Some people like to use the gizzards in their gravy; my mother and aunt freeze the liver for risotto. I give them to the dog.

❖ If you are not making stuffing, insert into the body cavity of the bird(s) something that will flavor the meat: a halved lemon or orange, a stalk of celery, a few garlic cloves, and/or a halved onion and a bay leaf. Rub the bird with oil or softened butter and season with salt and pepper.

- ❖ Cook unstuffed poultry at 325°F for about 15 minutes per pound, or until a meat or instant-read thermometer inserted into the thickest part of the thigh registers at least 180°F. For turkey, you probably will have to cover the breast and possibly the drumsticks with foil if they brown too quickly. Baste with melted butter.
- ❖ If you stuff the chicken or turkey, cook it for about 20 minutes per pound; make sure that the stuffing inside registers at least 165°F on an instant-read thermometer.
- ❖ Remove the bird from the oven, cover with a tent of foil and let sit for about 10 minutes for the juices to collect (use this time to make gravy). Slice and serve. Cool, wrap, and refrigerate or freeze leftovers—including the carcass—as soon as possible.

Good Gravy

POUR THE PAN juices into a glass container and allow to sit for a few minutes. Skim off ¼ cup of the fat that rises to the top. Pour the fat into the roasting pan or a skillet, place over low heat and stir in the flour until a paste is formed. (If you are making the gravy in the roasting pan, stir up the browned bits on the bottom of the pan. If the bottom of the pan seems burned, use a skillet instead). Stir in about 4 cups of liquid: the remaining, defatted drippings and/or canned chicken broth or canned turkey broth. Keep stirring until the gravy is thickened, about 5 minutes. Taste and season with salt and pepper if needed. Any leftover gravy (dream on!) can be used in Pot Pie, page 48.

CAPONS

A capon is a rooster that has been "desexed" at a young age (people in the food world usually hate to use words like "castrated"). But if you think a rooster would make for stringy meat, think again. Capons have tender flesh and a large proportion of white meat. The supermarket where I shop only carries frozen capons, and carries them only around the holidays. If that's the case where you live, and your freezer is large enough, you might want to buy a few and stash them away. A capon usually weighs 8 to 10 pounds. Treat as you would a chicken or a turkey.

Barbarians at the Plate

THE ROTISSERIE CHICKEN

A rotisserie chicken from the supermarket, served with mini-cut carrots and steamed ears of corn, makes about the fastest dinner I can think of. But if you skin it and shred it you have nicely cooked chicken meat—about 3½ cups in an average rotisserie chicken—to work with in other recipes; try it with any in this book that call for cooked chicken.

CARLA FITZGERALD WILLIAMS—a mother of two and sometimes-desperate home cook—wrote an entire, and entirely useful, book about rotisserie chicken: *Rotisserie Chickens to the Rescue* (Hyperion, 2003).

◆ Chicken or Turkey Soup ◆

YIELD: 6 to 8 servings.

You don't have to be under the weather to enjoy this soup. And if you use star-shaped pasta or alphabet pasta, the kids will think it's "almost" as good as the stuff from the can.

1 or 2 carcasses of a large roasting chicken, or 1 turkey carcass, most
    (but not all) meat removed
cold water
1 (14.5-ounce) can chicken or turkey broth (optional)
1 bay leaf
2 tablespoons canola or other vegetable oil
1 onion, peeled and chopped
4 to 5 carrots, peeled and chopped
2 stalks celery, trimmed and chopped
2 to 3 cups cooked, shredded chicken or turkey
¾ cup brown or white rice, pearl barley, or small pasta (such as orzo)
dried basil
dried thyme
salt and pepper
chopped fresh parsley, for serving (optional)

PUT THE POULTRY carcass(es) in a pot and add the water and the broth (you can add straight water, but the broth will boost the flavor) until the carcass is almost covered. Add the bay leaf and bring to a boil. Lower the heat so that the liquid simmers, and cook, covered, for about 1 hour.

Once-A-Week Cooking   47

Remove the carcass and, when cool enough to handle, take off any remaining meat. Discard the bones and set the meat aside.

Heat the oil in a skillet set over medium and cook the onion, carrots, and celery, stirring, until they begin to soften, about 5 minutes. Put in the pot with the cooking liquid. Add the cooked chicken or turkey and the rice, barley, or small pasta. Season to taste with basil, thyme, salt, and pepper. Cover and simmer until rice, barley, or pasta is tender (20 to 30 minutes). Garnish with chopped fresh parsley, if desired.

ADDITIONS: Chopped fresh lemongrass (available in some supermarkets or in Asian specialty shops) can be simmered with the carcass for an exotic, lemony flavor. Chop the white parts into chunks and add them to the pot. Remove with a slotted spoon before serving. Some stores sell dried, chopped lemongrass, but it always seems tasteless to me.

ALSO: Hot red pepper flakes or hot sauce; chopped fresh or canned tomatoes.

MAKE AHEAD: Up to 2 days. Cool, cover and refrigerate.

FREEZE: Up to 2 months.

◆ Pot Pie with Leftover Chicken ◆ or Turkey

YIELD: 6 servings.

It's hard to find anyone who doesn't love chicken pot pie. This version, like all good ones, is creamy and flavorful. I make it in a Dutch oven.

> 4 tablespoons (½ stick) unsalted butter
> ¼ cup all-purpose flour
> 1 (14.5-ounce) can chicken or vegetable broth, or more, if needed
> 4 cups chopped cooked chicken or turkey
> 3 cups frozen mixed vegetables, thawed
> salt and pepper
> 1 recipe biscuits (page 190), OR 1 prepared 9-inch pie crust, OR 1 sheet (½ package) frozen puff pastry, thawed according to package directions

PREHEAT THE OVEN to 375°F.

In a large ovenproof pot (such as a Dutch oven) set over medium heat, melt the butter. Stir in the flour until a paste forms, and cook for a minute

Barbarians at the Plate

or two to get rid of the "raw flour" taste. Slowly add the broth, stirring constantly, until thickened (about 5 minutes). Start with 2 cups of broth, add more if you think you need it. Stir in the chicken or turkey and the vegetables. Season with salt and pepper to taste. If using biscuits, place the raw biscuits over the filling to cover. If using pie crust or pastry, shape, crimp or cut to fit the top of the pie.

Bake, uncovered, for 35 to 45 minutes, until the crust is brown and the filling is bubbling up from the sides.

FREEZE: Up to 2 months.

◆ Chicken or Turkey Salad ◆

YIELD: 4 servings.
Recipe from Gigi Durham, Iowa City, Iowa.

Honey is the key to the dressing, while pear and pecans add crunch to the salad.

FOR THE DRESSING:
½ cup regular or reduced-fat mayonnaise, OR ¼ cup mayo and ½ cup plain regular or reduced-fat yogurt
1 tablespoon honey
2 teaspoons cider vinegar
½ teaspoon dry mustard
salt and pepper

FOR THE SALAD:
3 to 4 cups chopped cooked chicken or turkey
¾ cup hazelnuts or pecans, toasted (see box) and chopped
1 pear or tart apple, peeled, cored, and chopped
4 scallions, trimmed and chopped

IN A SMALL bowl whisk together the mayonnaise (or mayo and yogurt), honey, vinegar, and mustard. Season with salt and pepper to taste, cover, and refrigerate.

Just before serving, combine the salad ingredients in a serving bowl. Pour the dressing over all and toss to combine.

ADDITIONS: A small handful of grapes (cut in half if large), lettuce, or fresh spinach, washed and drained, to line plates or a platter for serving.
MAKE AHEAD: Dressing can be made up to 1 day ahead.

Toast nuts in a preheated 350°F oven until they become fragrant and begin to darken slightly, 7 to 10 minutes. (Pine nuts, or pignoli, will toast in about 5 minutes.) To toast nuts in the microwave: Line a microwave-safe plate with several thicknesses of paper towel. Spread the nuts out in a single layer. Cook on HIGH for 2 to 3 minutes (the time will vary according to the size and power of your microwave oven). To toast sesame seeds or raw, hulled pumpkin seeds (pepitas), put them in an ungreased skillet and cook over medium-high heat, stirring occasionally, until they begin to pop and turn brown.

OTHER IDEAS FOR LEFTOVER CHICKEN OR TURKEY

❖ Wrap in a warm flour tortilla for a burrito.
❖ Add to Fried Rice (page 107).
❖ Mix with barbecue sauce and serve on a bun, as for Pulled Pork (page 27).
❖ Add to pasta with Sesame/Peanut Sauce (page 114).
❖ Use for Chicken Enchilada Casserole (page 126).
❖ Serve sliced on toast, topped with leftover (or canned) gravy for an open-faced sandwich.

◆ Master Recipe: ◆
Roast Beef

Beef cuts are confusing, and they can be expensive. If you have just won the lottery or are celebrating your recent appointment to the UN, buy a standing rib roast or a tenderloin and consult a good, basic cookbook about how to cook it—and not overcook it—properly. If it's an average weekend and you are trying to cook something that will give you one great dinner and a bunch of great leftovers, and leave you with enough money to pay the utility bill, go for a beef round (bottom round, top round or rump roast).

❖ A beef round roast is likely to weigh about 3 or 4 pounds; for extra leftovers, you may want to cook two simultaneously. A half pound of uncooked beef will, when cooked, feed one person generously.

Barbarians at the Plate

To Cook:

I LIKE TO cut small slits in the beef and stuff them with slivers of fresh garlic, but you can skip this. Rub the meat with vegetable oil and season sparingly with salt and quite generously with coarsely cracked pepper (you can buy coarse ground pepper or, if you have a pepper mill, grind it yourself). Press the pepper into the meat to make it stick.

Roast at 450° for 10 minutes, then reduce the heat to 250° and roast about 20 to 30 minutes per pound, or until a meat or instant-read thermometer registers at least 145°F (medium rare). If you like it rarer (more rare? Okay, less cooked), I won't tell, but be advised that 145°F is the minimum temperature considered safe by the USDA. Remove from the oven and cover loosely with foil for at least 5 minutes, allowing the juices to collect. Slice and serve, and refrigerate or freeze all leftovers as quickly as possible. Save any pan juices to pour over the meat or use in the Stroganoff-ish Leftover Roast Beef (below).

◆ Stroganoff-ish Leftover ◆ Roast Beef

YIELD: 4 to 6 servings.

This is a quick version of the creamy, meaty dish many of us grew up with.

> 2 tablespoons canola or other vegetable oil
> 1 onion, peeled and chopped
> 4 cups bite-sized chunks of cooked roast beef
> 1 cup beef gravy, homemade or canned
> 3 tablespoons ketchup
> 1 (4-ounce) can sliced mushrooms, drained
> salt and pepper
> 1 (8-ounce) tub of regular (not reduced-fat) sour cream
> salt and pepper
> 1 pound cooked, buttered egg noodles or mashed potatoes (page 163),
>   for serving

IN A SKILLET set over medium heat, heat the oil. Add the onion and cook, stirring, until it begins to soften, about 5 minutes. Add the roast beef, gravy, ketchup and mushrooms and simmer for 10 minutes. Just before serving, add the sour cream, and cook a few minutes until everything is nice and hot. Season to taste with pepper; remember that canned gravy is often very salty, so make sure you taste before adding any salt. Serve over egg noodles or mashed potatoes.

MAKE AHEAD: Prepare up the point that the mushrooms have been added. Cool, cover, and refrigerate for up to 1 day. Just before serving, reheat and add the sour cream.

◆ Leftover Roast Beef Hash ◆

YIELD: 4 to 6 servings.

You can substitute cooked corned beef, chicken, turkey, or steak for the roast beef.

1½ pounds potatoes, scrubbed
3 tablespoons canola or other vegetable oil
2 onions, peeled and chopped
1 green bell pepper, stemmed, seeded and chopped
1 stalk celery, trimmed and chopped
4 cups chopped cooked roast beef
1 teaspoon dried thyme
1 teaspoon dried basil
½ teaspoon white pepper (optional)
salt and pepper
4 eggs, poached or otherwise cooked as desired, for serving (optional)
toast, for serving (optional)
hot sauce, for serving (optional)

FIT A LARGE pot with a steamer basket and pour in water to a depth of 1 to 2 inches. Bring the water to a boil while you cut the potatoes into ½-to-1-inch cubes. (The smaller you cut them, the quicker they will cook.) Steam the potatoes for 10 to 15 minutes, until very tender when pierced with a fork. Drain.

Heat 1 tablespoon of the oil in a large skillet set over medium heat. Cook the onions, green pepper, and celery, stirring often, until they begin to soften, about 5 minutes. Scrape into a mixing bowl.

Add the beef, the cooked potatoes, the thyme, basil, and white pepper (if using). Season to taste with salt and black pepper. Stir to mix thoroughly.

To cook the hash, heat the remaining 2 tablespoons of oil in the skillet over medium high heat. Add the hash. Cook until a crust begins to form on one side, then flip sections of the hash with a spatula so that the sides brown evenly. The hash will be loose, not like a solid cake.

Barbarians at the Plate

Serve with cooked eggs on top, if desired, and toast on the side. Pass the hot sauce.

IF YOU HAVE TIME: Omit the oil and cook 3 strips bacon, chopped, in the skillet. When crisp, remove and set aside. Substitute the bacon fat for the oil, and add the crumbled bacon to the hash when you add the potatoes.

MAKE AHEAD: Assemble but do not cook up to 1 day ahead. Store it in the refrigerator, covered, until needed.

◆ Roast Beef, Tomato and Onion ◆ Salad with Horseradish Dressing

YIELD: 4 servings.

This makes a light, tasty supper on a hot night; pack the leftovers for your lunch, and you will be the envy of your coworkers.

FOR THE DRESSING:
⅔ cup regular or reduced-fat mayonnaise
¼ cup prepared horseradish, drained
juice of 1 lemon (3 to 4 tablespoons)
2 tablespoons mustard
generous pinch sugar
pepper, preferably coarsely ground (you can buy coarsely ground pepper
   in the supermarket if you don't have a peppermill)

FOR THE SALAD:
16 thin slices roast beef (generous pound)
¾ pound tomatoes (2 regular tomatoes), stemmed and sliced
¼ to ½ red onion, peeled and thinly sliced
2 to 3 tablespoons bottled, chopped pimientos, drained
2 tablespoons capers, drained
salt and pepper

MAKE THE DRESSING: Combine all the ingredients in a small bowl or in a jar with a lid, whisking or shaking to mix well. Taste and adjust seasonings, if needed. Cover and refrigerate.

On a serving platter, arrange the roast beef and tomatoes in overlapping circles. Scatter the onions, pimientos, and capers on top. Season with salt and pepper and drizzle the dressing over all. Serve with French or Italian bread.

MAKE AHEAD: The dressing can be made up to 3 days ahead.
SUBSTITUTIONS AND ADDITIONS: Substitute leftover, cooked, cold salmon or thin slices of smoked salmon for the roast beef. Add a small handful of chopped fresh basil or parsley, or salad greens (for those with "adult" tastes, try watercress or arugula).

◆ Master Recipe: Baked Ham ◆

"Someone defined eternity as a ham and two people," wrote Irma S. Rombauer and Marion Rombauer Becker in the Joy of Cooking *(Penguin, 1997). Bad news if you are one of the two people; good news if you are trying to cook something on a weekend that will provide meals for a good part of the week: Pea Soup, Stuffed Peppers, and Ham-balaya among them.*

A whole ham weighs somewhere between 10 and 20 pounds (sounds like eternity to me!), and half-hams (called the shank end) are 5 to 8 pounds. This is the size most readily available in the supermarket, and will make at least 12 to 16 servings. (See note on canned hams, page 55.)

To Cook:

THE HAM YOU buy will either be fully cooked or partially cooked. Read the labels carefully and follow the instructions. Fully cooked hams should be baked at 325°F for 10 to 12 minutes per pound, or until an instant-read thermometer inserted in the thickest part of the meat reads at least 140°F. Partially cooked hams should bake for 15 to 20 minutes per pound, or until the internal temperature reaches at least 160° F. If you plan to glaze the ham, cut a crosshatch pattern in the top layer of fat before you start cooking.

TO GLAZE A HAM: Remove it from the oven about one hour before you think it is done. Spoon a glaze over the ham (if you have crosshatched the top, the glaze will sink in better), then return it to the oven, basting occasionally.

When the ham is done, cover it with a tent of aluminum foil and let it rest for about 10 minutes for the juices to collect. Slice and serve. Cool, cover, and refrigerate or freeze all leftovers, including the bone (for soup).

Quick Glazes

- ❖ Mix ½ cup orange marmalade with 2 tablespoons orange juice. Add ½ teaspoon ground ginger, if desired, and about ¼ teaspoon pepper.

- Mix ¼ cup red wine, ¼ cup rum, ¼ cup brown sugar, ¼ teaspoon ground cloves, ¼ teaspoon cinnamon, and the grated zest from an orange.
- Mix ½ cup red currant jelly with ½ teaspoon ground ginger
- Mix one (8-ounce) can of crushed pineapple with ½ teaspoon ground ginger, ⅛ teaspoon cloves, and ½ cup brown sugar.
- Mix ½ cup of pure maple syrup with 2 teaspoons Dijon mustard.

CANNED HAMS

Personally, I've never loved the texture of canned hams, but I always thought they were useful because you could keep them in the pantry as a hedge against unexpected company. Not always so. Many canned hams, especially those imported from Denmark, Holland, or Poland, must be refrigerated even before they are opened. Make sure you read the label and follow both storage and cooking directions.

◆ Pea Soup ◆

YIELD: 8 to 10 servings.

The meatier the ham bone, the better the soup.

    1 pound split peas
    1 ham bone (see note)
    4 or 5 carrots, peeled and chopped
    2 stalks celery, trimmed and chopped
    2 cloves garlic, peeled and chopped (optional)
    1 onion, peeled and chopped
    1 teaspoon dried thyme
    8 cups cold water, or more, if needed
    salt and pepper
    homemade or store-bought croutons, for serving (see box)

RINSE THE PEAS and pick out any stones or weird-looking ones.

Place the ham bone, peas, carrots, celery, garlic, onion, thyme and water into a large pot. You want the water to almost cover the bone; if it doesn't, add more. Cover and bring to a boil; reduce the heat so that the soup simmers and let cook for 1½ to 2 hours, or until the peas are very tender. Let the soup cool until it is easier to work with.

Remove the bone and remove any meat from it. Chop the meat and discard the bone. Set the meat aside.

Working in batches, puree the soup in a food processor or blender until it is the consistency you like. Return to the pot. Add the meat and stir. Taste and add salt and more pepper if needed. Serve hot.

NOTE: If you want to make this soup but don't have a ham bone, buy a smoked ham hock instead.

IF YOU HAVE TIME: Cook the carrots, celery, garlic, and onion, stirring, in about 1 tablespoon of canola or other vegetable oil, until they begin to soften, about 5 minutes, then add to the soup with the remaining ingredients. This will caramelize the vegetables and add flavor to the soup.

VEGETARIAN VARIATION: Omit the ham bone and substitute 4 cups of vegetable broth for 4 cups of the water. Increase the amount of onion, carrots, and celery to your taste.

MAKE AHEAD: Up to 2 days. Cool, cover and refrigerate.

FREEZE: Up to 3 months.

SERVING SUGGESTION: Serve with homemade rolls (page 193) or Irish soda bread (page 191).

HOMEMADE CROUTONS

Preheat a broiler. Lightly spray a cookie sheet with nonstick cooking spray. Brush both sides of slices of stale French, Italian, or sandwich bread (any kind) with olive oil, and cut the bread into small cubes. Spread on the cookie sheet in one layer, and season with salt, pepper, and Italian herb blend, or other seasonings of your choice. Broil until golden brown, turning once, 2 to 3 minutes per side. Allow to cool.

◆ Bell Peppers Stuffed ◆ with Leftover Ham

YIELD: 6 servings

Many people stuff peppers with ground beef and rice, but my mom always stuffed them with ham, and that's the way I like them. Count on one half of a pepper for each child, and two for each hungry adult.

6 large green or red bell peppers
1 tablespoon canola oil or other vegetable oil
2 cloves garlic, peeled and finely chopped
1 onion, peeled and finely chopped
3 cups finely chopped cooked ham (use a food processor to chop it)
½ cup fresh parsley leaves
½ cup bread crumbs (seasoned or plain)
1 large egg
1½ cups shredded regular or reduced-fat Cheddar, Colby or Jack cheese
hot sauce (optional)

PREHEAT THE OVEN to 350°F.

Bring a large pot of water to a boil. While it's heating, cut the peppers in half lengthwise. Carefully remove the seeds, leaving the pepper halves intact so that you can stuff them. Place them, cut-side up, in a baking pan with sides and pour the boiling water over the peppers so that they are mostly covered. Let sit for 7 to 10 minutes to soften.

While the peppers are softening, heat the oil in a skillet set over medium heat. Add the garlic and onion and cook, stirring, until they start to soften, about 5 minutes.

In a large bowl combine the garlic and onion with the ham. Add the parsley, bread crumbs, egg, and 1 cup of the cheese. Mix well. Season with hot sauce, if using. Drain the peppers and the baking pan, and stuff each half pepper with the ham mixture. Arrange the stuffed halves in the baking pan and top with the remaining ½ cup cheese.

Pour water to a depth of about ¼ inch and bake, uncovered, for 30 minutes, or until the stuffing is hot and the cheese is melted and beginning to bubble.

VARIATION: You can substitute loose sausage for the ham; cook it with the onions and garlic until no longer pink, drain off the excess fat, and then proceed with the recipe.

FREEZE: Bake the peppers, then cool and wrap well. Freeze up to 1 month. Reheat in microwave.

HAM SPREAD

The stuffing for this recipe makes a wonderful sandwich spread. Omit the bread crumbs, egg, and cheese and add a spoonful of mustard and enough mayonnaise to bind the ham mixture together. Add a dash or Worcestershire sauce and hot sauce to taste. Spread on those small "cocktail" slices of pumpernickel or rye bread; serve cold or sprinkle with shredded cheese and broil until the cheese melts. You can also add a few tablespoons of finely chopped bell pepper to the mix.

◆ Ham-Balaya ◆

YIELD: 6 servings

Don't you hate cutesy recipe titles? I do. But for this take-off on jambalaya, I just couldn't help myself. It's a variation on the well-known Creole dish of rice, vegetables, and meat or fish.

2 tablespoons canola or other vegetable oil
2 stalks celery, trimmed and chopped
2 cloves garlic, peeled and chopped
1 onion, peeled and chopped
1 green bell pepper, stemmed, seeded, and chopped
2 teaspoons dried thyme
1 bay leaf
½ teaspoon hot red pepper flakes (optional)
salt and pepper
6 ounces fresh tomatoes chopped to make 1 cup, or 1 cup diced canned
    tomatoes
1½ cups long grain white rice
2 (14.5-ounce) cans chicken broth
1½ cups water
1 pound chopped cooked ham (2 cups)
½ pound raw shrimp, shelled and thawed if frozen
hot sauce, for serving

HEAT THE OIL in a saucepan set over medium-high heat. Add the celery, garlic, onion, bell pepper, thyme, bay leaf, and hot pepper flakes (if using), and season with salt and pepper. Cook, stirring, until the vegetables begin to soften, about 5 minutes.

Add the tomatoes, rice, chicken broth, water, and ham and stir well. Bring to a boil. Reduce the heat to medium-low, cover and simmer without stirring for 30 minutes, or until the rice is tender. There should be some liquid left in the pan, but it should not be soupy. Add the shrimp, stir, and cook until pink, 3 to 5 minutes.

Remove the pot from the heat and let rest, covered, 10 minutes before serving. This ensures that the rice fully absorbs the liquid and is nice and fluffy. Serve in bowls, and pass the hot sauce.

MAKE AHEAD: Prepare up to the point when the ham has been added and cool, cover and refrigerate up to 2 days. Add the shrimp after reheating and finish cooking as directed.
FREEZE: Prepare as for making ahead and freeze up to 1 month. Add shrimp after thawing and reheating.

BUYING SHRIMP

Most shrimp sold in this country are frozen, which is fine because, as one cookbook says, "shrimp freezes brilliantly." Buy it frozen, and still in its shell; shrimp that has been thawed, shelled, and/or deveined in the market will have lost some of its flavor and firmness and will have a much shorter shelf life. Keep the shrimp frozen until you need it, and then thaw under cold running water, or in a colander sitting in a bowl in the refrigerator.

Shrimp are sold according to size (hence the oxymoronic phrase "jumbo shrimp"). If the sign at the fish counter says U-8, it means that it takes fewer than 8 shrimp to make a pound. Those in the 20-to-30-per-pound range are perfect for most home cooking.

Should you devein shrimp? The vein, according to some cookbooks, may impart a bitter taste. According to others, removing it is purely an aesthetic choice. If you want to devein shrimp, snip the shell along the vein with scissors, then remove the vein with your fingers. I never bother.

❖ Use in place of bacon in the Potato-Bacon Frittata (page 118).
❖ Add to Macaroni and Cheese (page 110).
❖ Add to Fried Rice (page 107).
❖ Use in making a Cuban sandwich (page 24).
❖ Add to Blackirican Rice and Beans.

THE UN-PICKY EATER

WE WERE ENJOYING a rare (for our family) elegant meal at a "fancy" restaurant on Prince Edward Island in Canada. Our daughter Emma, then fourteen, scanned the menu with a furrowed brow; she doesn't eat seafood, so that nixed the mussels, salmon, the arctic char, and the lobster. She doesn't eat beef or lamb, two more entrées that were out of the question. She found vegetarian ravioli, but with a mushroom ragout and—you guessed it—she doesn't eat mushrooms. The waitress obliged by saying the chef would leave the ragout off the plate. Emma was, if not happy, at least mollified.

Her friend Erin, who was with my husband, daughter, and I on this vacation, had a somewhat different take: "So many choices!" she crowed.

"I'll have the oysters to start," she said, indicating a dish of steamed oysters with a Japanese seaweed salad, "and then the grilled salmon."

Where had I gone wrong? After our first daughter, Hannah, was born, I was so pleased to see that she ate widely that I was startled when Emma, our second, started rejecting foods early on. Along with the aforementioned beef, lamb, mushrooms, and all seafood (including fish sticks and canned tuna), Emma eschews: most pork (except ham and bacon), chicken on the bone (boneless breasts are okay), and several vegetables including fresh tomatoes, cooked spinach, and (a favorite of mine) fennel. Compared to the child who will only eat plain noodles, she's not that picky. But I think she's missing a lot.

When I asked Erin how she became such an adventuresome eater, she shrugged. "I guess it's because of my dad. He always said: 'You don't like it? *Learn* to like it.' "

When we returned home, I talked with Erin's dad.

"That saying came from *my* dad," said Matt Shippee. His father, an ex-Marine who received a Purple Heart in the Philippines in World War II, raised eight kids and didn't put up with much whining at the table. "He'd say it with a smile on his lips, but we knew he pretty well meant it." Matt used the technique on Erin and her older sister and brother.

"I'm not mean about it, but maybe I am a little stricter than some parents," he said. "If the kids would say at dinner, 'I don't like this, and I don't

like that and that and that,' then I'd say 'Gee, that's what we're having for supper. See you at breakfast.' And at breakfast they'd be ready to eat."

"There's nothing wrong with pushing kids a little," said Matt. It works for him. Erin spent the vacation with us chowing down on mussels, smoked mackerel, lobster, and other foodstuffs, some of which she was trying for the first time.

Diann Neal, a cash-strapped single mother of six in Cromwell, Oklahoma, has a similar approach. She offers food with a "You'll like this," rather than a "Try it, see if you like it." It works for her. "I've never had a picky eater," she says.

My husband and I thought the "no-thank-you bite" routine ("try one bite, and if you don't like it, just say 'no thank you' ") was a good approach, but now I'm not so sure. On the plus side, our daughters have occasionally changed their minds about foods: Emma now loves asparagus, Brussels sprouts (if roasted), "weird" lettuce (frisée, arugula, radicchio), sun-dried tomatoes, and feta cheese, all of which she once professed to dislike. On the minus side, there is a whole array of foods that she still rejects.

I've always tried to follow the advice of Dr. Benjamin Spock, who began his classic 1946 volume, *Baby and Child Care*, with the words "Trust yourself." When it comes to mealtime rules, you have to do what works for you. But I think we owe it to our children, and the world at large, not to make them tyrants at the table. Don't allow your children to turn you into a short-order cook by leaping up to prepare them something special while the rest of the family enjoys the meal and yours gets cold. Put the kibosh on culinary demands ("Get me . . . !" "I want . . .") and insults ("I hate this!" It's yucky!"), which are disrespectful to the cook. You may be willing to offer a self-help alternative, such as allowing children to pour themselves a bowl of cereal or make a peanut butter sandwich; my husband and I are not. I always try to include at least one food in each meal that I know the kids like; if they don't want the fish, they can fill up on the potatoes and green beans. If your kids hate spicy foods try adding the strong spices to the "adult" portions after you have served the children.

If you can enforce reasonable rules about teeth-brushing and homework, you can establish rules for reasonable eating behavior.

And it helps to be flexible. Matt Shippee and Erin, for example, both remember the incident with the peas.

"I made her try them once, and she gagged them down . . . and up they came again," says Matt. "I backed off on peas real fast."

◆ Master Recipe: ◆
Roast Leg of Lamb

Buy a bone-in leg of lamb (5 to 7 pounds). A half pound of uncooked, bone-in lamb will, when cooked, feed one person generously.

To Cook:

I LIKE TO cut small slits in the lamb and stuff them with slivers of fresh garlic, but you can skip this step. Rub the meat with olive oil and season sparingly with salt and generously with coarsely cracked pepper (you can buy coarse-ground pepper or, if you have a pepper mill, grind it yourself). Sprinkle with chopped fresh or dried rosemary leaves, pressing the leaves (and the cracked pepper) into the meat with your hands. Roast at 450°F for 10 minutes, then reduce the heat to 325°F and roast about 12 minutes per pound, or until a meat or instant-read thermometer registers at least 145°F (medium rare). Remove from the oven and cover with a tent of foil for about 10 minutes, allowing the juices to collect. Slice and serve, refrigerating or freezing all leftovers—including the bone—as soon as possible. Save any meat juices to pour over the lamb.

◆ Lamb, Barley and Carrot Soup ◆
YIELD: 8 servings.

I think of this the way most people think of homemade chicken soup: it's a definite pick-me-up when you feel a bit out-of-sorts. A great winter meal.

> 1 lamb bone (see note) from roast leg of lamb
> 10 cups cold water
> 1 bay leaf
> ¾ cup pearl barley
> 6 carrots, peeled and sliced
> 2 onions, peeled and sliced
> 2 stalks celery, trimmed and chopped
> 4 tablespoons ketchup or tomato paste
> dried thyme
> salt and pepper

PLACE THE LAMB bone, water, and bay leaf in a large pot set over high heat. Bring the water to a boil, then reduce the heat so that the liquid simmers. Cover and simmer for 2 hours. Remove the bone and, when cool enough to handle, cut off any remaining meat. Discard the bone. Remove the bay leaf from the pot and return any chopped meat to the cooking liquid.

Add the remaining ingredients and simmer until the barley and carrots are tender, at least 30 minutes. Serve hot.

NOTE: If you don't have a lamb bone from a roast leg of lamb, use two fresh lamb shanks. Sauté them first in a bit of oil.

MAKE AHEAD: Up to 2 days. Cool, cover and refrigerate.
FREEZE: Up to 2 months.

♦ Leftover Lamb, Feta Cheese ♦ and Tomatoes

YIELD: 4 servings.

This is an amazing dish, and it can be made with fresh shelled shrimp (see "Buying Shrimp," page 59) or cubes of chicken breasts. If you use either of these, make sure you cook them through. Shrimp take 3 to 5 minutes to cook, a small cube of chicken should cook in 5 to 7 minutes.

> 2 tablespoons olive oil
> 1 onion, peeled and sliced
> 2 cloves garlic, peeled and minced
> ½ teaspoon hot red pepper flakes
> 3 to 4 cups cubed leftover lamb
> ¾ pound tomatoes (2 regular tomatoes), stemmed and chopped
> finely chopped zest of 1 lemon (optional)
> dried oregano
> salt and pepper
> 1 cup crumbled feta cheese
> ¼ cup chopped fresh parsley
> at least 3 cups cooked rice (from 1 cup uncooked) or 1 (10-ounce) box
>   couscous, prepared according to package directions, for serving

PREHEAT THE OVEN to 400°F.

Heat the oil in an ovenproof skillet set over medium heat. Add the onion, garlic, and red pepper flakes and cook, stirring, until they begin to soften, about 5 minutes. Add the lamb, the tomatoes, and the lemon zest

(if using) and season with oregano, salt and pepper. Cook, stirring, until heated through. Top with the crumbled feta and transfer the skillet to the oven for about 5 minutes, or until the cheese begins to melt. Sprinkle with parsley and serve with rice or couscous.

◆ Lamb Salad ◆
with Yogurt Dressing
YIELD: 4 servings.

You can turn this into a sandwich by stuffing the salad into pita bread. Do that at the last minute; otherwise the pita will get soggy and break apart.

FOR THE DRESSING:
- 1 cup regular or reduced-fat plain yogurt
- ½ cucumber, peeled, seeded, and grated
- 2 teaspoons lemon juice
- pinch of sugar
- salt and pepper

FOR THE SALAD:
- 1 (7-ounce) package fresh baby spinach leaves (about 6 cups), washed and drained
- 16 thin slices of cooked lamb
- ¾ pound tomatoes (2 regular tomatoes), sliced
- ¼ to ½ red onion, peeled and sliced
- ½ cucumber, peeled and thinly sliced
- chopped fresh mint (optional)
- toasted pine nuts (optional; page 50)
- 2 (8-inch) pita breads, or more, cut in half and heated according to package directions, for serving

IN A SMALL bowl, whisk together the yogurt, cucumber, lemon juice, sugar, and salt and pepper. Taste and correct seasonings, if needed.

Place the spinach on a serving platter and top with sliced lamb, tomatoes, onion, and cucumber slices. Scatter mint and toasted pine nuts on top, if using. Drizzle with the yogurt dressing and serve with warm pita bread.

MAKE AHEAD: The dressing can be made up to 1 day ahead. Cover and refrigerate until needed.

Barbarians at the Plate

THE COOKBOOK SHELF:

Gunst, Kathy. *Leftovers: 50 Simple Master Preparations and 150 Delicious Variations for the Second Time Around*. HarperCollins, 1991. Out of print but worth finding.

Urvater, Michele. *Monday to Friday Cookbook*. Workman, 1991. Look for "Sunday Start-Up" recipes.

Freezer Feeds

FREEZER BASICS

YOU CAN FREEZE almost any food, except for canned foods and eggs in their shells. Make sure that you wrap it well, in freezer-quality plastic, foil, or paper, removing as much air as possible. Double wrapping is usually a good idea. Be aware that food quality doesn't *improve* with freezing, but with care, you can maintain it. If you follow these guidelines, you are more likely to find edible food in your freezer as opposed to unidentifiable, frosted, shriveled lumps.

- ❖ Keep the freezer at 0°F or lower to protect food quality. Remember that freezing does not kill bacteria, but only inactivates it. As long as food is kept solidly frozen, it will not become unsafe to eat.
- ❖ Freezer burn occurs when air touches the food and moisture begins to evaporate. To prevent it, remove as much air as possible from the package. Freezer burn is a *food quality* issue, not a *safety* issue.
- ❖ Remember that liquids expand when frozen. Leave about an inch of headroom between the liquid and the lid.
- ❖ Make sure all precooked food is thoroughly cooled before freezing. Then, freeze as quickly as possible.

- The safest way to defrost foods, to discourage the growth of bacteria, is in the refrigerator.
- You can freeze a baked or unbaked casserole. You can bake a frozen casserole without thawing it first, but it may take almost twice as long. Start by baking it covered with foil, then remove the foil and bake until it is heated through, and an instant-read thermometer registers at least 165°F when inserted in the center.
- Do not try to thaw or heat frozen bread, biscuits, rolls, etc. in the microwave; they will get tough. Instead, wrap in aluminum foil and heat in a preheated 425°F oven for 3 to 5 minutes.

THINGS YOU CAN FREEZE THAT YOU MIGHT NOT HAVE THOUGHT OF FREEZING

FRESH GINGER: Peel large chunks of ginger. When needed, just grate it, frozen.

GRATED ZUCCHINI: Add to baked goods or stews for moisture and bulk.

COOKED RICE: Store it in plastic freezer bags in usable portions; then pop it in the microwave before serving.

MASHED POTATOES AND TWICE-BAKED POTATOES: Treat as for rice above.

COOKED GROUND BEEF AND COOKED, SHREDDED CHICKEN: Treat as for rice, above.

DAIRY PRODUCTS: You can freeze light and heavy cream, half-and-half, milk, buttermilk, sour cream, and yogurt for one month. First, remove them from their original packaging and freeze in glass jars or plastic freezer containers, leaving one inch of headroom. Defrost in the fridge. Many dairy products will separate; whisk them to restore their proper consistency, and use in cooking, not for serving as is. Frozen heavy cream will usually not whip after thawing. Firm cheeses (like Cheddar or Jack) can be cubed or grated before freezing. Soft cheeses (like goat cheese and cream cheese) do not freeze well. Butter freezes beautifully for up to a year.

EGGS: Break the eggs and add one tablespoon milk or water per egg and a dash of salt. Scramble well and pour into freezer container. Thaw in the refrigerator and use for scrambling or baking.

WATERMELON: Slice and freeze it for a short time (several hours or overnight), and eat as a summer treat.

GRAPES AND BERRIES: Stem or hull, if needed, rinse and drain, and freeze in one layer on a cookie sheet. When frozen, transfer to an appropriate container. Berries can be used in baking, smoothies, and frozen desserts; grapes can be eaten, out of hand, as an icy treat.

FROSTED CAKES, IF THE FROSTING IS MADE WITH BUTTER.

PIES: Most pies can be frozen baked or unbaked for at least 4 months. You can bake them frozen if they are in a freezer-to-oven pie plate.

GRAPE OR CHERRY TOMATOES: Freeze them as you would grapes, above, and use in cooking.

BANANAS: When a banana starts to blacken in the fruit bowl, throw it into the freezer, peel and all. To use, run under hot water and scrape off the peel with a table knife. (Great in smoothies, banana bread, and the banana "ice cream" on page 182.)

THINGS THAT DON'T FREEZE WELL

SAUCES AND GRAVIES THICKENED WITH FLOUR OR CORN-STARCH: For best results, freeze the stock for gravy unthickened and add thickener when you reheat it. (The reason packaged frozen entrées with gravies freeze well is that the manufacturers use commercial thickeners not available to the home cook.)

ANY DISH WITH COOKED EGG WHITES.

MARGARINE AND WHIPPED BUTTER.

MAYONNAISE: Use "salad dressing" (like Miracle Whip) instead of mayonnaise when you make sandwiches or other dishes for freezing.

LETTUCE, CELERY, AND GARLIC.

FROSTED CAKES WITH EGG-WHITE OR COOKED FROSTINGS.

Dinner with the Knoxes
STURBRIDGE, MASSACHUSETTS

LOOK IN MARY Kay Knox's upright freezer in the basement of her Sturbridge, Massachusetts, home and you will find quarts and quarts of her signature, homemade tomato sauce. It's the sauce she learned to make from her mother, the sauce that jump-starts some of her family's favorite meals: chicken parmigiana, pizza, baked ziti.

"My mom taught me to plan," she says. "She was always thinking ahead."

Knox is such a planner that, she says laughing, "my friends all hate me." A bulletin board that she and her husband, Stephen, call "Command Central" hangs in the kitchen, bearing a shopping list, and a list of nonroutine chores ("change lightbulb in garage"). A basket sits in her kitchen, holding her coupon file. The cellar in the Knoxes traditional Cape is lined with industrial-quality metal shelves stacked with packaged foods. Her upright freezer is crammed, not only with containers of sauce, but with chicken breasts, ground meat, pork tenderloin, homemade soup.

For Mary Kay, being organized is simply a matter of survival.

"I couldn't do the jobs I do—teaching, mothering—without being organized," she says. "Life as I know it would grind to a halt." The couple moved to Sturbridge—a once-rural town about sixty miles east of Boston—so that they would be equidistant from their jobs: Stephen's in Worcester, Massachusetts, where he works in health-care finance, and Mary Kay's in Tolland, Connecticut, where she teaches sixth grade.

Their day begins early. Mary Kay gets up at 4:30 every morning to have some "alone time." She reads a bit for pleasure, has her coffee, plans her day, packs lunches for nine-year-old Katie and six-year-old Sam, and for herself. She wakes her husband and kids at 6 a.m., and is out the door a half hour later. Stephen takes the kids to their before-school daycare, arriving by 7 a.m.

Mary Kay's teaching day ends at 2:25 p.m. but between teacher's union duties and curriculum committee work, she rarely gets home before 4, picking up the kids on the way. The first thing they want when they get home is a snack: Chex Mix, carrots and dip, clementines, raw string beans or red pepper slices, a bowl of cereal, or Fruit Roll-Ups are favorites. If she's wearing something "uncomfortable" (heels, panty hose) Mary Kay will change before attacking dinner.

She still remembers talking with a colleague about cooking dinner when the colleague remarked, "Oh, I don't do that."

"What do you mean, you don't do that?" Mary Kay recalls saying. "That's not an option!"

A tall, lean thirty-seven-year-old with a cascade of dark hair, there is a slightly old-fashioned air about Mary Kay Knox. When she and Stephen became engaged, for example, she began learning to cook, using a roommate as a guinea pig. "I wanted to be a good wife," she says. "And I thought a good wife should provide good meals." She never saw this as un-feminist. "It seemed silly to not cook because of a cause," she said.

But she is also a take-charge kind of person, who manages with aplomb her career, a local softball team (she is the pitcher as well), the teacher's union (she's vice president of her local), her church's Sunday school (she's the superintendent), and her children's schedules. She "laughed out loud," however, when she received a notice from a mother at her children's school asking her to produce a pie for a bake sale. The note, she recalls, read: "If you must use a store-bought crust, roll it out so the creases don't show."

"She gives me almost no notice, and expects me to go out, get the ingredients, and then make the crust from scratch, or waste time disguising a packaged crust," Knox says, shaking her head. "Clearly, this is a person who does not work outside the home."

When I visited the family, arriving just before dinner, the kitchen was spic and span, the house fragrant with the smell of chicken parmigiana and garlic bread, and the kids in high gear. Petey, the ten-year-old boxer, sniffed the air hopefully. Later, when Stephen was stacking the dishwasher after dinner, Petey sidled over to the machine and licked the plates.

Katie, slender and bespectacled, practiced ballet stretches—arching her leg up behind her to almost touch her head—while Sam zoomed around the house airplane fashion. He zoomed up to his mother, assumed a winning smile and a wheedling tone, and begged for a predinner treat. "Mom, I am

Barbarians at the Plate

completely dying for garlic bread," he said. He grasped his stomach theatrically. Mary Kay was not buying it.

Katie brought Katrina Elizabeth, her brown-haired American Girl doll, down from her room for my inspection, and proudly paged through *The Mix-It-Up Cookbook*, published by the doll company.

"I love to cook," she said, describing how she helps her mom make lemon chicken, cakes, and cookies.

Stephen, arriving home in a suit and tie, joined the family in time for dinner, which was served on a long, cloth-covered table almost in the center of the house. The kids were giggly in the presence of a stranger (me), asking a bit self-consciously for their mom or dad to "please pass" the salt, the chicken, the salad.

"I'm proud that they know how to behave at the table," said Mary Kay. "Learning to chew with your mouth closed is a big milestone for a child." This made Sam laugh. He slid out of his chair and attempted an escape.

"You're not finished yet, buddy," Stephen said gently. Sam returned to his seat.

Mary Kay says she learned to love food from her mother, an Italian American, and her dad, who is Jewish by birth.

"Growing up, I had the best of both worlds," she says of her culinary heritage. "I was raised by people who loved food and who saw making good food as a way to express love."

After dinner the kids took their baths in a bathroom just off the kitchen, while Stephen cleaned up and Mary Kay sipped a glass of red wine, checking tomorrow's "to-do" list. Sam reappeared, wearing plaid pajama bottoms and a white T-shirt, in record time—"Did you wash your hair and body?" his mother asked. Katie emerged in a pink nightie. "He did!" she said. "I saw him!"

Mary Kay was already planning ahead for the weekend. She would be entertaining a friend, and planned to make an eggplant and artichoke pizza, an entrée that is a bit more exotic than Stephen, who favors plain, mildly spiced, foods, would like.

"Once a month this friend and I get together and try something new," said Mary Kay. "She cooks for me, and I cook for her."

Later in the weekend she will probably cook up some sauce.

◆ Mary Kay Knox's Tomato Sauce ◆ and Meatballs

YIELD: about 12 cups.

This is one of those sauces that is better than the sum of its parts. You can use it, as Mary Kay does, for everything—pizza, pasta, soups, and stews—that calls for tomato sauce.

FOR THE SAUCE:
- 2 to 3 tablespoons olive oil
- 1 or 2 onions, peeled and finely chopped
- 3 to 4 cloves of garlic, peeled and finely chopped
- 1 tablespoon dried basil or about 2 tablespoons chopped fresh basil leaves
- 1 tablespoon dried oregano or about 2 tablespoons chopped fresh oregano leaves
- 1 #10 can (6 pounds, 6 ounces) crushed tomatoes, or four 28-ounce cans crushed tomatoes (Mary Kay prefers Pastene brand)
- 2 tablespoons sugar or red wine
- salt and pepper

HEAT THE OLIVE oil in a large pot set over medium heat. Cook the onion, stirring, until nearly translucent, about 7 minutes. Add the garlic and cook, stirring for a minute or two, making sure that it does not brown. Add basil and oregano. Stir briefly, until onion, garlic, and herbs are mixed. Add the tomatoes. If the sauce looks too thick, add a bit of water. Add sugar or wine (this cuts the bitter acid taste). Bring to a boil, stirring constantly so that the sauce does not stick to the bottom of the pot. Once the sauce boils, adjust the heat so that it simmers. If you want a rich, winter sauce, simmer for about two hours. If you are making this sauce in the summer, turn the heat off right after it boils. You can also substitute or add chopped fresh tomatoes to this sauce.

Mary Kay writes: "If I am going to add meatballs, I do so right after the sauce boils. If the sauce has not boiled yet, the meatballs fall apart."

FOR THE MEATBALLS
YIELD: About 70 meatballs.

- 2 pounds of high-quality, low-fat ground meat
- 2 large eggs
- 1 cup bread crumbs, seasoned or plain, or more if needed

½ cup grated Parmesan cheese
¼ cup garlic powder
1 tablespoon dried parsley flakes or about 2 tablespoons chopped fresh
     parsley
a few tablespoons milk, as needed
salt and pepper

IN A LARGE bowl, using your hands, mix together the meat, eggs, bread crumbs, Parmesan, garlic powder, and parsley. If the mixture feels too stiff, add some milk, a tablespoon at a time. If the mixture feels too mushy, add more bread crumbs, a bit at a time. Season with salt and pepper.

Roll the meatballs in your palms. The size is your choice, but Mary Kay uses about a tablespoon of meat per meatball, which makes a meatball about 1½ inches in diameter. Drop the meatballs into boiling tomato sauce. Continue this process until all of the meat is shaped and in the pot. Stir gently, every so often, so that the sauce does not stick. Once all of the meatballs are in the pot, lower the heat to a simmer, and allow the meatballs to cook for about 1 hour. If the meat is high in fat, you may need to skim the top of the sauce. Otherwise, the sauce is ready to be served, with the meatballs.

MAKE AHEAD: Up to 2 days. Cool, cover, and refrigerate.
FREEZE: Up to 4 months.

DISHES THAT FREEZE WELL

Soups and Stews:

Chicken or Turkey Soup, page 47
Pea Soup, page 55
Lamb, Barley and Carrot Soup, page 62
Sausage, Spinach, and Rice Soup, page 82
White Bean and Tomato Soup, page 83
Black Bean Soup, page 84
Slow-Cooker Curry, Page 28
Mexican Pork and Hominy Stew, page 31
Slow-Cooker Bourgignon, page 34
Meatless Chili, page 88

Pasta and Casseroles:

Chicken or Turkey Pot Pie, page 48
Macaroni and Cheese, page 110
Chicken Enchilada Casserole, page 126

THE COOKBOOK SHELF:

DISHES THAT LEND themselves to freezing include soups, stews, and casseroles. Many of the recipes in this book freeze well, and are so marked. Here is a very short list of cookbooks that contain plenty of recipes for good, freeze-ahead, one-pot meals.

Main, Jan. *The Best Freezer Cookbook: Freezer Friendly Recipes, Tips and Techniques.* Robert Rose, 2001.

Valenti, Tom and Friedman, Andrew. *Tom Valenti's Soups, Stews and One-Pot Meals.* Scribner, 2003.

Villas, James. *Crazy for Casseroles: 275 All-American Hot-Dish Classics.* Harvard Common Press, 2003.

Vollstedt, Maryana. *The Big Book of Casseroles: 250 Recipes for Serious Comfort Food.* Chronicle Books, 1999. Also *The Big Book of Soups & Stews: 262 Recipes for Serious Comfort Food* (2001).

FOOD. FAST

Strategies for
Last-Minute Cooks

Soup and Salad Suppers

THE QUICK FIX

Soups and salads make terrific last-minute meals: They need no accompaniment (except for, perhaps, some good bread), and are, if you make them right, full of good things that some people in your family might not eat if they were presented differently. (For example: My kids won't eat cooked carrots served by themselves, but will eat them in soup; conversely, they claim to hate mushrooms, except raw, in salads).

The soup recipes here make thick, hearty, main-dish soups; if you like your soup more soup-y, add broth or water. The salads, too, are fairly hefty.

Things to keep in mind:

❖ For soups, a well-stocked pantry is essential (see Appendix 3: Stocking the Civilized Pantry, page 208). At the very least, you need to have on hand canned broth, canned beans, canned tomatoes, frozen spinach, onions, garlic, carrots, rice, and small pasta.

❖ Canned beans should be drained, rinsed, and drained again before using, or the beans will have an unappealing viscous texture. Also, I'm told that rinsing the beans helps reduce the gas-producing properties that everyone makes fun of.

- Soups often benefit from a sprinkling of chopped fresh parsley, cilantro, or other herbs. If you don't keep fresh herbs on hand, some are now sold in spice jars in the freezer section of the supermarket.
- A teaspoon of cider vinegar or sherry added to a serving of a bean soup just before serving can really improve flavor. This works for canned soups as well.
- Some soups call for a dollop of sour cream, plain yogurt, or shredded cheese. The cheese is the easiest to keep on hand: Buy it in bulk, repackage it into smaller servings, and freeze it.
- Keep some French or Italian bread or those dark round "peasant" loaves in the freezer if you have room, and heat them in the oven at about 200 degrees while you make the soup or salad. Homemade rolls (page 193), soda bread (page 191), and corn bread (page 192) are wonderful with soups and salads, and can be made ahead and frozen.
- Frozen onions and bell peppers will disappear in a long-cooking soup or slow-cooker recipe but are fine for the quick soups in this chapter. Thawed, they are too limp to use in fresh salads.
- The salads here require no chilling time, but *can* be refrigerated, covered, if you want to make them ahead.
- Salads are the perfect medium for introducing your children (or partner) to an unfamiliar vegetable. If the vegetable gets a thumbs-down, it can just be picked out of the salad and set aside, and the rest of the meal can still be enjoyed.

Dinner with the Millers
LAWRENCEVILLE, NEW JERSEY

GRAYSON MILLER, AGE 18 months, is trying desperately to climb into the refrigerator. He is naked, except for a hat.

Mia Miller, his mom, is chopping vegetables on the clean white kitchen counter. She swoops down, grabs Grayson gently with one arm and slings him over her shoulder as she continues prepping vegetables for dinner. He wriggles, and Mia sets him on the floor, where he clings, wobbling, to her leg, then makes another mad dash for the fridge. This time he's lost the hat.

"Well, you see, it's always an . . . an adventure, cooking with an eighteen-month-old underfoot," Mia says, smiling as she hoists the sturdy child again. Cooking with an eighteen-month-old underfoot is—let's be frank—a nightmare. It's enough to make you want to throw in the (kitchen) towel and feed the tyke SpaghettiOs for the rest of his days.

But Mia perseveres. Nearly every night she comes home from her work in the development office at nearby Princeton University and cooks dinner for her husband, Matthew, their four-year-old daughter, Sophia, and son, Grayson.

"I don't know how she does it," says Matthew of his wife's kitchen skills. "Give her thirty minutes and she'll produce something wonderful."

What makes this culinary feat even more impressive is that the Millers could, quite easily, eat out every night. For free. Their apartment, a spacious two-bedroom in a stately nineteenth-century brick building on the grounds of Lawrenceville School, the private prep school where Matthew teaches interdisciplinary studies, is a stone's throw from the school cafeteria, which is open to faculty and their families. No shopping, no cooking—"No mess in the kitchen," says Mia, sounding a bit wistful. But the Millers usually opt for homemade instead.

"I like food too much," Mia says, tucking a strand of blond hair behind her ear as she continues whisking salad dressing. "I like to eat what I'm in the mood for, not just what's being served. I like to serve foods that are healthy. And the cafeteria—which is full of students, who are great with our kids—is a very distracting place. It's hard to get the children to sit and eat."

On the evening I visited, Mia threw together a Salade Niçoise, having steamed the vegetables a few nights before. With no room in the kitchen for a table, the Millers eat regularly at the large oak table in the dining room, a room that might look formal if not for the child's easel, the bulletin board crowded with artwork, and a metal stand holding plants spilling over their pots. Mia served the salad with crusty French bread and, for the adults, a glass of wine. Grayson, fully clothed for the dining table (after a brief and fruitless struggle with his dad), sat placidly—for a few minutes at least—in his booster seat, munching on the green beans and hard-boiled eggs from the salad. Sophie, very much the "big girl," sat demurely at her spot, delicately eating her salad from a bright pink plate shaped like a flower.

"I am really fortunate to have two good eaters," says Mia. The kids eat fish, chicken, California rolls, Mexican food. She sometimes tries to plan ahead, turning Sunday night roast beef into a Monday night stroganoff, for example, but generally she admits she's a "last-minute" kind of cook; she tends to stop at the store a few times a week on her way into work to pick up ingredients. She tried using a slow cooker a couple of times, "but I just don't get it," she says. A chicken recipe she made turned out with a "funky texture," and she wound up dirtying a skillet in preparing the dish. She's more comfortable cooking up a pork tenderloin or grilling some salmon. She is "constantly trolling" for recipes, often online at Web sites like epicurious.com, and keeps a big binder full of her favorites. She and Matthew are so finicky about their coffee that they roast their own beans (sometimes putting the roaster on the roof outside their apartment, to avoid setting off the smoke alarms) and brew their own espresso in an impressive-looking machine that presides over the kitchen counter. Mia is no food snob though: mac and cheese (homemade) is a staple in her repertoire, and her children "lick the plate" when she serves them Bird's Eye Broccoli with Cheese Sauce. She also stocks up on the frozen meatballs sold at a nearby Sam's Club, and a dish she grew up on, "Chicken Spectacular," (cooked chicken, Uncle Ben's Wild Long Grain & Wild Rice, Cream of Celery soup, frozen French-cut green beans, and a can of water chestnuts) makes at least one annual appearance on the family table.

"When I grew up, we ate family-style from a lazy Susan at the center of the table," says Mia. "Matthew grew up with dinner already portioned out on individual plates." She now plates the food first. Matthew, in turn, will now eat brown rice—which is Sophie's favorite, not his—at least "sometimes."

After a few minutes in his high chair Grayson was ready for his mom's lap, where he sat gravely watching while she finished her meal. The kids then scooted down the hallway to their parents' bedroom, where they made a tent out of the comforters from the bed. Bath time seemed a quiet affair until Grayson, once again in his natural state, slipped out of Matt's grasp. He zigzagged down the hall, chortling loudly and dripping water.

◆ Sausage, Spinach, and Rice Soup ◆

YIELD: 4 servings.

My mother and aunt often make this soup, without the sausage, for lunch and serve it with toasted cheese on English muffins. Follow their lead if you are feeding vegetarians.

> 1 tablespoon olive oil
> 1 onion, peeled and chopped
> ½ pound smoked sausage, such as kielbasa or andouille, sliced into ½-inch rounds
> 1 (10-ounce) package frozen chopped spinach, thawed
> 2 (14.5-ounce) cans of broth, with water added to make 4 cups, or 4 cups broth made with bouillon cubes and water
> ½ cup quick-cooking brown rice, or regular brown or white rice

HEAT THE OIL in a saucepan set over medium heat. Cook the onion, stirring, until it begins to soften, about 5 minutes. Add the sausage slices to the skillet and cook, turning, until the sausage is browned. Drain any excess fat and add the remaining ingredients. Bring to a boil, then adjust the heat so that the broth simmers. Cover and cook until the rice is tender, about 20 minutes for quick-cooking brown or regular white rice, or 45 minutes for regular brown rice.

MAKE AHEAD: Up to 1 day. Cool, cover and refrigerate.
FREEZE: Up to 1 month.

◆ White Bean and Tomato Soup ◆

YIELD: 4 main-course servings.

Vegetarian friendly (when made with vegetable broth)

This is truly a last-minute soup that I "invented" out of desperation. My kids like it so much that one year my younger daughter requested it as her special birthday dinner. Use a good-quality, flavorful spaghetti sauce.

1 (26-ounce) jar spaghetti sauce
1 (14.5 ounce) can vegetable or chicken broth
1 cup water, plus more if needed
½ cup orzo, ditallini, elbows, or other small pasta
1 (19-ounce) can cannellini beans (white kidney beans), drained and
    rinsed
dried oregano and/or basil
salt and pepper
4 slices French or Italian bread (optional)
¼ cup prepared pesto (optional)

COMBINE ALL INGREDIENTS in a pot and bring to a low boil. Cover and simmer for 15 or 20 minutes, until pasta is just tender. Taste and add more herbs, or salt and pepper, if needed. Serve hot. If desired, toast French or Italian bread and top each with pesto (available in the section of the supermarket where fresh pasta is sold). Float on top of the soup or serve on the side. Alternatively, swirl a spoonful of pesto through each bowl of soup just before serving.

> **IF YOU HAVE TIME:** For added flavor, cook a finely chopped onion and a clove or two of finely chopped garlic in a tablespoon of olive oil in the soup pot until they begin to soften, about 5 minutes, then proceed with recipe.
> **INCREASE THE VEGGIES:** Add 1 (10-ounce) package frozen, chopped spinach, thawed, or a cup of cubed carrots to the soup with the rest of the ingredients and cook as directed.
> **FREEZE:** Up to 1 month.

◆ Black Bean Soup ◆

YIELD: 6 to 8 servings.
Vegetarian friendly (when made with vegetable broth)

It's amazing how delicious this soup is, considering it only requires opening a few cans.

1 (16-ounce) jar salsa, medium, mild or hot according to your taste
2 (15-ounce) cans black beans, drained and rinsed
2 (14.5-ounce) cans vegetable or chicken broth
1 (15-ounce can) whole peeled tomatoes, chopped, juices reserved
2 cups frozen or canned corn kernels
1 or 2 canned (1 to 2 tablespoons) chipotle chilies in adobo sauce,
    chopped (optional; see box on following page)
salt and pepper

FOR SERVING:
cider vinegar
any or all of the following: chopped scallions, chopped chili peppers,
    chopped onions, chopped fresh cilantro, low-fat or no-fat sour cream,
    shredded regular or reduced-fat Cheddar, Colby, or Jack cheese, hot
    sauce

IN A SAUCEPAN set over medium heat, combine all of the ingredients, reserving the juice from the tomatoes. Cover; reduce the heat so that the liquid simmers, and cook for about 15 minutes. If the soup seems too thick, add some of the reserved tomato juice.

Taste and adjust the seasonings, if necessary. Ladle into bowls, and pour a teaspoon of cider vinegar on each serving; this brings out the flavor. Serve with desired toppings.

FOR THE CARNIVORES: Add crisp, cooked bacon (page 91) smoked, cooked sausage such as andouille or kielbasa, or leftover cooked ham, cut into bite-sized chunks.
MAKE AHEAD: Up to 1 day.
FREEZE: Up to 1 month. Cool, cover and refrigerate.
SERVING SUGGESTION: Serve with corn bread (page 192) or warm flour or corn tortillas, heated according to package directions and lightly brushed with melted butter.

Chipotle chilies in adobo sauce are smoked jalapeños, very hot and savory. They are available, canned, in the supermarket; check the Hispanic, international, or "gourmet" aisle. Transfer the unused portion to a jar or other container; covered and refrigerated, it will keep for weeks. Consider adding a bit of chipotles in adobo to any chili or other Mexican dish you make. They add great depth of flavor.

◆ Tortellini Soup ◆

YIELD: 6 to 8 servings.

This recipe was sent to me by Chris Vineis, a friend since grade school and working mother of two in Columbus, Ohio. Chris, who runs her own consulting business, is a dedicated cook who would never think (as I would) of using store-bought chicken stock or buying grated Parmesan for this dish. I adapted her recipe, which she had adapted from Cold Weather Cooking *by Sarah Leah Chase (Workman, 1990). To make up for my laziness in the chicken stock and grated cheese department, I use a really good-quality broth (an organic broth sold in aseptic packaging at my supermarket) and good quality Parmesan, which I buy shredded in the specialty cheese section.*

4 slices thick-cut bacon, chopped
1 onion, peeled and chopped
3 cloves garlic, peeled and chopped
1 tablespoon dried Italian herb blend
6 cups canned chicken broth or vegetable broth
1 (28-ounce can) crushed tomatoes
8 to 10 ounces fresh or frozen spinach or cheese tortellini
1 (7-ounce) package fresh baby spinach (6 cups), washed and drained
salt and pepper
grated Parmesan cheese

IN A LARGE pot set over medium-high heat, cook the bacon until the fat is rendered and the bacon is cooked, but not crisp. Add the onion, garlic, and herbs and cook, stirring, until the onions begin to turn a bit brown, about 10 minutes. Add the broth and tomatoes, cover and bring to a boil. Add the tortellini and cook until just "al dente" ("to the tooth"), that is, not raw-tasting but still firm (consult the package directions for time). Add the spinach and cook until wilted, about 3 minutes. Serve hot, with grated Parmesan.

◆ Simple Fish Soup ◆

YIELD: 4 to 6 servings.

This uncomplicated soup showcases the ingredients without an overwhelming "fishy" flavor.

> 2 tablespoons olive oil or unsalted butter
> 1 onion, peeled and chopped
> 2 stalks celery, trimmed and chopped
> 2 cloves garlic, peeled and chopped
> 1 pound potatoes, scrubbed and cut into small pieces (3 cups)
> 5 cups water and 2 cubes fish bouillon (available in supermarkets) OR 5
>   cups canned chicken broth
> 6 ounces tomatoes diced to make 1 cup, or 1 cup canned diced toma-
>   toes
> 1½ pound any white-fleshed fish, such as haddock, cod, scrod, pollock,
>   or ocean perch, cut into small chunks
> pepper
> chopped fresh parsley, for serving

HEAT THE OIL or melt the butter in a saucepan set over medium heat and cook the onion, celery, and garlic, stirring, about 3 minutes. Add the potatoes and stir. Add the water and bouillon, or the broth, along with the tomatoes; cover and bring to a simmer. Cook until potatoes are almost tender (5 to 10 minutes, unless you have cut large chunks).

Add the fish and simmer for about 10 minutes, or until the fish flakes easily. Season with pepper. Serve with chopped parsley, if desired.

MAKE AHEAD: The soup can be prepared to the point just before the fish is added, then covered and refrigerated up to 1 day. Reheat the soup, add the fish, and cook as directed.

Barbarians at the Plate

Real Food for Real Kids

THE PUBLIC RELATIONS representative for a soup company once called me to pitch a story on kids and soup. Her idea was to make soup more enticing by adding . . . gummi worms.

Call me close-minded. Call me a food snob. I thought it was one of the worst ideas I had ever heard.

It seems to me that food manufacturers, with parents' complicity, are hell-bent on turning every meal into dessert, and our kids into mealtime tyrants. All kinds of foods—from breakfast cereals to frozen dinner entrées—are cut into cartoon shapes, tricked out in colored sprinkles, or coated in chocolate. The end result is two-fold: First, we're giving kids way too much power at the grocery store and the dinner table; and second, we are denying them the experience—and the pleasure—of sampling all the edible glories of the earth.

I spoke to a grade-school teacher in Vermont who has cleaned and cooked squid in her classroom, and smoked salmon and cooked venison sausage, and found her students to be incredibly receptive. "One of them told me he eats pizza every single night for supper," she said. "And I mean *every* night. And there he was eating squid and loving it. Wouldn't his Mom have been surprised?' "

It probably never occurred to Mom to put some squid on the table (or on the pizza) but that's just the point. We've so narrowly defined what kids "will" and "won't" eat that we've excluded hundreds of wonderful, natural foods from their lives. My older daughter shocked me when, as a young child, she said that the grape she was eating didn't "taste like grape." What she meant, of course, was that it didn't taste like that industrial "grape" flavor of a lollipop. So in addition to becoming worried about my daughter's nutrition, I started worrying about her palate: What if she grew up actually preferring the "grape flavor" to actual grapes?

And I worry about my children's perspective on eating in general: If every meal is a party, how will they learn to truly celebrate?

It's our job, as adults, to help kids understand that that when it comes to food—or to life, for that matter—"fun" does not come in a box, or have sprinkles on it or marshmallows mixed in. Real fun can be had by trying something new, stretching a little, allowing ourselves to be surprised.

So bring on the soup. But hold the gummi worms.

◆ Meatless Chili ◆

YIELD: 4 servings.
Vegetarian friendly (of course)

Bulgur, also called "bulgur wheat," is a nutritious staple in the Middle East and is available in many supermarkets as well as in natural foods stores. Here, it supplies the bulk and texture of meat in this flavorful chili.

1 tablespoon canola oil or other vegetable oil
3 onions, peeled and chopped
1 (4-ounce) can mild or hot chilies, drained and chopped
1 tablespoon chili powder or to taste
2 teaspoons paprika
1 teaspoon ground cumin
1 teaspoon sugar
1 (28-ounce) can plus 1 (14-ounce) can chopped tomatoes, with juice
2 (15-ounce) cans red kidney beans, drained and rinsed, or 1 (15-ounce)
    can kidney beans and 1 (15-ounce can) hominy (with liquid)
⅓ cup bulgur
salt and pepper
For serving (any or all): chopped scallions, chopped chili peppers,
    chopped onions, chopped fresh cilantro, low-fat or no-fat sour cream,
    shredded regular or reduced-fat Cheddar, Colby, or Jack cheese, hot
    sauce.

HEAT THE OIL in a large pot set over medium heat. Add the onions and cook, stirring, until beginning to soften, about 5 minutes. Add the remaining ingredients, and simmer until the chili is thickened, about 20 minutes. Taste and adjust seasonings.

Serve hot with the toppings of your choice.

INCREASE THE VEGGIES: Chop 1 or 2 carrots and a bell pepper (any color) and cook with the onions.
MAKE AHEAD: Up to 2 days. Cool, cover and refrigerate.
FREEZE: Up to 2 months.
SERVING SUGGESTION: Serve with corn bread (page 192) or warm flour or corn tortillas, heated according to package directions and lightly brushed with melted butter.

Barbarians at the Plate

◆ Salade Niçoise ◆

YIELD: 4 to 6 servings.

This dish has its origins in the city of Nice, on the French Riviera, where I've read that to be considered truly "à la Niçoise" ("as prepared in Nice"), a dish must contain tomatoes, black olives, garlic, and anchovies. This salad fits the bill. The key is to be liberal with the oil and vinegar, and to use the best olive oil you can afford. My kids have always loved this salad, probably because I arrange it on a platter and they can pick and choose what they want. (Since neither will eat tuna or anchovies, I put these items way at the edge of the platter, or on a separate plate.)

1½ pounds small red potatoes, scrubbed but not peeled
salt and pepper
good-quality olive oil
4 large eggs
¾ to 1 pound green beans, trimmed
red wine vinegar, preferably balsamic
1 cup black olives, preferably Niçoise olives, pitted (see note)
¾ pound tomatoes (2 regular tomatoes), cut into wedges, or 2 cups
    cherry or grape tomatoes
2 tablespoons drained capers
2 cloves garlic, peeled and finely chopped
2 (6.5-ounce) cans tuna packed in water, drained
1 (2-ounce) can anchovy filets, drained (optional)
fresh basil leaves, shredded (optional)

IF USING LITTLE, golf-ball-sized new potatoes, leave them whole. If using larger red potatoes, cut them in halves or quarters. Fit a large pot with a steamer basket and pour in water to a depth of 1 to 2 inches. Bring the water to a boil and steam the potatoes until tender when pierced with a fork, about 20 to 25 minutes depending on how large they are. (If using the tiny new potatoes, start checking after about 10 minutes.) Drain and arrange on a serving platter. Season immediately with salt and pepper and drizzle generously with olive oil.

Meanwhile, bring a pot of water to a boil, and boil the eggs for 10 minutes. Remove them with a slotted spoon and set them aside to cool, but keep the water boiling. Add the green beans and cook until just tender, 5 to 10 minutes, depending on the thickness of your beans. Drain and arrange on the platter with the potatoes. Season with salt and pepper and drizzle with olive oil and vinegar.

Scatter the olives, tomatoes, capers, and garlic over the potatoes and green beans. Add the tuna, in a mound, and drizzle generously with oil. Add the anchovies, if using, to the tuna mound. Shell and halve or quarter the hard-boiled eggs, place around the edge of the platter, and season them with salt and pepper. Scatter basil leaves (if using) over all.

Serve at room temperature with lots of good bread for sopping up the oil and vinegar.

MAKE AHEAD: The potatoes, eggs, and beans can be cooked in the morning; store them in the refrigerator and assemble the salad in the evening.

PITTING OLIVES

Place olives on a cutting board, a few at a time, and press down on them with the flat side of a wide knife (cleaver or chef's knife). If you don't have time to do this, warn your family that the olives have pits.

◆ BLT Salad ◆

YIELD: 4 servings.

Tell your kids you are serving them a sandwich-salad. If they find this funny enough, they may eat it.

FOR THE DRESSING:
- ½ cup buttermilk
- ¼ cup regular or reduced-fat mayonnaise
- 1 teaspoon onion powder
- 1 teaspoon dried dill
- generous pinch of sugar
- salt and pepper

FOR THE SALAD:
- 1 (8-to-10-ounce) iceberg, romaine, or combination lettuce (about 8 cups) washed and drained
- ¾ pound tomatoes (2 regular tomatoes), cut into wedges, or 2 cups grape tomatoes
- ½ bell pepper (any color), seeded and chopped

Barbarians at the Plate

1 cup cubed or shredded regular or reduced-fat Cheddar, Colby, or Jack cheese

¼ to ½ red onion, peeled and chopped

4 hard-boiled eggs, peeled and chopped (optional)

12 slices bacon, cooked (see box)

4 slices whole grain bread

mayonnaise

Make the dressing: Combine all the ingredients in a small bowl or in a jar with a lid, whisking or shaking to mix well. Taste and adjust seasonings. Cover and refrigerate.

Make the salad: In a large bowl, toss the lettuce, tomatoes, bell pepper, cheese, onion, and eggs (if using). Add the bacon and drizzle with the dressing and toss.

Toast the bread and spread it lightly with mayonnaise. Cut into cubes and add to the salad. Drizzle with more dressing and toss.

Make Ahead: The dressing can be made up to four days ahead. Whisk or shake well to mix before using. Cook the eggs and refrigerate them in their shells for up to 1 day.

Cooking Bacon

- ◆ **In the microwave:** Separate the slices and place them on several layers of paper towels on a microwave-safe plate. Cover with more towels. Cook on HIGH for 2 minutes, then check; if not crispy, continue to cook, checking at 30-second intervals.
- ◆ **In the broiler or toaster oven:** Adjust the broiler rack so it is 5 inches from the heat source. Place the bacon on a rack set in a shallow pan and broil, turning often, for 10 to 15 minutes. The fat will accumulate in the drip pan.
- ◆ **In the skillet:** Set a skillet over medium heat and cook the bacon, turning once, until crisp, about 15 minutes. Transfer to a plate lined with paper towels and drain.

◆ Pizza Salad ◆

YIELD: about 6 servings.

Kids will like the name, which is a giant step toward getting them to like the salad. If they don't like mushrooms or olives or tomatoes, make the salad in stages and serve out their portions before you add the offending ingredients.

1 pound penne, rotini (corkscrew), or farfalle (bow-tie) pasta or other
    pasta of similar size

1 tablespoon red wine vinegar

3 tablespoons olive oil

2 cups shredded regular or part-skim mozzarella cheese

6 ounces cubed pepperoni (a generous cup), or loose, cooked Italian
    sausage, drained (see note)

½ red or green bell pepper, seeded and chopped

1 (8-ounce) jar marinated mushrooms (available in the condiment,
    canned-vegetable, or "international" aisle of the supermarket)

1 (2.25-ounce) can sliced pitted black olives, drained

¾ pound regular tomatoes (2 tomatoes), cut into wedges, or 2 cups
    grape or cherry tomatoes

dried oregano

dried basil

hot red pepper flakes (optional)

BRING A LARGE pot (4 quarts) of salted water (page 96) to a boil. Add the pasta, cover the pot and bring the water back to a boil. Remove the cover and cook, boiling, according to package directions for "al dente" ("to the tooth"); that is, not raw-tasting but still firm. Drain.

Place the pasta in a bowl and immediately drizzle with the vinegar and oil. Toss. Add the cheese and pepperoni (or cooked sausage) and toss again. The cheese will begin to melt a bit. Add the remaining ingredients, sprinkling just a bit of oregano and basil and hot pepper flakes (if using) over all. Toss to combine.

NOTE: You can buy pepperoni already sliced, but I think the pepperoni is chewier if you cut it into thick rounds and then quarter the rounds. Remember to peel the casing off the pepperoni before you chop it.

MAKE AHEAD: The salad can be made up to a day ahead, but add the tomatoes at the last minute. Store covered, in the refrigerator, and allow to come to room temperature before serving.

SERVING SUGGESTION: Serve with warm, store-bought, or homemade focaccia (flatbread; page 151) to enhance the pizza-ness of this meal.

◆ Meat-and-Potato Salad ◆

YIELD: 4 to 6 servings.

My friend Susan Stuck of Charlotte, Vermont, developed this recipe. In her version the potatoes are cooked whole and then sliced. The texture is better her way, but my version is faster. Take your pick.

This is a great way to make a relatively small piece of beef go a long way. You can use leftover roast beef or steak, or grill a small sirloin or 2 New York strip steaks.

FOR THE DRESSING:

2 tablespoons Dijon mustard
juice of 1 lemon
3 tablespoons red or white wine vinegar
salt and pepper
½ cup olive oil
¼ cup mixed chopped fresh herbs—flat-leaf parsley, chives, scallion greens, and/or thyme

FOR THE SALAD:

2½ to 3 pounds potatoes, preferably Yukon Gold, scrubbed but not peeled
¼ cup white wine, dry vermouth (see page 211) or white wine vinegar
¼ cup canned beef or vegetable broth
½ red onion, peeled, thinly sliced, and separated into rings
8 to 12 ounces cold grilled or roast beef, thinly sliced
3 or 4 sour gherkins, thinly sliced, or 1 tablespoon capers, drained
6 ounces tomato (1 regular tomato), cut into wedges, or 1 cup cherry or grape tomatoes

MAKE THE DRESSING: Combine all the ingredients in a small bowl or in a jar with a lid, whisking or shaking well to mix. Taste and adjust the seasonings. Cover and refrigerate.

Fit a large pot with a steamer basket and pour in water to a depth of 1 to 2 inches. Bring the water to a boil while you cut the potatoes into 1½-inch cubes. Steam the potatoes until tender, 15 to 20 minutes. Drain. Transfer to a mixing bowl and sprinkle with the white wine (or vermouth or vinegar) and broth. Toss gently and set aside to allow the potatoes to absorb the liquid.

Put the sliced onion in a small bowl and add enough of the dressing to coat. Toss the sliced beef and gherkins or capers with the remaining dressing. Set aside to marinate for a few minutes.

When you are ready to serve the salad, spread the potatoes on a platter. Sprinkle with salt. Top with the sliced beef and gherkins alternating with the sliced onions. Garnish the edge of the platter with tomato wedges and any optional vegetables.

SUBSTITUTIONS AND ADDITIONS: Substitute your favorite Italian or balsamic dressing for the dressing here, enlivening it with the fresh herbs. Add green beans, broccolini (also sold as "baby broccoli"), or beets, cooked and cooled, or canned or marinated artichoke hearts, drained. Toss them with the dressing, as you did the onions, before serving.

MAKE AHEAD: The dressing can be made—up to the point that the fresh herbs are added—up to four days ahead. Cover and refrigerate. Add the herbs and whisk, or shake well before using.

THE COOKBOOK SHELF:

Chesman, Andrea. *Salad Suppers*. Houghton Mifflin, 1999. Out of print, but worth looking for.

Fiszer, Louise and Ferrary, Jeannette. *A Good Day For Salad*. Chronicle Books, 1999. Also: *A Good Day For Soup*, 1996.

Hanson, Jeanne. *The Everything Soup Cookbook*. Adams Media, 2002.

Schlesinger, Chris and Willoughby, John. *Lettuce in Your Kitchen*. William Morrow, 1996. Out of print, but worth looking for.

Schwartz, Arthur. *Soup Suppers: More Than 100 Main-Course Soups and 40 Accompaniments*. HarperPerennial, 1994.

Stovetop Suppers:
Skillet Dinners,
Stir-frys, and Pasta

STOVETOP SAVVY

MY NEIGHBOR JAMIE Cherington says that when her kids were young, she used to come through the door from work, grab a skillet, and start cooking with her coat still on. It's actually not a bad strategy: If you put the onions on to sauté, and the meat to defrost in the microwave, you can buy yourself a few minutes to get your coat off and maybe even change out of your work clothes.

Here are some other hints to speed stovetop suppers along:

❖ Preheat the skillet or wok. If you watch chefs cook, they almost always throw a pan on the burner before adding oil or butter. Allowing the pan to preheat makes everything cook more quickly.

❖ Assemble ingredients and utensils before hand. This is a good idea for any culinary project, but is absolutely necessary for stir-frys and for grilling; once the cooking starts, you had better be able to move fast.

❖ Cut all vegetables that you are sautéing to approximately the same size so they will cook at the same time.

❖ If you don't have a wok, use a deep skillet instead.

❖ For cooking pasta:

- ◆ Buy dry pasta made with durum wheat semolina; it produces a firmer cooked pasta because of the high gluten content. You can use fresh pasta, but it cooks *very* quickly and is easily overcooked.

- ◆ A large amount of water helps all of the pasta cook at the same rate; boil at least 4 to 5 quarts.

- ◆ Salt the pasta water: My mom always did, but I thought it just increased the salt content of the dish. A chef has persuaded me that salting the water not only adds taste but helps the pasta retain its shape. Once again, it turns out that Mom knows best. For 4 to 5 quarts of water, add 2 to 3 teaspoons salt, once the water has come to a boil and before you add the pasta.

- ◆ Add the pasta all at once. Then raise the heat and stir briefly with a wooden spoon. Cover the pot until the water returns to a boil, then uncover it for the duration of the cooking time, stirring occasionally to keep the pasta from sticking. Drain and toss immediately with sauce. There should be no need to run the pasta under water.

Dinner with the Brancos
BELLEVUE, OHIO

THE SCREEN DOOR to the kitchen of the Branco house opens and the smell of chicken and chili peppers wafts out. Ben Branco, fifteen, a broad-shouldered young man wearing a Bellevue Football T-shirt and a base-ball cap, welcomes a visitor with a firm handshake. A greeting from Ben's thir-teen-year-old brother, Dustin, is drowned by the whirring of a food processor as it transforms fresh peppers and tomatoes into salsa. Courtney, age ten, is setting the table for dinner. It's "Mexican Night" at the Brancos.

"Theme" nights, planned menus, cooking contests—the Branco kids are involved on a daily basis in cooking. Their mom, Karen, has made a point of it, especially since her husband, Mark, died in 1996.

"The kids have been amazing," says Karen, who lost the man she describes as the "love of her life" to a sudden and largely unexplained illness. She was thirty-five when she found herself "suddenly thrown into single motherhood," with three kids under the age of eight.

The Brancos live in a tidy, two-story home with a brick facade and a wrap-around porch off the tired-looking main street of Bellevue, Ohio, a town probably most famous for being twenty-two miles from Sandusky. Karen grew up in Bellevue, as did Mark, who worked in a local fertilizer plant before his death. She is first to credit her relatives—especially her mom and her dad—and her church with helping her survive her grief and loss. But she is also proud of the way her two boys (Courtney was only two when Mark died) began taking on household chores, including cooking. Nowadays, they often make dinner; Ben also cleans the kitchen, Courtney vacuums and sets the table, and Dustin (who "hates" emptying the dishwasher) takes out the trash. Ben has also stepped up to other household chores, such as balancing his mother's checkbook and paying bills.

"I would never consider myself an organized person, but I've had to become one, I guess," says Karen. She now keeps a shopping list on her computer, and prints out the week's menus, posting them on the refrigerator door. A kitchen cabinet serves as the pantry and is crammed with canned goods. A bank of cookbooks, including a large white binder containing family favorites, spills out of a bookcase in the dining room.

When Mark died, the congregation of St. Paul's United Church of Christ kept Karen and her children fed, bringing in meals—"even several months later," recalls Karen. Back at work, as a finance clerk at the local hospital, and learning to manage alone, Karen relied heavily on her slow cooker so that something was ready when she and the children returned home from work, school, and day care.

Nowadays, the boys are likely to start a meal when they arrive home after school, consulting the posted menu so they know what's planned. This week's menu: chicken enchiladas tonight, spaghetti tomorrow, then, in sequence, pork chops, chicken Parmigiana, leftovers. Dustin, who is thinking of becoming a professional chef, watches the cooking shows with his mother and won a prize in a school contest with his grandmother's recipe for apple pie. He sometimes grinds his own meat for another family favorite, meatballs (and meatball subs).

"Meals are important, and not just for what you are eating," says Karen. "I wanted the kids to get in the habit of sitting down with each other and having a meal. They get a chance to hear each other's stories. When you are forced to sit next to that brother or sister you just had a big fight with, well . . . it makes you more tolerant."

The family manages to squeeze dinner in between other activities: Karen teaches yoga, and is president of the Christian Education Board at her church, sews quilts, and has recently taken up the craft of stamping. Ben has played football (after an injury, he was planning on switching to tennis) and is active in high school theater (he played the police inspector in *Les Misérables*). Courtney pitches and plays outfield on her softball team; Dustin is a center on the junior high football team. All three Branco kids are involved in church activities, including choir.

The family eats, enthusiastically talking about school, about recipes, about the possibility of the three kids attending church camp in the summer. After cleaning up, Ben and Courtney grab baseball gloves and a softball and head outside to play catch. Dustin settles in the den watching television. Karen sits in the living room, near a photograph of Mark—warm smile, salt-and-pepper beard—taken the Thanksgiving before he died. "He used to do all the kitchen cleanup," she says. "After he died, I bought a dishwasher."

She pauses. "I hope it goes without saying I'd rather have him."

SKILLET, STIR-FRY, AND PASTA RECIPES

❖

BONELESS, SKINLESS CHICKEN BREASTS FOUR WAYS

Boneless, skinless chicken breasts always *seem* like a good idea. They are a blank slate, absorbing and showcasing the ingredients you cook them with, which can be both a blessing and a curse. You take them out of the wrapper and throw them in a skillet and then you say: *Now* what?

Here is a basic recipe for sautéing chicken breasts, along with four recipes for variations. Remember that a full chicken breast equals two of the pieces that many people refer to as one breast. Thus, the recipe below calls for "chicken breast halves." All recipes yield four servings.

◆ Basic Sautéed Chicken Breasts ◆

YIELD: 4 servings

4 boneless, skinless chicken breast halves (1½ to 2 pounds)
⅓ cup all-purpose flour
1 teaspoon salt
½ teaspoon pepper
2 tablespoons olive or canola oil

PLACE THE CHICKEN breasts between two sheets of waxed paper or plastic wrap and flatten by pounding with a rolling pin or the bottom of a heavy skillet.

Combine the flour, salt, and pepper on a plate or in a heavy-duty plastic bag, stirring or shaking to mix. Dredge or shake each chicken breast in the seasoned flour until coated. Shake to remove excess coating and set aside.

Heat the oil in a skillet set over medium-high heat. When hot, add the chicken breasts and cook until they are browned on both sides and no longer pink in the center (slice one to test), 6 to 8 minutes per side. Proceed with one of the variations on the following pages.

Barbarians at the Plate

◆ Lemony Chicken Breasts ◆

YIELD: 4 servings.

There's nothing bland about chicken breasts when they are topped with this flavorful sauce.

    1 recipe Basic Sautéed Chicken Breasts (page 100)
    ½ onion, peeled and chopped
    1 or 2 cloves garlic, peeled and finely chopped
    ⅓ cup dry white wine, white vermouth, or chicken broth
    zest of 1 lemon
    juice of 2 lemons
    ¼ cup drained capers

REMOVE THE BREASTS from the skillet and set them on a platter. Cover the platter with aluminum foil and set aside.

Add the onion and garlic to the skillet and cook, stirring, until soft, about 3 minutes. Add the wine, zest, lemon juice, and capers. Bring the sauce to a simmer and cook for a few minutes until the sauce thickens slightly. Pour the sauce over the chicken and serve.

NOTE: This recipe also works well on veal cutlets.

◆ Chicken Breasts with Creamy ◆ Mustard Sauce

YIELD: 4 servings

The cream mellows the piquant flavors of mustard and tarragon.

    1 recipe Basic Sautéed Chicken Breasts (page 100)
    ½ onion or 2 shallots, peeled and finely chopped
    ½ cup heavy (whipping) cream or half-and-half
    2 tablespoons Dijon mustard
    1 teaspoon dried tarragon

REMOVE THE BREASTS from the skillet and set them on a platter. Cover the platter with aluminum foil and set aside.

Add the onion (or shallots) to the skillet and cook, stirring, about 2 minutes. Add the cream, mustard, and tarragon. Cook, whisking, until thickened, about 1 minute. Pour over the chicken and serve.

NOTE: This also makes a good sauce for fish.

◆ Chicken Breasts with ◆
Apricot Glaze

YIELD: 4 servings.

All you need is jam and mustard—what could be more simple?

> ⅓ cup apricot or peach jam
> 3 tablespoons Dijon mustard
> pepper
> 1 recipe Basic Sautéed Chicken Breasts (page 100), prepared to the
> point where you have just turned the chicken breasts over to cook on
> the other side

IN A SMALL bowl combine the jam and mustard and stir well. Season with pepper to taste.

Spoon the glaze over the just-turned chicken breasts. Cover the skillet and cook until the glaze is melted and the chicken is no longer pink inside—slice one to test—about 5 minutes. Serve immediately.

NOTE: This recipe also works well on pork chops.

◆ Chicken Breasts ◆
with Orange Chili Glaze

YIELD: 4 servings.

The canned chipotle chiles add a rich, smoky flavor.

> ⅓ cup orange marmalade
> 1 canned chipotle chili in adobo sauce, chopped (page 85)
> salt
> 1 recipe Basic Sautéed Chicken Breasts (page 100), prepared to the point
> where you have just turned the chicken breasts over to cook on the
> other side

IN A SMALL bowl combine the marmalade and the chili, stirring well. Season with salt to taste.

Barbarians at the Plate

Spoon the glaze over the just-turned chicken breasts. Cover the skillet and cook until the glaze is melted and the chicken is no longer pink inside—slice to test—about 5 minutes. Serve immediately.

NOTE: This recipe also works well on steak.

CHICKEN-ON-A-STICK

Carole Naquin, mother of two in Montpelier, Vermont, says this was her go-to recipe when she was desperate: Cut boneless, skinless chicken breasts into 1-inch strips. Thread the strips on skewers, winding them around the skewers as you thread: "This makes them look more interesting," she says. "I think kids respond to the way food looks on the plate." Sprinkle with salt and pepper (Carole uses a garlic-pepper blend) and any other spices that your children like. Sauté in olive oil for perhaps 10 minutes, turning to cook on all sides. Slice to make sure the chicken has cooked through; it should no longer be pink.

Karen Branco of Bellevue, Ohio, dredges chicken strips in flour seasoned with ground cumin, salt, and pepper, and frys them in ½ inch of oil.

◆ Sautéed Ham Steak ◆ with Cabbage and Apples

YIELD: 4 servings.

Cabbage-haters may change their minds when it's cooked with maple syrup, cider and apples.

2 tablespoons canola or other vegetable oil, if needed
1 (1½-pound) ham steak
1 (10-ounce) bag shredded red cabbage (about 5 cups)
1 tart baking apple (such as Granny Smith), cored and chopped
1 cup apple cider or apple juice
2 tablespoons pure maple syrup or brown sugar
salt and pepper

Heat a skillet large enough to hold the ham steak over medium-high heat. If the ham is very lean, heat 1 tablespoon of the oil in the skillet. If there is some fat on the ham, put it in an ungreased skillet.

Cook the ham until beginning to brown on one side, about 7 minutes. Discard any liquid that accumulates in the pan. Turn and cook on the other side until beginning to brown; the edges should be a bit crispy. Transfer the ham to a platter, cover with aluminum foil and keep warm.

If there is some grease in the skillet, add the cabbage and apple. If the skillet seems dry, add the remaining tablespoon of oil first and heat it; then add the cabbage and apple. Pour in the cider (or juice), add the syrup (or brown sugar) and stir to mix. Bring to a boil, reduce the heat to medium low and cook, covered, until the cabbage is tender, about 10 minutes. Season with salt and pepper and serve with the ham.

Serving Suggestion: Serve with corn bread (page 192), plain or cheese grits, or a side of macaroni and cheese (page 110).

◆ Shrimp Creole ◆

Yield: 4 servings.

My mother clipped this recipe from a newspaper years ago, and it's still a family favorite.

4 tablespoons (½ stick) unsalted butter
2 stalks celery, trimmed and chopped
2 cloves garlic, peeled and chopped
1 onion, peeled and chopped
1 green bell pepper, stemmed, seeded, and chopped
1 (28-ounce) can whole tomatoes, chopped, juices reserved
2 teaspoons Worcestershire sauce
several dashes hot sauce (optional)
1 teaspoon dried marjoram
1 pound raw shrimp (see Buying Shrimp, page 59)
3 cups cooked rice (from 1 cup uncooked), or 1 recipe Funji (page 165)
    for serving

Melt the butter in a saucepan set over medium heat. Add the celery, garlic, onion, and bell pepper and cook, stirring, for 5 minutes. Add the tomatoes, reserving some of the juice. Stir in the Worcestershire sauce, hot sauce (if using), and the marjoram. Adjust heat so the mixture simmers;

Barbarians at the Plate

cover and cook for 15 minutes. If the mixture seems too thick, add some of the reserved tomato juice. Add the shrimp and cook until pink, about 5 minutes. Serve hot over rice.

PREP AHEAD: Up to 1 day ahead, chop the celery, garlic, onion, and bell pepper. Cover and refrigerate. Cook the rice. To serve, reheat it on the stovetop or in the microwave.

SERVING SUGGESTION: Serve with sautéed greens (page 172).

MUSSELS TWO WAYS

MUSSELS ARE, BY shellfish standards, incredibly cheap. They are also quick-cooking and delicious. Serve the mussels and sauce alone in warm bowls, or serve them over cooked linguine. Either way, have hunks of bread on hand to mop up the sauce.

◆ Mussels in Spicy Red Sauce ◆

YIELD: 4 servings.

My dad called this dish "Mussels Diavolo" as in "devil." Lots of flavor, lots of spice.

½ cup olive oil
8 cloves garlic, peeled and minced
1 teaspoon hot pepper flakes
1 (28-ounce) can whole, peeled Italian tomatoes in puree
2 tablespoons tomato paste
2 teaspoons dried oregano
1 teaspoon dried basil
¼ cup drained capers
2 tablespoons dry red wine
salt and pepper
4 pounds mussels, bearded and washed (box, page 106)

HEAT THE OIL in a skillet set over medium high heat. Add the garlic and hot pepper and stir, cooking, about 2 minutes. Add all of the remaining ingredients but the mussels, and cook, uncovered, stirring occasionally, for about 15 minutes.

Add the mussels to the hot, bubbling tomato sauce. Cover and cook 8 to 10 minutes, until the mussels have opened. Discard any mussels that remain closed. Stir well so that the tomato sauce and mussel juices are well combined.

◆ Mussels in White Wine ◆

YIELD: 4 servings.

¼ cup olive oil or 4 tablespoons (½ stick) unsalted butter
  (or combination)
4 cloves garlic, peeled and finely chopped
1 onion, peeled and chopped
¾ cup dry white wine or white vermouth
4 pounds mussels, bearded and washed (see box)

HEAT THE OIL or butter (or oil and butter) in a large pot set over medium heat. Add the garlic and onion and cook, stirring, until they begin to soften, about 5 minutes.

Add the wine and mussels, cover the pot and turn the heat to high. Cook 8 to 10 minutes, until the mussels have opened. Discard any mussels that remain closed. Stir well so that the mussel juices and sauce are well combined.

BUYING, STORING, AND CLEANING MUSSELS

One pound of mussels will serve one person.

Store mussels in a bowl or colander, loosely covered with a damp paper towel until ready to use. Do not store in a plastic bag.

It is likely that any mussels you buy in the supermarket will be farm-raised; this means they usually don't have "beards," the tough weedy growths that can be stuck between the shells. If the mussels you buy do have beards, tug them off, using a clean dish towel for a better grip. Rinse the mussels under cold water and discard any that don't close tight when their shells are tapped.

Barbarians at the Plate

◆ Fried Rice ◆

YIELD: 4 to 6 servings.
Vegetarian friendly when made with tofu.

This is a good use for leftover rice; or rice that you have made and frozen (and thawed). I like it for breakfast.

2 eggs
2 teaspoons Asian sesame oil (made with toasted sesame seeds)
3 tablespoons peanut, canola, or other vegetable oil
1 tablespoon chopped, peeled fresh ginger
2 cloves garlic, peeled and chopped
6 scallions, trimmed and chopped (white and green parts)
2 cups finely chopped (¼-inch cubes) vegetables such as broccoli, carrots, and celery
2 cups diced cooked meat (chicken, pork, beef, or lamb)
3 cups leftover rice (from 1 cup uncooked), brown or white, or a combination
soy sauce
1 cup roasted but unsalted peanuts (optional)

IN A SMALL bowl beat the eggs and the sesame oil together with a fork. Set aside.

Heat 1 tablespoon of the oil in a wok or a deep skillet set over high heat. When very hot, add the ginger, garlic, and scallions and stir-fry for about 1 minute. Remove from the wok with a slotted spoon and set aside. Heat the remaining 2 tablespoons oil and add the vegetables, stirring and cooking 2 to 3 minutes. Add the meat and stir to heat through. Add the rice and drizzle with soy sauce. Cook, stirring and tossing the rice with a spatula so that it does not stick. When very hot, add the beaten eggs, cooking and stirring until they look like scrambled eggs but are distributed throughout the rice. Add the peanuts and toss. Serve with extra soy sauce on the side.

VARIATION (TOFU): Drain a 1-pound package of extra-firm tofu and cut into 1-inch cubes. In a bag combine ½ cup cornmeal, ¼ cup all-purpose flour, ½ teaspoon salt and ¼ teaspoon pepper. Working in batches, place the tofu cubes in the bag and shake to coat. Discard extra cornmeal mixture. Increase the total amount of oil in the recipe to 5 tablespoons and, before you fry any vegetables, heat 2 tablespoons of the oil until very hot. Fry the tofu until crisp on all sides, about 4 minutes. Remove from the wok and continue as directed.

◆ Stir-fry with Cashews ◆

YIELD: 4 to 6 servings.

Don't forget to be hyperorganized and have all the ingredients at hand and pre-measured, because stir-frying goes fast.

4 cups broccoli florets
⅔ cup orange juice
2 tablespoons cornstarch
2 tablespoons soy sauce
2 teaspoons rice-wine vinegar or cider vinegar
½ teaspoon Asian chili paste (available in supermarkets, sometimes as "Chili Paste with Garlic") or hot red pepper flakes (optional)
3 tablespoons peanut oil, canola oil, or other vegetable oil
6 scallions, trimmed and chopped
4 cloves garlic, peeled and chopped
1 tablespoon grated peeled fresh ginger
1 pound steak, boneless chicken, or pork, thinly sliced against the grain
1 (8-ounce) can sliced water chestnuts, drained (optional)
1 cup salted, roasted cashews
at least 3 cups cooked rice (from 1 cup uncooked), for serving

BRING A POT of water to a boil. Add the broccoli and cook 2 minutes. Drain and immediately run under cold water to stop the cooking. Set aside.

Combine the orange juice, cornstarch, soy sauce, vinegar, and chili paste (or red pepper flakes) in a small bowl, whisking with a fork to minimize lumps. Set aside.

Heat 1 tablespoon of the oil in a wok or large skillet set over high heat. Add the scallions, garlic, and ginger and cook, stirring, for 30 seconds. Add the broccoli and cook, stir-frying 1 to 2 minutes more. Using a slotted spoon, remove the broccoli mix from the wok. Add the remaining 2 table-spoons of oil and allow it to get hot. Add the beef (or chicken or pork) and stir-fry until cooked through, 3 to 5 minutes. Add the orange juice mixture and cook, stirring, until thickened, about 1 minute. Add the broccoli-scallion-garlic mixture and the water chestnuts (if using) and stir to heat through. Scatter with cashews and serve over rice.

PREP AHEAD: Up to 1 day before, chop and cook the broccoli as directed. Cover and refrigerate. Make the orange juice mixture; cover and refrigerate. Chop the scallions, garlic and ginger and cover and refrigerate. Cook rice for serving (reheat on stovetop or in microwave).

Barbarians at the Plate

SERVING SUGGESTION: Sliced oranges are a healthy dessert, and are often served in Chinese restaurants at the end of a meal. You can also buy fortune cookies at the supermarket.

SHARING THE WORK

COOKING SEEMS MUCH less like hard labor if you share the chores. If your partner hates to cook, perhaps he or she will do the shopping or the cleanup. (Teenagers newly possessed of drivers' licenses will usually be thrilled to be sent to the supermarket; we make it a condition for using the family car.) Even small children can wash lettuce, mix things, and—with supervision, of course—chop vegetables and stir pots.

Nancy Wolf of Glide, Oregon, gave every one in her family—herself, her husband, and her son and daughter (now grown)—responsibility for two dinners a week. The kids took on this responsibility in junior high.

"The deal was: They had to make out a detailed grocery list and cook the meals. Whoever cooked didn't have to clean up that night," says Nancy. If they didn't want to, or couldn't (due to schedules) cook for two nights, they had to make sure that they made enough on the first night for leftovers. "The doubling—sometimes tripling—of recipes helped the kids with their math and with following directions," she says.

They were also quite adventuresome, trying Vietnamese, Korean, Chinese Mexican, and Indian food. "I found they were more likely to try something new if they made it themselves," she says.

Another strategy is to share the cooking with another family. Ellen Brodsky, of Cambridge, Massachusetts, discovered the benefits of this tactic when her kids were little and she would pick them up, along with some friends' children, from day care. In exchange for doing the driving, the friends would often ask Ellen and her two girls to stay for dinner. With a husband whose travel schedule often keeps him away from home, Ellen happily accepted.

"When the girls and I eat at home by ourselves, our level of civility plummets," says Ellen, a documentary filmmaker. "We'll find ourselves eating with our hands." When they eat with friends, she says, "Conversation is more elevated." She said that among her network of working parents, she has shared many "accidental dinners."

Now that the children are older (Emma is five, Mia nearly nine), and the day care run finished, the families still share meals regularly. On a Monday night when I visited, Ellen packed up some fresh strawberries she had found at the market, and some fillet of sole she had marinated in a bottled orange-soy marinade, and drove to the nearby home of Julie Reuben and Lisa Lovett, mothers of 5-year-old Charlotte and 8-year-old

Stovetop Suppers 109

Phoebe. The long dining table was set with a blue cloth and matching cloth napkins. Lisa opened a bottle of chardonnay for the grown-ups ("we don't have wine *every* Monday," said Lisa), and Julie was tossing a huge salad made with lettuce, red peppers, tomatoes, toasted pecans, dried cranberries, and avocados and dressed with a tangy, homemade vinaigrette.

With a filmmaker (Ellen), a Harvard professor (Julie), and a social worker (Lisa) at the table, one would expect a *highly* elevated discussion, but talk centered mostly on the kids. Phoebe, at school in a dual-immersion Spanish-English school, volunteered a song in Spanish from a play entitled *The Girl Who Hugged Trees.*

"I got a solo," she said proudly. Mia reported on "clown class," a program in circus arts offered at her school. Emma discussed the recent loss of her two front teeth. Charlotte, thoughtfully lifting a forkful of dinner to her mouth, said, "Isn't this fish *yummy*?"

When dinner was over, the girls cleared the plates quickly, then dashed outside to play with Sophie, an energetic part-lab, part-who-knows-what. The adults put the food away and began to collect the forks and knives. All of them had, in fact, been used; apparently no one had eaten with their hands.

❖ ❖ ❖

◆ Macaroni and Cheese ◆

YIELD: 4 servings.

A box of mac and cheese requires you to cook the noodles in a pot, add the powdered cheese stuff, milk, and butter (or margarine). This recipe requires you to cook the noodles in a pot, and add flour, cheese, and milk. If you buy the cheese already shredded, this recipe takes exactly the same time to prepare as the boxed kind, but the flavor is way better.

As a bonus, one serving—if made with reduced-fat cheese and low fat (1%) milk—has about one-third of the fat and twice of the protein of the stuff from a box, even when the boxed stuff is prepared with 1% milk.

A newspaper editor I once worked with gave me this recipe when I was trying to meet a deadline and whining that I still had to make dinner. I have always thought of him fondly every time I make this—which, when my kids were little, was at least once a week.

8 ounces (½ pound) elbow noodles or other small-shaped pasta
2 tablespoons all-purpose flour
1 cup regular, reduced-fat, or skim milk
2 cups shredded regular or reduced-fat Cheddar cheese

Barbarians at the Plate

Bring a large pot of salted water (page 96) to a boil over high heat, add the noodles, cover, and bring back to a boil. Remove the cover and cook, boiling, according to package directions for *al dente* ("to the tooth"); that is, not raw-tasting but still firm. Drain well.

Return the noodles to the pot and sprinkle with the flour, stirring well to coat the noodles. Return the pot to the stove, and set the heat to low. Add the milk and stir until slightly thickened, about 2 minutes. Add the cheese and stir until melted and creamy, 2 minutes or so.

Serve hot.

Additions: Add several tablespoons of salsa, drained, when you add the cheese, or add 1 (4-ounce) can of green chilies, drained and chopped. Also:

Add any or all of the following: frozen peas (thawed), frozen chopped bell peppers (thawed), frozen chopped onions (thawed), chopped fresh tomato.

Add chunks of leftover ham or sausage, or crumbled crispy bacon or real bacon bits.

Add a teaspoon of prepared mustard.

Freeze: Up to 1 month.

Seven Quick Pasta Sauces

The beauty of cooking pasta is that it's simple, and both children and adults love it. If the kids don't like the sauce that you are having, serve them first, adding whatever they like on plain noodles (butter and cheese, store-bought spaghetti sauce). This way you're not technically acting like a short-order cook, and everybody's happy.

◆ Barely Cooked Tomato Sauce ◆

YIELD: about 1½ cups, or enough for 1 pound of pasta, cooked.
Vegetarian friendly, when made with vegetable bouillon

1 tablespoon unsalted butter
1 tablespoon olive oil
1 (8-ounce) can tomato sauce
3 tablespoons tomato paste
½ cup of water, or more, if needed
1 beef or vegetable bouillon cube
dried oregano and dried basil

COMBINE ALL OF the ingredients in a saucepan set over low heat, adding
the herbs to your taste. Add more water (if cooking pasta at the same time,
use some of the pasta-cooking water) until the sauce is the consistency
you like, at least 15 minutes.

> **IF YOU HAVE TIME:** Peel and finely chop an onion and a clove
> or two of garlic. Heat the butter and olive oil and add the onion and
> garlic and cook, stirring, until it begins to soften, about 5 minutes.
> Proceed with the recipe.
> **ADDITIONS:** Add about ¼ teaspoon hot pepper flakes for a bit of
> zing. For a heftier sauce, add ½ pound of cooked ground beef,
> turkey, pork, veal, or a combination.

◆ No-Cook Tomato Sauce ◆

YIELD: 4 cups, enough for 1 pound of pasta.

Use the best-quality olive oil you can afford, and make sure the tomatoes are really ripe.

1½ pounds tomatoes (4 regular tomatoes), coarsely chopped to make 4
    cups
½ cup good-quality extra-virgin olive oil or more as needed
1 tablespoon balsamic vinegar
salt, preferably coarse salt such as kosher salt or sea salt
coarsely ground black pepper (available in the spice aisle of the super-
    market, if you don't own a peppermill)
a pinch of ground white pepper (optional)
chopped fresh herbs such as oregano, basil, or parsley

IN A MEDIUM bowl, toss all the ingredients together. Let sit at room temperature for at least 15 minutes.

Barbarians at the Plate

◆ Tuna Topping for Pasta ◆

YIELD: About 1½ cups, or enough for 1 pound of pasta, cooked.

When my friend Mario's fourteen-year-old son Paolo came to stay with us from Rome for two weeks one summer, he lived on pasta and tuna. I thought he was crazy, until I tried it.

> ¼ cup extra-virgin olive oil, plus more if needed
> 2 (6.5-ounce) cans tuna (drained)
> hot red pepper flakes
> chopped tomatoes (optional)
> chopped fresh basil (optional)
> salt and pepper

IN A MEDIUM bowl, toss all the ingredients together.

◆ Lemon Sauce for Pasta ◆

YIELD: About ½ cup, or enough for ½ pound pasta, cooked.

The fresh flavors in this sauce really wake up the taste buds.

> ¼ cup fresh lemon juice
> 2 tablespoons soy sauce
> 1 to 2 teaspoons chopped, peeled fresh ginger
> 2 teaspoons Asian sesame oil (made with toasted sesame seeds)
> 1 garlic clove, finely chopped
> chopped fresh cilantro
> zest from 1 lemon (optional)

IN A SMALL bowl, combine all of the ingredients.

◆ Chickpeas and Spinach ◆
Pasta Sauce

YIELD: About 2 cups, or enough for 1 pound of pasta, cooked.

You may want to use some of the pasta-cooking water in making this sauce, for added flavor and liquid. Remember to reserve a cup or so when you drain the pasta.

¼ cup olive oil, plus more if needed
3 garlic cloves, peeled and chopped
¼ teaspoon hot red pepper flakes (optional)
1 (19-ounce) can of chickpeas (garbanzo beans), drained and rinsed
1 (10-ounce) package chopped, frozen spinach, thawed and drained
cooking water from pasta
grated Parmesan cheese, for serving

HEAT THE OIL in a skillet set over medium heat. Add the garlic and hot pepper flakes (if using) and cook, stirring, about 2 minutes. Add the chickpeas and spinach and cook, stirring until heated through. Make the topping more "saucelike" by adding more oil or some of the pasta-cooking water, or both.

Toss with pasta and serve with grated Parmesan.

◆ Sesame-Peanut Sauce for Pasta ◆

YIELD: About 1 cup, or enough for ¾ pound pasta, cooked and chilled.

There's a reason this dish seems to turn up at every potluck supper: it's delicious and everyone seems to like it.

1 tablespoon Asian sesame oil (made with toasted sesame seeds)
½ cup tahini (sesame paste) or smooth peanut butter
1 tablespoon honey
2 tablespoons soy sauce
1 tablespoon rice wine vinegar or cider vinegar
dash hot sauce
hot water, if needed

COMBINE ALL INGREDIENTS, thinning the sauce with hot water if needed. Taste and add more of anything as needed. Serve slightly chilled or at room temperature.

Barbarians at the Plate

ADDITIONS: Chopped scallion greens or chives; cooked shredded chicken; chopped red bell pepper.

◆ Anchovy Sauce for Pasta ◆

YIELD: About 1½ cups, or enough for 1 pound pasta, cooked.

If you love anchovies this dish is for you. If you don't, skip it.

½ cup olive oil
8 cloves garlic, peeled and chopped
¼ teaspoon hot red pepper flakes
1 (2-ounce) can flat anchovy fillets packed in oil, drained and chopped
1 (10-ounce) package frozen, chopped spinach, thawed and drained well

HEAT THE OIL in a skillet set over medium heat. Add the garlic and cook, stirring, until beginning to soften, about 5 minutes. Do not let the garlic brown. Add the red pepper flakes and the anchovies and stir until the anchovies more or less dissolve. Add the spinach and stir to heat through.

❖ ❖ ❖

◆ Pasta with Chicken, Sun-Dried ◆ Tomatoes and Capers

YIELD: 4 to 6 generous servings.

This is an absolute favorite at our house, based on a dish served to us by Carol Beatty Owens, a good friend and great cook in our neighborhood. It will cook in about the time it takes to bring a pot of water to a boil and cook the pasta. You can make this sauce in stages, serving the "picky" family members before any ingredients they object to are added.

1 pound pasta (linguine, bow ties, or any other)
4 tablespoons olive oil
2 to 4 cloves garlic, peeled and chopped
3 or 4 boneless, skinless chicken breast halves (about 1½ pounds total),
    cut into bite-sized pieces
1 teaspoon dried oregano
1 teaspoon dried basil
½ teaspoon dried hot red pepper flakes (optional)
1 (8-ounce) can tomato sauce
1 (10-ounce) jar sun-dried tomatoes, packed in oil (see note)
2 (6-ounce) jars marinated artichoke hearts, drained
2 tablespoons capers
½ cup pitted black olives, preferably Calamata olives
salt and pepper
grated Parmesan cheese, for serving

BRING A LARGE pot (4 quarts) of salted water (page 96) to a boil. Add the pasta, cover the pot and bring the water back to a boil. Remove the cover and cook, boiling, according to package directions for al dente ("to the tooth"); that is, not raw-tasting but still firm. Drain.

Meanwhile heat the oil in a skillet set over medium heat. Add the garlic and chicken and cook about 10 minutes (depending on the size of the chicken pieces) until the chicken is no longer pink inside; slice a piece to test.

Add all of the remaining ingredients, reduce heat to a simmer, cover and cook for 15 minutes or more.

Serve over pasta and pass the grated Parmesan.

NOTE: Dried tomatoes packed in oil are expensive, but quick. You can buy dried tomatoes loose or packaged in small quantities. Soften them by soaking them in very hot water for about 20 minutes, or by putting them in water in a microwave-safe bowl and nuking them for 20 seconds on HIGH.

Barbarians at the Plate

◆ Veggie Home Fries ◆

YIELD: 4 to 6 servings.
Vegetarian-friendly

This is another recipe from my friends Jimmy and Maya Kennedy at River Run restaurant in Plainfield, Vermont. I've taken a number of shortcuts here that a chef like Jimmy would never take, but the dish is still delicious. This is also a great way to use leftover, cooked potatoes.

> 2 pounds potatoes, raw or cooked
> 3 to 4 tablespoons canola or other vegetable oil
> 1 onion, peeled and chopped (optional, but nice)
> salt and pepper
> 4 cups frozen mixed vegetables, cooked according to package directions
> 1½ to 2 cups shredded regular or reduced-fat Cheddar, Colby, or Jack cheese
> hot sauce, for serving

IF USING RAW potatoes: Fit a large pot with a steamer basket and pour in water to a depth of 1 to 2 inches. Bring the water to a boil while you cut the potatoes into ½-to-1-inch cubes. (The smaller you cut them, the quicker they will cook.) Steam the potatoes for 10 to 15 minutes, until very tender when pierced with a fork. Drain. If using cooked potatoes, cut them into small cubes.

Heat 1 tablespoon of the oil in a large, broiler-proof skillet set over medium high heat and cook the onions (if using), stirring, until they begin to soften, about 5 minutes. Remove with a slotted spoon and set aside. Add the remaining 3 tablespoons oil, allow it to get hot, and add the potatoes, seasoning them with salt and pepper. Cook the potatoes until they are crisp on one side, about 10 minutes. Flip and cook on the other side, seasoning that side of the potatoes as well.

While the potatoes are cooking, set an oven rack about 5 inches from the heat source of your broiler, and preheat the broiler.

Top the potatoes with the vegetables and top the vegetables with the cheese. Slide the skillet under the broiler, and broil until the cheese is melted, bubbling and beginning to brown, about 3 minutes. Serve with hot sauce on the side.

FOR THE CARNIVORES: Omit the oil and cook 4 strips bacon, chopped, in the skillet. When crisp, remove and set aside. Substitute the bacon fat for the oil, and add the crumbled bacon to the potatoes when you add the cheese.

◆ Potato and Bacon Frittata ◆

YIELD: 4 servings.

A frittata is like an omelet, only heftier. If you have any leftover, cooked potatoes on hand, the meal will be even quicker to prepare.

8 eggs
salt and pepper
¾ pound potatoes, raw or cooked
4 strips thick-cut bacon, chopped
1 or 2 tablespoons olive oil or unsalted butter, if needed
½ onion, peeled and chopped
6 ounces tomato (1 regular tomato), chopped, or 1 cup cherry or grape
    tomatoes, halved
1 cup shredded regular or reduced-fat Cheddar or Jack cheese

LINE A PLATE with paper towels. Beat the eggs together in a large bowl. Season with salt and pepper and set aside.

If using raw potatoes: Fit a large pot with a steamer basket and pour in water to a depth of 1 to 2 inches. Bring the water to a boil while you cut the potatoes into ½-to-1-inch cubes. (The smaller you cut them, the quicker they will cook.) Steam the potatoes for 10 to 15 minutes, until very tender when pierced with a fork. Drain. If using cooked potatoes, cut them into small cubes.

While potatoes are cooking, cook the bacon in a large, broiler-proof skillet set over high heat, stirring until fat is rendered and the bacon is crisp. Using a slotted spoon, transfer the bacon to the prepared plate.

Add the onion to the skillet and cook, stirring, 3 minutes. If the pan looks dry, add the oil or butter. Add the potatoes, season generously with salt and pepper and cook until starting to brown, about 5 minutes. Scatter the bacon and tomatoes over the potatoes and cook, stirring, for about 3 minutes, until tomatoes start to soften.

Position a rack about 6 inches from the source of heat in the broiler, and preheat the broiler.

Pour the eggs over the mixture and cook, stirring and tilting the pan so the eggs spread evenly, until the bottom of the frittata is set. Scatter the cheese evenly over the top (out to the edges) and broil until melted and just beginning to brown, 2 to 3 minutes. Serve hot.

INCREASE THE VEGGIES: Add ½ bell pepper (any color) when you add the onions. Add 1 cup lightly steamed broccoli florets (cut small) when you add the tomatoes.

Barbarians at the Plate

THE COOKBOOK SHELF:

DeMane, Erica. *Pasta: Williams-Sonoma Collection*. Free Press, 2001.

Dojny, Brooke and Barnard, Melanie. *A Flash in the Pan: Fast, Fabulous Recipes in a Single Skillet*. Chronicle Books, 2003.

Fullan, Joanne G. *Better Homes and Gardens Cooking for Today: Stir-Fries*. Better Homes and Gardens, 1994.

Start Your Ovens

CASSEROLES AND BAKED DISHES

GONE ARE THE days (thankfully) when home cooks were forced to regulate the heat of their ovens by adding more wood or coal, working the dampers, and keeping their fingers crossed. But even today individual ovens are notoriously unreliable; many are said to be typically 25 degrees out of whack in either direction, and most have a "hot spot." Buy an oven thermometer—one cookbook author recommends buying *two* and placing them in different parts of the oven—to determine how your oven stacks up. You can reset the thermostat (the directions should be in the owner's manual, which you have, of course, neatly filed away), or have it reset by a service person. Or, you can do as I do, and just live with it, adjusting recipes as you cook.

Also, always remember to preheat the oven for at least 10 minutes. Make sure you set a timer—many microwave ovens have a "kitchen timer" function in case you don't have one on your oven.

Finally, as long as the oven is on, think about sticking in potatoes (white or sweet potatoes), winter squash (halved, seeded, and seasoned with some butter and brown sugar), or root vegetables such as beets.

Note: All recipes here were tested in a conventional gas oven, not a convection oven. If you have a convection oven, follow the manufacturers' instructions about adjusting cooking time.

Dinner with the Hills
SAN DIEGO, CALIFORNIA

FOUR-YEAR-OLD CAROLINE HILL and her six-year-old sister Madeline are standing upside-down on their heads on the couch in the home they share with their mother and dad in the Balboa Park area of San Diego. From the depths of the cushions, slightly muffled by their hair (blond for Caroline, red for Madeline) comes the sound of full-bore giggling; the kind of little-kids' laugh that makes me wish I could bottle it, the kind that makes me wish my own two daughters were little again. I say this to Stephen Hill, the girls' father. He looks at me kind of funny.

"I know you're right," he says. "But sometimes it feels like we're just getting through the day, just surviving."

I remember that look, that feeling; probably every parent does. A friend of mine once sent me a Christmas card when his kids were about the same ages as the Hills'. "The kids are fun . . . in a relentless sort of way," he wrote. I used that line for several years to describe my own children.

Steve and his wife, Catherine, are cleaning the kitchen of their classic California bungalow-style home after supper. Steve has spent the last ten minutes in a ritual he shares with his daughters: making fresh vegetable juice (apple, carrots, ginger, beets, parsley), using the Juiceman machine on the kitchen counter. Madeline has dragged a kitchen chair over to reach the juicer while Caroline perched next to it. It was clear that they love the fresh juice and were excited about serving some to a visitor (me) who has never tasted such an exotic combination. It was clear that they got a thrill out of doing this project with their dad. Nevertheless, Steve was called on to referee a seemingly endless series of minor squabbles: who gets to put the carrots in, who gets to add the parsley, whose turn is it to turn the machine on, who will drink out of which glass.

"So much," he says, rolling his eyes, "for a father-daughter bonding moment." But how many four-year-olds do you know who are happy to drink their beet juice?

I had arrived at the house earlier in the day, as Catherine, who runs a consulting business from an office off of the kitchen, drove in from picking up the girls—Madeline was at her Montessori school, Caroline was at her grandmother's house. Caroline dashed into the house to prepare a turkey breast (a little olive oil, a little rosemary, salt and pepper) and pop it into the oven. A pan of cornbread, from a Marie Callendar mix, went in with it, and the combined fragrances of toasting corn and fresh rosemary filled the kitchen. She prepared a side dish of asparagus, sautéing them in butter and olive oil, and put a pot of brown rice—her husband's favorite—on the stove. Caroline had made dessert at her grandmother's house—brightly-colored "haystacks" of coconut and jelly beans—and had brought them home with pride and appropriate fanfare.

A petite woman with Michele Pfeiffer-esque looks, Catherine darted through the house like a dynamo, simultaneously making dinner, retrieving Caroline's shoe from the rose bushes (how it got there was unclear), finding a Scooby-Doo Band-Aid for a scrape on Madeline's foot, hunting for a lost tennis ball, and combing a particularly nasty-looking snarl out of Madeline's curls. Setting the table, and sensing storm clouds, she quickly hunted up two matching Ariel "the Little Mermaid" dinner plates to forestall an incipient dispute.

Steve, quiet-spoken and bespectacled, returned home from his job in the city's deputy mayor's office just in time to eat. The girls said grace ("God is great, God is good . . ."). Madeline reported on her role as an acorn in the recent production of Acorns to Oaks, a play performed by her church class. She showed off a loose tooth ("my first!") and laughed about how, when she was a "baby," she used to call broccoli "broccobee." Caroline, clearly casting around for a conversational gambit, stood on her seat and announced "I have a tummy!!" Her mother pointed to her chair. She sat.

"May I be excoosed?" she asked a few minutes later. She was.

With two unpredictable schedules—Stephen's job often requires late nights, Catherine's long hours on the road—Catherine keeps her meal plans simple. "Burger Night" (featuring veggie burgers because Catherine doesn't eat red meat) and "Burrito Night" are regular events on the Hill's culinary calendar. When speed is of the essence, she bakes chicken tenderloins in barbecue sauce, or mixes up a batch of Annie's brand macaroni and cheese.

Catherine credits the members of both her and Steve's families, many who live close by, with helping out often. "It's that 'it takes a village to raise a child,' concept," says Catherine. "It works."

After dinner and juice-making, the girls are watching a *Veggie Tales* video, happily singing the words to a song about "Barbara Manatee" ("Barbara Manatee/ You are the one for me . . ."). They dissolve again into giggles. Stephen looks at me.

"I know, I know," he says. "I'm enjoying this."

◆ Chicken Nuggets ◆

YIELD: 4 servings.

Like the Macaroni and Cheese recipe on page 110, this is one of those recipes that your kids will clamor for. You'll like it, too.

2 eggs
⅓ cup milk
dash of hot sauce (optional)
2 cups crushed corn flakes (see note) or seasoned bread crumbs
salt and pepper
garlic powder
2 tablespoons canola or other vegetable oil
4 boneless, skinless chicken breast halves, cut into bite-sized pieces
ketchup, barbecue sauce, or honey-mustard, for dipping

PREHEAT THE OVEN to 450°F. Line a cookie sheet with waxed paper.

Mix the eggs, milk, and hot sauce (if using) in a shallow bowl.

In another shallow bowl, combine the corn flakes (or bread crumbs) and season generously with salt, pepper, and garlic powder. Mix well.

Pour the oil into a 9-by-13-inch baking pan. Slide the pan into the preheated oven and allow the oil to get hot, about 5 minutes. The surface of the oil should look wavy.

Meanwhile, working quickly, dip the chicken nuggets into the egg mixture, and then dredge in the breading. Shake off excess crumbs and place the coated chicken on the prepared cookie sheet as you work.

Remove the pan with the hot oil from the oven and, working carefully to avoid oil splatters, add the breaded chicken pieces. Bake 10 minutes, turn the pieces over with a spatula, and bake 5 minutes more. Slice a nugget to make sure it is no longer pink inside (if it is, cook it a bit more).

Serve with dipping sauce of your choice.

NOTE: You can buy crushed corn flakes in a box at the grocery store, or crush your own: place the cereal in a plastic bag, seal the bag, and crush the corn flakes with a rolling pin.

VARIATION: Substitute ½ cup sesame seeds for ½ cup of the corn flakes or breadcrumbs. Use soy sauce mixed with a bit of sugar and sesame oil as a dipping sauce. OR: Substitute a thick fillet of mild-tasting white fish for the chicken.

◆ Parmesan Chicken ◆

YIELD: 4 to 6 servings.

Recipe from Mia Miller, adapted from Gourmet, *December 2001.*

Incredibly simple and absolutely delicious, and pleasing to both adults and children. Who could ask for anything more?

    4 to 6 skinless boneless chicken breast halves
    3 tablespoons Dijon mustard
    1 tablespoon white-wine vinegar
    ½ teaspoon salt
    ½ teaspoon pepper
    about 1 cup bread crumbs
    ¾ cup finely grated Parmesan cheese, preferably Parmigiano-Reggiano
    1 tablespoon unsalted butter, melted (optional)

CENTER A RACK in the oven and preheat the oven to 450°F. Line a 9-by-13-inch baking pan or a cookie sheet with baking parchment or foil.

Trim any fat from chicken. If the breasts are especially thick, place between two sheets of waxed paper or plastic wrap and pound with a rolling pin.

Combine the mustard, vinegar, salt, and ¼ teaspoon of the pepper in a large bowl and add the chicken breasts, tossing to coat well.

Combine the bread crumbs, cheese, butter (if using), and the remaining ¼ teaspoon pepper in a shallow soup bowl or pie plate.

Dredge the chicken, 1 piece at a time, in the crumbs, coating completely and pressing the crumbs on gently. Transfer the chicken to the prepared baking pan. Bake until golden brown and cooked through, 15 to 20 minutes.

MAKE AHEAD: Prepare the marinade a day ahead and refrigerate. You can marinate the chicken breasts, covered and refrigerated, for up to 2 hours before dredging and cooking. Combine the bread crumbs, cheese, and butter mixture up to a day ahead. Cover and refrigerate.

◆ Chicken Enchilada Casserole ◆

YIELD: 4 servings (if everyone is really hungry) and 8 if they are not.
Recipe from Jeff and Mary Jackowski, Brighton, Michigan.

This is a one-dish meal with a lot of heft, but with enough vegetables that you'll feel virtuous.

 1 to 2 tablespoons canola or other vegetable oil
 1 pound boneless chicken breast cut into ½-inch cubes
 1 onion, peeled and chopped
 2 cloves garlic, peeled and finely chopped
 2 cups mild picante sauce or salsa
 1 (14-ounce) can whole tomatoes, drained and chopped
 1½ cups chopped broccoli florets
 1 tablespoon ground cumin
 2 cups shredded regular or reduced-fat Cheddar cheese
 8 (8-inch, "burrito size") flour tortillas
 sour cream, for serving (optional)
 chopped fresh cilantro, for serving (optional)

PREHEAT THE OVEN to 350°F. Lightly oil a 9-by-13 inch baking pan.

Coat the bottom of a large skillet with oil and set the skillet over medium heat. Add the chicken, onion, and garlic and cook until the chicken is no longer pink, about 7 minutes.

Add ½ cup of the picante sauce (or salsa), the chopped tomatoes (no juice), broccoli, and cumin. Mix well. Bring to a boil, then adjust the heat so that the mixture simmers; cover, and cook for 5 minutes. Uncover, increase the heat, and cook at a rapid simmer, stirring frequently, until most of the liquid has evaporated. Stir in 1 cup of the cheese.

Spoon a generous ½ cup of the mixture down the center of each tortilla, then roll up and place seam-side down in the prepared pan. Spoon remaining 1½ cups picante sauce (or salsa) over the tortillas. Bake 20 minutes or until hot.

Scatter the remaining 1 cup cheese over the top. Return to oven for 2 minutes, or until the cheese melts.

Serve hot, with sour cream and/or cilantro, as desired.

MAKE AHEAD: Up to 1 day, to the point where the rolled tortillas are arranged in the pan. Cover and refrigerate.

FREEZE: Prepare to the point where the rolled tortillas are arranged in the pan; cover and freeze up to 2 months.

Barbarians at the Plate

◆ Tacos in Pasta Shells ◆

YIELD: 4 to 6 servings.
Recipe from Mary Jackowski, Brighton, Michigan.

A *twist on plain tacos, with all the same flavors. Tortilla chips add the crunch.*

18 jumbo pasta shells (½ pound)
1¼ pounds ground beef, pork, turkey, or combination
1 (3-ounce) package cream cheese with chives, cut into ½-inch cubes
1 teaspoon salt
1 teaspoon chili powder
1 (8-ounce) jar taco sauce
1 cup shredded regular or reduced-fat Cheddar cheese
1 cup shredded regular or reduced-fat Monterey Jack cheese
1 cup crushed tortilla chips (place chips in a plastic bag, seal, and crush
    with a rolling pin; or crush them in the food processor)
1 cup regular, low- or no-fat sour cream, for serving
3 scallions, trimmed and chopped, for serving

BRING A LARGE pot (4 quarts) of salted water (page 96) to a boil. Add the pasta, cover the pot, and bring the water back to a boil. Remove the cover and cook, boiling, according to package directions for al dente ("to the tooth"); that is, not raw-tasting but still firm. Drain. Run the shells under warm water and drain well again.

Preheat the oven to 350°F. Butter a 13-by-9-inch pan.

In a large skillet set over medium-high heat, cook the meat until browned, stirring to separate. Drain any fat from the pan.

Reduce the heat to medium-low, add the cream cheese, salt, and chili powder. Simmer for 5 minutes, stirring occasionally.

Using a spoon, fill the shells with the meat mixture. Place the shells in the prepared pan. Pour taco sauce over each shell and cover with foil. Bake 15 minutes.

Uncover the pan, scatter the cheese and chips over the shells, and bake, uncovered, for an additional 15 minutes, or until cheese is bubbly.

Serve with sour cream and scallions as a garnish, if desired.

MAKE AHEAD: Prepare the filling up to 1 day ahead. Cover and refrigerate.
FREEZE: Up to 2 months.

◆ Ginger-Marinated Pork Tenderloin ◆

YIELD: 6 to 8 servings.

*Recipe adapted from Mia Miller, Lawrenceville, New Jersey,
who in turn adapted it from the November, 2003 issue of* Gourmet *magazine.*

Pork tenderloins are a wonderful treat and cook really quickly. They usually come
2 to a package. This recipe uses 2, or a total of 1½ to 2 pounds.

 1 (14.5-ounce can) chicken broth
 ¼ cup soy sauce
 ¼ cup packed brown sugar
 3 tablespoons ketchup or 2 tablespoons tomato paste
 3 tablespoons grated peeled fresh ginger
 3 garlic cloves, peeled and finely chopped
 1 tablespoon cider vinegar or balsamic vinegar
 2 pork tenderloins (around 2 pounds) (see note)
 1 tablespoon olive oil

WHISK TOGETHER ⅔ cup of the broth, the soy sauce, brown sugar,
ketchup (or tomato paste), ginger, garlic, and vinegar and pour into a large
sealable plastic bag. (If you prop the bag open in a bowl or a quart measuring cup, you can mix the marinade right in the bag and not even dirty
a bowl!) Add the pork, turn to coat, and seal the bag. Refrigerate at least
2 hours and up to 10, turning the bag over if you think of it.

Center a rack in the oven and preheat the oven to 425°F.

Remove the pork from the marinade and pat dry with a paper towel.
Reserve the marinade.

Heat the oil in a large ovenproof skillet over moderately high heat, until
hot but not smoking. Brown the pork on all sides, about 3 minutes total.
Transfer the skillet to the oven and roast the pork until a meat or instant-
read thermometer inserted diagonally into center of the meat registers
160°F; start checking at about 15 minutes. Transfer the meat to a cutting
board, cover loosely with foil, and let sit while you make the sauce.

Return the skillet to the stove over medium-high heat and pour in the
reserved marinade, scraping up any browned bits in the skillet as you stir.
Add the remaining broth (there should be about 1 cup) and simmer for
ten minutes, or until thickened.

Slice the pork and serve it with the sauce.

MAKE AHEAD: The marinade can be made a day ahead, covered,
and refrigerated. The pork can be placed in the marinade in the
morning, and cooked in the evening.

Barbarians at the Plate

◆ Pork Chops Baked ◆
with Apples and Pears

YIELD: 4 servings.

These days, pork chops are often so lean that they often dry out with cooking. This recipe keeps them moist and flavorful.

2 tart apples (such as Granny Smith) stemmed, cored, and sliced
2 firm pears (slightly underripe is better than overripe), stemmed, cored, and sliced
1 tablespoon brown sugar
ground cinnamon
ground ginger
4 thick, boneless pork chops (about 1¼ pounds total)
salt and pepper
2 tablespoons unsalted butter, cut into small pieces

PREHEAT THE OVEN to 375°F. Line an 8-inch square pan with aluminum foil.

Place the apple and pear slices in the prepared pan. Sprinkle with sugar, cinnamon and ginger to taste. Season both sides of each pork chop the pork chop with salt and pepper and nestle the chops in the fruit, so that the chops are partially covered by the apples and pears. Scatter the butter over the top and cover the baking dish with foil.

Bake for 40 minutes. Remove the foil and bake, uncovered, for about 20 minutes more, until the fruit is very tender and the pork is beginning to brown.

Serve each chop with a scoop of apples, pears, and pan juices.

——— COOKING WITH KIDS ———

GIGI DURHAM WAS making muffins with her six-year-old daughter Sonali when it came time to combine ¾ cup of one ingredient with ¾ cup of another. "That's one and one half" Sonali announced proudly. Yes, kids who cook can do the math.

Cooking teaches young children all sorts of skills: sequencing, measuring, telling and keeping track of time.

But cooking is also fun. Look at it from a child's point of view: You get to make a mess and play with fire and sharp knives; it doesn't get much better than that. And when you make something good to eat, and your family likes it, well, it's a huge boost to self-esteem.

When you're cooking with your kids, don't "cook down" to them:

They can do way more than chocolate chip cookies, and will probably surprise you by being more capable and interested in making main courses and vegetable dishes than you think. For a couple of years I taught cooking classes at my daughter's grade school, and after the initial, predictable reactions ("yuck," "gross," etc.), the kids were enthusiastically making—and eating—fresh salsas, artichokes with vinaigrette, pesto, vegetable soup. And in your own home, kitchen time—time spent trimming green beans, chopping celery, washing lettuce, doing dishes—can turn into great talking time; like driving and folding laundry, it's when the important stuff often comes out.

One of my least favorite television commercials depicts a woman apparently so inept in the kitchen that her idea of "making cookies" is to break apart premade squares of dough and put them in the oven. She sits at the table in her immaculate kitchen tousling the hair of her young children, while the voice-over informs the viewer that this woman—liberated from the odious chore of actually mixing ingredients—now has "more time" to spend with her children. I don't know about your kids, but mine would rather be breaking eggs into cookie dough than sitting around having their hair tousled.

Maybe the announcer meant that the *kids* would have more time . . . no doubt they'll need to spend it on homework, so they can learn to do the math.

❖ ❖ ❖

THE COOKBOOK SHELF:

THERE ARE LOTS of really awful children's cookbooks out there, cutesy volumes in which most of the recipes are for desserts and the rest involve food smothered with gobs of cheese. Here are some books that don't "cook down" to children.

Dodge, Abigail Johnson. *Williams-Sonoma: The Kid's Cookbook.* Time Life Books, 2000.

Jones, Judith and Evan. *Knead It, Punch It, Bake It: The Ultimate Breadmaking Book for Parents and Kids.* Houghton Mifflin, 1998. A great introduction to breadmaking for adults as well.

Raab, Evelyn. *Clueless in the Kitchen: A Cookbook For Teens.* Firefly Books, 1998. Also, *The Clueless Baker (2001).*

Waters, Alice. *Fanny at Chez Panisse: A Child's Restaurant Adventures with 46 Recipes.* HarperCollins, 1992.

Zanzarella, Marianne. *The Good Housekeeping Illustrated Children's Cookbook.* Morrow Junior Books, 1997.

◆ Cheater Lasagne ◆

YIELD: 6 servings.
Vegetarian-friendly

Lasagne flavor with only a fraction of the work.

¾-pound (1 12-ounce box) fusilli (long spiral pasta) or other long pasta
1½ cups store-bought or homemade tomato-based spaghetti sauce
  (page 112)
1 (8-ounce) carton regular or reduced-fat ricotta cheese
2 cups shredded regular or reduced-fat mozzarella
grated Parmesan cheese

PREHEAT OVEN TO 350°F. Lightly oil an ovenproof casserole dish (see note). Bring a large pot of salted water to a boil over high heat, add the noodles, cover, and bring back to a boil. Remove the cover, and cook, boiling, according to package directions for al dente ("to the tooth"); that is, not raw-tasting but still firm. Drain well and toss into the prepared casserole. Stir in the pasta sauce, ricotta, and mozzarella, mixing well. Sprinkle with grated Parmesan. Bake, covered (use aluminum foil if the dish has no cover) for 25 minutes. Remove the cover and bake 10 minutes more.

NOTE: A Dutch oven (a large, ovenproof pot) will work for boiling the noodles and for baking. Otherwise, boil the pasta in a pot and bake in a 9-by-13-inch pan.
FOR THE CARNIVORES: Add 1 pound of cooked ground beef, pork, turkey, veal, or a combination.
MAKE AHEAD: Prepare up to the point of baking. Cook, cover and refrigerate up to one day.
FREEZE: Up to 1 month.

◆ Baked Shells with Broccoli ◆

YIELD: 4 to 6 servings.

My mother and aunt make this dish for my kids all the time, and it's always a big hit. Using whole-milk mozzarella, no surprise, gives a much creamier texture.

1 pound large pasta shells
3 to 4 cups broccoli florets
2 cups shredded or cubed regular or reduced-fat mozzarella
grated Parmesan cheese
1 to 2 tablespoons unsalted butter, cut into tiny pieces

PREHEAT THE OVEN to 325°F. Grease a 9-by-13-inch baking pan. Set aside.

Bring a large pot of salted water (page 96) to a boil over high heat. At the same time bring a smaller pot of water to a boil.

Add the noodles to the large pot, cover and bring back to a boil. Remove the cover and cook, boiling, according to package directions for al dente ("to the tooth"); that is, not raw-tasting but still firm. Drain well and return to the pot.

Meanwhile, add the broccoli to the boiling water in the smaller pot and cook just until it can be pierced with a fork, 4 to 5 minutes. Drain and combine with the cooked shells. Stir in the mozzarella. Spoon into the prepared pan. Sprinkle with Parmesan and dot with butter.

Cover with foil and bake 15 to 20 minutes. Remove foil and bake another 5 to 10 minutes, until the edges just begin to turn brown and crispy.

MAKE AHEAD: Up to 1 day. Cover and refrigerate.
FREEZE: Up to 1 month.

◆ Foolproof Fish ◆

YIELD: 4 servings.

This stovetop-to-oven method ensures that the fish will be neither raw in the middle nor dry and overcooked. The method also works on steak and other similar cuts of meat.

> canola oil
> 1½ pounds fish fillets or fish steaks—salmon, tuna, mahi-mahi,
>   halibut—about 1 inch thick
> salt and pepper
> topping or glaze of your choice (optional; page 148)
> lemon wedges, for serving

PLACE A LARGE ovenproof skillet over high heat for 2 minutes, until very hot. Add a spoonful of oil and tilt the pan to spread it over the bottom. Return to the heat for 30 seconds or so. Add the fish, flesh side down and cook for a minute or two until well seared. Carefully turn and sear the skin side of the fish.

Transfer the skillet to the oven and top the flesh side of the fish with a glaze or topping, if using. Bake about 10 minutes (see note). Check for doneness: the inside should be opaque; return to the oven for a few minutes if not done.

Serve immediately, with lemon wedges.

NOTE: The fish will take about 10 minutes per inch of thickness; if your fillets or fish steaks are thicker or thinner, adjust the cooking time.

◆ Roasted Vegetables ◆

YIELD: 6 to 8 servings.

This is not an inexpensive meal (unless all the vegetables come from your own garden) but it is a gorgeous one, and one that you can feel good about serving. My younger daughter wouldn't touch Brussels sprouts until she had them roasted; now they are among her favorite vegetables. It's probably because roasting brings out the sugars. Clearly, if everyone in your family gags over one of the suggested vegetables, leave it out. But one of the nice things about this dish is that the vegetables cook separately on the pan, so everyone can choose according to his or her own taste. The garlic can be squeezed like butter onto the polenta, the other vegetables, or bread. If you used all of the vegetables below, you would have enough for at least 6 main-course servings, and you would want to use 2 tubes of polenta. You can also serve this with mashed potatoes (page 163). And if anyone in your family feels a dinner is not complete without meat, cook up some sausage (hot Italian sausage goes well) and serve on the side.

ANY OR ALL OF THE FOLLOWING:
- 4 carrots, peeled
- 4 parsnips, peeled
- 1 large turnip, trimmed, peeled and halved
- 1 pound Brussels sprouts
- 2 sweet potatoes, scrubbed but not peeled
- 1 bunch beets (about 4), leaves removed, roots trimmed
- 2 onions, peeled
- 1 bulb fennel, leafy tops removed
- 1 bunch asparagus
- olive oil as needed
- salt and pepper, preferably coarse salt such as kosher or sea salt, and coarsely ground pepper
- 1 or 2 heads garlic
- 1 or 2 (1-pound) tube(s) ready-to-cook polenta (depending on how many people you are serving)

Preheat the oven to 500°F.

Cut the carrots on the diagonal into ½-inch-thick slices. Do the same with the parsnips or, if using turnip, slice each turnip half into ¼-inch-thick half-moon slices. Halve the Brussels sprouts. Cut the sweet potatoes in ¼-inch-thick rounds. Do the same with the beets. Cut each onion into wedges and do the same for the fennel. Trim the woody ends of the asparagus. Slice about ¼ inch of the top off the head of garlic, exposing

Barbarians at the Plate

the cloves, and roughly peel off any loose skin (you don't have to get it all off). Leave the root end intact. Wrap in aluminum foil.

Line a large baking sheet (or sheets, depending on how many vegetables you are cooking) with heavy-duty aluminum foil. Spread all the vegetables out in one layer on the baking sheet(s). Drizzle generously with olive oil and toss to coat; season with salt and pepper. Place the wrapped heads of garlic on the pan.

Bake for about 30 minutes, until all vegetables are tender. (If using very thin asparagus, you may need to remove them sooner, or put them in the oven 10 or 15 minutes later).

Meanwhile, prepare the polenta according to package directions. You can bake or broil it; I usually pan-fry it in a lightly-oiled non-stick pan until it is crispy on both sides (about 20 minutes, total).

ADDITIONS: Other vegetables that roast well include winter squash (sliced thin), zucchini, or summer squash (sliced into ½-inch rounds), and bell peppers, seeded and cut into chunks.

THE COOKBOOK SHELF:

Grunes, Barbara. *The Williams-Sonoma Collection: Roasting.* Free Press, 2002.
Kafka, Barbara. *Roasting: A Simple Art.* Morrow Cookbooks, 1995.
See also the casserole and one-pot cookbooks, page 130.

Fire Up the Grill

THE JOY OF GRILLING

KIDS WILL TRY an amazing array of food that has been grilled, especially if the grilling involves barbecue sauce and pointy sticks (kids *love* stuff on pointy sticks). Kebobs of any kind—meat, vegetables, or fruits—are surefire winners, and I'm sure there are children out there (alas, mine not among them) who love grilled fish.

Grilling is a vast subject; entire cookbooks have been written about it. Here are a few very basic tips:

- ❖ Get to know your grill. Understand how to prepare the fire for "direct" grilling (right over the coals or heat source) and "indirect" grilling (away from the heat source) and how to tell the difference between high, medium, and low heat. If you have a charcoal kettle grill, learn how to adjust the vents properly.
- ❖ If you have a covered grill, use the cover. If grilling over a hibachi or open fire, you may have to increase cooking times for most grill recipes.
- ❖ Use a meat thermometer. Instant-read thermometers are inexpensive (about $10) and available at the supermarket. Since I do a lot

Barbarians at the Plate

of grilling, and am paranoid about either burning the meat or killing everyone by undercooking it, I use a digital thermometer—it has a cord attached to a probe that you stick in the meat. You can set it for a certain length of time, or you can set it to sound its alarm when the internal temperature reaches a certain point. Mine is a Bonjour brand, and it cost about $30 several years ago. It's also handy for oven-roasted meats. See Appendix 6: Food Safety.

❖ Get extra-organized. Grilling is like cooking in a wok—things go fast once you get started. Make sure you have all ingredients and equipment (mitts, tongs, etc.) on hand.

❖ If using bamboo skewers, soak them in water for at least 5 minutes (longer is better) to delay burning.

❖ Ixnay on the mesquite. A few years ago, every grilled food seemed to be infused with mesquite smoke. The trouble is that mesquite is so pungent it tends to overwhelm the flavors of the food. Try hickory, apple wood, or oak.

Dinner with the Masons
SAN DIEGO, CALIFORNIA

"SUNDAY DINNERS WERE sacred," says Sarah Mason, recalling the meals of her childhood. "No matter where you were, what you were doing, you made sure you were home for dinner on Sunday night."

Divorced, with one son—nine-year-old Mason Church—Sarah remarried last year. Her husband is Brad Roberts, a man with three kids of his own: Elana, five, Emily, twelve, and Jason, seventeen. Nowadays, it's Friday nights that are "sacred" in Sarah's household. With all four children in attendance, Sarah and Brad preside over the Shabbat, the traditional Jewish Friday night meal.

"It was the kids who asked us to reinstitute Shabbat," says Sarah. "They wanted us all to be together."

She said that the children often invite friends to dinner on Friday night, "a meal they rarely miss."

On this particular Friday evening it is just family, gathered at the striking green marble table that dominates one end of the large modern kitchen in a Carmel Valley section of San Diego, in a neighborhood of spacious new houses about two miles from the ocean. Sarah has placed a number of hors d'oeuvres on the counter: spinach pies (bought frozen at the supermarket), steamed baby artichokes left over from the night before, and a community-cookbook standard: tiny hot dogs in a heated sauce of grape jelly and mustard. Brad, a landscape architect who sports a trim beard and mustache, is outside tending the chicken on the gas grill in a yard that promises to be a landscaped wonder but which is, with construction going on, a sand pit. The family's dog, Diamond, an enthusiastic retriever, fetches a ball whenever she can importune upon a visitor (me) to throw it.

Sarah, a lawyer, threw the chicken into a lemon-pepper marinade when she got home from work, and pulled the rest of the meal together—asparagus cooked in the microwave, and rice in the rice cooker—at the same time.

"You have to think about it, plan ahead, consider what you have in your freezer, what's on special at the grocery store," she says. Tall and lean, she moves about the kitchen quickly but with composure. She has abandoned any hopes of reliving the dinners of her youth made by her dad, a doctor, who found it relaxing to whip up dishes like chateaubriand and coq au vin on a daily basis.

"The kids don't really like anything that fancy," she says. "And working around their schedules is difficult." They are a busy crew. Mason plays lacrosse and basketball. Jason is involved in drama; his high school, with 3,500 students, is acclaimed for its elaborate productions. Emily, still in middle-school, is also interested in theater, and plays basketball and volleyball.

The meal begins with the traditional Hebrew blessing of the wine, and Brad and Sarah, launching their own tradition, walk around the table, whispering a quiet blessing or word of praise to each child.

"It's fun to watch everyone's face while they listen," says Emily as she awaits her message. "We usually look embarrassed, but we like it."

While Brad's family did not have the "gourmet" traditions that were Sarah's, he says "food galvanized our family events." He recalls large Sunday brunches at his grandmother's house, feasts of smoked fish, salami, and eggs.

"For my grandmother and Sarah's father, food was about love," says Brad. "It was 'Eat this, you've received my love.' What could be more powerful?"

Conversation at the table is lively. Mason seeks permission to sleep at a friend's house (denied due to prior commitments), Emily discusses her upcoming transition from middle to high school, and Jason talks about his plans to pursue a career in the theater. Elana, tiny and blonde, is the quietest, but after dinner she proudly points out the family's job chart, which hangs in the kitchen and lists not only the jobs that the kids are responsible for, but those that Sarah and Brad perform as well.

"We wanted them to realize, in a palpable way, that in a family, everybody works," says Brad. Near the job chart hangs a device called the "Wheel of Dreaded Consequences," which Sarah purchased on-line (at www.consequences.ca). Spin the dial and the wheel doles out consequences ("vacuum;" "bathroom duty") for misdeeds and rewards ("one rental video" or "$5 cash") for good behavior.

"Anything but the Wheel of Dreaded Consequences!" shrieks Emily in mock despair. Mason rolls his eyes.

Though Sarah is not Jewish, she is quite comfortable with the rituals of Shabbat. Her parents, she said, immigrated from England, and since they had no relatives in the United States, they "adopted" a family of Polish Jews with whom they shared weekly Sunday night feasts and holidays.

"Sometimes you feel like you come full circle," says Sarah. "My dad wasn't Jewish, but it was he who cooked the Seder every Passover."

GRILL RECIPES

Marinades and Rubs

A MARINADE USUALLY consists of something acidic (citrus juice, vinegar, tomatoes, wine), salt, herbs, and spices. The acid tenderizes the meat and the salt, herbs and spices flavor it. Often, oil is added to protect the meat a bit, and keep it from losing too much moisture. Experiment with the flavors you like.

- ❖ Always use a nonreactive pan (page 4) when marinating foods. A sealable, heavy-duty plastic bag works well; discard after using.
- ❖ Discard any marinade that held raw food, and never put cooked food back on a platter that held raw food. If you want to use the marinade as a sauce after the food is cooked, boil it vigorously for at least 5 minutes before serving. Or make extra and store it separately.
- ❖ Although most cookbooks will tell you otherwise, I have found that most foods (including fish) can be placed in a marinade in the morning and cooked in the evening. Some foods, like bone-in beef, pork, lamb and chicken, can keep 24 hours in the marinade. If you are worried about a delicate fish breaking down in the marinade, just bathe it for about 30 to 60 minutes.

SALAD DRESSINGS AS MARINADES

- ❖ Kathy Schulz of Escondido, California, swears by Catalina dressing for grilling salmon: She places the salmon on foil, pours dressing over it, and tops it with chopped red onions, chopped garlic, salt and pepper. Then she wraps it up, and "bakes" it on the grill for about 20 minutes, without turning.
- ❖ Diann Neal of Cromwell, Oklahoma, tosses chicken breasts in Italian salad dressing; other folks use the dressing as a marinade for shrimp.
- ❖ For an Asian flavor, I like Annie's Naturals brand Shiitake & Sesame Vinaigrette. There are lots of bottled marinades available; read the labels if you want to avoid certain additives like MSG.

Here are some ideas to get you started. All make enough marinade for at least 1½ to 2 pounds of meat, poultry or fish.

◆ Red Wine Marinade ◆

½ cup dry red wine
¼ cup olive oil
4 cloves garlic, peeled and finely chopped
2 teaspoons dried oregano
1 teaspoon dried basil
¼ teaspoon dried hot pepper flakes
pinch of sugar

MIX ALL INGREDIENTS together. Use for beef, lamb, or portobello mushrooms.

◆ Lemon Caper Marinade ◆

6 tablespoons lemon juice
3 tablespoons olive oil
4 cloves garlic, peeled and finely chopped
1 tablespoon capers, with juice
1 teaspoon salt
½ teaspoon pepper
zest of 1 lemon, finely chopped
red hot pepper flakes (optional)

MIX ALL INGREDIENTS together. Use for poultry or fish.

◆ Buttermilk Marinade ◆

1 cup buttermilk
½ onion, peeled and grated
2 garlic cloves, peeled and finely chopped
1 tablespoon dried dill
1 teaspoon sugar
¼ teaspoon cayenne

MIX ALL INGREDIENTS together. Use for poultry or pork.

◆ Tandoori Marinade ◆

1 cup plain regular or reduced-fat yogurt
2 tablespoons lemon juice
½ onion, peeled and grated
3 cloves garlic, peeled and finely chopped
2 teaspoons curry powder
½ teaspoon cumin
pinch of sugar

Mɪx ᴀʟʟ ɪɴɢʀᴇᴅɪᴇɴᴛꜱ together. Use for lamb, pork, beef or poultry.

◆ Lemon-Soy Marinade for Salmon ◆

Recipe from Mary and Jeff Jackowski, Brighton, Michigan

¼ cup packed brown sugar
3 tablespoons chicken broth
3 tablespoons canola or other vegetable oil
1 tablespoon soy sauce
2 teaspoons dried minced onion

Mɪx ᴀʟʟ ɪɴɢʀᴇᴅɪᴇɴᴛꜱ together. Sprinkle a salmon fillet with dried dill, lemon pepper, and garlic powder and marinate in the lemon-soy mixture before grilling.

RUBS

Rubs are dry marinades. You can sprinkle them on the food 15 minutes before grilling, or leave them on for up to an hour. Store any leftover rub, covered, with your other spices.

◆ Cajun Rub ◆

2 tablespoons chili powder
2 teaspoons salt
2 teaspoons brown sugar
1 teaspoon onion powder
1 teaspoon garlic powder
½ teaspoon ground cumin
½ teaspoon cayenne

MIX TOGETHER. Excellent on pork, beef, or poultry.

◆ Sage Rub ◆

1 tablespoon dried sage
1 tablespoon dried thyme
1 teaspoon dried rosemary
1 teaspoon sugar
1 teaspoon salt
½ teaspoon pepper

MIX TOGETHER. Excellent on poultry or pork.

◆ Cracked-Pepper Rub ◆

2 cloves garlic, peeled and chopped
2 tablespoons dried rosemary
1 teaspoon dried thyme
3 tablespoons whole black peppercorns, or whole varicolored peppercorns (red, green, and black)
2 teaspoons coarse salt, such as kosher salt or sea salt
zest of 1 orange or 1 lemon

MIX IN A SPICE grinder, clean coffee grinder, mini-food processor, or mortar and pestle. Excellent on beef or pork.

Barbarians at the Plate

◆ Mixed Grill ◆

YIELD: 4 to 6 servings.

The idea here is to get meat—bone-in steak and chops, sausage—that cook in approximately the same time.

> 3 pounds meat: T-bone steak, pork chops, lamb chops, and/or sausage
> store-bought or homemade marinade (pages 142–143)
>
> **FOR SERVING:**
> barbecue sauce, mayonnaise spiked with hot sauce, or flavored mayon-
> naises (such as French's GourMayo: wasabi, chipotle, Caesar ranch, or
> creamy Dijon)

PLACE THE MEAT in a shallow, nonreactive pan (page 4). Pour the marinade over all, turning to coat. Cover and refrigerate up to 1 day, turning
the meat whenever you think about it.

Remove the meat from the refrigerator and let sit at room temperature
for about 30 minutes before grilling. If using sausage, pierce each sausage
link several times with a fork.

Prepare a charcoal fire or preheat a gas grill for direct grilling over high
heat.

Remove the meat from the marinade and discard the marinade.

Grill the meat 12 to 15 minutes, turning once. An instant-read thermometer inserted in the center of the steak, pork, and lamb should read
at least 145°F for medium-rare; the sausage should register at least 160°F.
Let the meat rest for about 5 minutes, then slice and serve with the sauces
of your choice.

SERVING SUGGESTION: Serve with any of the Four Slaws (page 169)
and corn on the cob or Almost-Instant Mashed Potatoes (page 163).

MEALTIME RITUALS

EVERY VALENTINE'S DAY when my kids were little, I would get up extra-
early (which I hate) and make a special breakfast; sometimes eggs and a
coffee cake, sometimes pancakes (yes, I shaped them—or tried to—like
hearts) and, one memorable year, brownie sundaes. A few years ago, with
the girls both in high school, I had more or less forgotten about Valentine's
Day. But the night of February 13 both kids announced that they would
be getting up early so we could all share our "special" breakfast. Clearly, I
wasn't going to get off the hook. I realized I didn't want to.

Most of us instinctively create rituals around the holidays—and we get help from the culture, which spells them out for us to some extent (turkey at Thanksgiving, fireworks on the Fourth of July). But it is those daily rituals that really establish communication and solidify our bonds to each other. The note in the lunchbox, the nighttime story, and yes . . . the family meal. If your ritual is that meals are used as a time when parents critique kids' school-work, so be it. It's still a ritual, and one that your kids will remember as they grow up. Think about rituals you would be happy to have them look back on.

❖ Setting the table: Kids often count on using their "special" plate or cups, napkin, napkin rings, or utensils, just as they often "have" to sit in the same exact place at the table each night. Just the act of setting the table—not with crystal and china but with an identifiable place setting—signals that the meal is a family "event" and not just a time for calories to be consumed.

❖ Saying grace: Lots of families say grace, or hold hands and observe a moment of silence right before the meal starts. Some ask children to take turns in leading the grace. Sarah Mason and Brad Roberts, of San Diego start the Shabbat—the Friday night meal in the Jewish tradition—with prayers, but then walk around the table, whispering into the ear of each of their four children a quiet word of praise. While saying grace adds an obvious spiritual note to the meal, Diann Neal, a devout Baptist and mother of six in Cromwell, Oklahoma says it has an additional benefit: "It makes the kids shut up," she says, laughing. "And gives me control of the table."

❖ Candles, flowers, music: "There's something about lighted candles," says Ellen Brodsky, mother of two in Cambridge, Massachusetts. "It calms everyone down and makes everyone feel a little special." If you are eating in the kitchen where you just prepared the food, and if you can dim the lights, there is the bonus of not seeing quite so much of the kitchen mess while you eat. (Of course, the kids may fight about whose turn it is to light or blow out the candles; think of it as another lesson in sharing.) A small bouquet of flowers—fresh, dried, or silk—or a centerpiece of children's artwork, or the playing of music can signify to the family that meal times are something to be appreciated.

❖ Weekly specials: Designate one night a week as a "special" meal, and your children will grow to depend on and look forward to it. Sarah Mason says it was the four children in her newly blended family, who insisted on celebrating Shabbat each Friday night. Jacquie Wayans of the Bronx has a special Sunday dinner after church each week. The Knoxes, of Sturbridge, Massachusetts, designate Friday as "Family Movie and Pizza Night"; and others have a celebratory weekend breakfast or brunch. Special foods—challah for Shabbat, roast chicken for Sunday dinner, home-made muffins for brunch—help cement the ritual. Some families designate a special plate—one in a bright color or a pretty pattern—to mark an achievement: a good grade in a tough subject, a special project completed at work, learning to ride a two-wheeler.

❖ Ending rituals: Family therapists say that it's a good idea to establish a routine for ending a meal. It doesn't have to be elaborate: "May I be excused?" can work just fine. Blowing out the candles, clearing the plates—these all sound the final note to this period of family time. The idea is to avoid ending the meal with arguing, phone calls, or just drifting away.

THE COOKBOOK SHELF:

Doherty, William J. *The Intentional Family: How to Build Family Ties in Our Modern World*. Addison-Wesley Publishing, 1997.

GRILLED FISH

YOU CAN USE a grill basket for fish, you can wrap it in foil, or you can grill it directly on the grill. I prefer the latter method, so I use only fillets or steaks that are at least 1-inch thick—salmon, tuna, mahi-mahi or halibut—because they will not fall apart when placed directly on the grill.

Here's a basic method (for thick fillets or steaks)

❖ Prepare your grill for direct grilling over medium heat.
❖ Using a pastry brush, brush both sides of the fish with olive oil. Place it on the grill, flesh-side down. (This is important if you are going to add a glaze or other topping.) Cover the grill and cook 5 to 7 minutes, turn carefully, and add a glaze (if using). Cover the grill and cook 4 to 5 minutes more, until the topping has heated through.
❖ To test for doneness: Prod the center of the fish gently with a knife (try not to mutilate it); it is done when opaque inside. If you, like me, like it a little more well done, cook it longer, until it flakes easily when prodded with a fork (that's when the experts say it is overcooked and dry).

◆ Maple Orange Glaze ◆

¼ cup pure maple syrup
2 tablespoons orange juice
2 tablespoons balsamic vinegar
zest of 1 orange
1 tablespoon grated fresh ginger
¼ teaspoon hot red pepper flakes (optional)
salt and pepper

◆ Three-Citrus Topping ◆

zest from 1 orange
zest from 2 lemons
zest from 1 lime
2 tablespoons chopped cilantro
salt and pepper
1 tablespoon lemon juice

◆ Creamy Mustard Glaze ◆

½ cup mayonnaise
¼ cup mustard, preferably Dijon
2 teaspoons fresh or 1 teaspoons dried dill
pinch of sugar
salt and pepper

GRILLED PIZZA

GRILLED PIZZA MAY sound tricky, but it's really simple and tastes like the kind made in wood-burning ovens in trendy restaurants. Once you've figured out the method, you can add any toppings you want. And, don't worry, I've included directions (see box) for baking pizza in the oven as well.

General Tips:

- ❖ Store-bought pizza dough costs about $1 a pound and comes bagged in plastic in the bakery or deli section of the supermarket. I

find it is more resilient than homemade dough, but feel free to make your own. The store-bought kind is best used within a day or so, but it will keep for several days in the refrigerator (it tends to rise in the bag, and gets very yeasty-smelling, but is still good) and for weeks in the freezer. (Defrost it on the counter; the microwave toughens it). Note: The brands I've found do contain those nasty trans-fatty acids (page 201). If you are lucky enough to have a friendly neighborhood pizzeria or bakery that will sell you dough, go for it.

❖ I usually roll out the dough into an irregular rectangle, maybe 15 inches long and 8 to 10 inches wide. I transfer it to the grill with a long-handled spatula and my hands. You could also divide the dough into equal pieces and roll each piece into an 8-inch round, for easier handling. Transfer the uncooked rounds to the grill with a spatula or your hands, and use tongs to flip them over.

❖ Grilling pizza is a very quick process. Make sure you have everything you need on hand: spatulas, tongs, grill mitts, and all of the toppings (chopped and pre-measured and cooked if required).

❖ If using a gas grill, you can adjust the temperature if you think the crust is cooking too quickly. If using a charcoal grill, you will have to try to find a cooler section to work over, if needed.

The Method

❖ Prepare a covered gas or charcoal grill for direct grilling over high heat.

❖ Using a pastry brush, slather one side of the rolled-out dough with oil. Transfer the dough—oiled side down—to the grill. If a tiny hole develops during the transfer, don't worry. Cover and cook for 3 to 5 minutes, checking occasionally. It is done when streaked with dark grill marks. If bits of the crust look burned, that's okay, it's "rustic."

❖ Once one side is grilled, transfer the dough to a work surface, slather the uncooked surface with oil, and put the dough—oiled-side down—back on the grill. Working quickly, add all toppings, ending with the cheese. Cover the grill and cook until the toppings are hot and the cheese is melted, 3 to 5 minutes.

❖ After you remove the pizza from the grill, let it sit for a minute or two before slicing.

YIELD: 1 pound of dough will make a pizza large enough to feed three hungry people or four with smaller appetites. I usually make two and keep leftovers for breakfast.

Fire Up the Grill 149

◆ For Mexican Pizza ◆

⅓ cup salsa, mild, medium or hot
1 tablespoon chopped canned chipotles in adobo sauce (optional; page 85)
1 to 2 cups canned black beans, drained and rinsed
1 to 2 cups fresh or frozen corn kernels, cooked and drained
1 (2.25-ounce) can sliced black olives, drained
chopped scallions (optional)
chopped fresh cilantro (optional)
1 to 2 cups grated regular or reduced-fat Monterrey Jack or Cheddar
    cheese, or "Taco" blend sold in bags in supermarket

MIX THE SALSA and chipotle in adobo (if using) in a small bowl. Spoon the salsa onto the pizza, spreading outward from the center, but leaving a rim of plain dough around the edges. Distribute the other ingredients evenly on top, in the order listed.

◆ For Steak and Cheese Pizza ◆

2 tablespoons canola oil or other vegetable oil
2 onions, peeled and sliced
½ to ¾ pound cooked steak, thinly sliced
salt and pepper
bottled hot pepper rings, drained (optional)
1 to 2 cups regular or reduced-fat Cheddar or Jack cheese

HEAT THE OIL in a skillet and cook the onions, stirring, until quite soft, about 7 minutes. Add the steak to the skillet and heat through. Season with salt and pepper. Spoon the cooked onions and meat onto the pizza, leaving a rim of plain dough around the edges. Top with hot peppers (if using) and cheese.

◆ For Mushroom and Sage Pizza ◆

2 tablespoons olive oil
1 large onion, peeled and sliced thin
2 garlic cloves, peeled and finely chopped
1 pound mushrooms: shiitake, portobello, cremini (also sold as "baby
    bellas"), white button mushrooms, or a mixture

salt and pepper
small handful of fresh sage leaves, or 2 to 3 teaspoons dried sage
1 to 2 cups shredded regular or reduced-fat mozzarella cheese

HEAT THE OIL in a skillet and cook the onions and garlic, stirring, until quite soft, about 7 minutes. Add the mushrooms, sprinkle with salt and pepper, and add the sage. Cover and cook until mushrooms are soft, about ten minutes. Spoon onto the pizza and top with the cheese.

◆ For Pesto Pizza ◆

1 (8-ounce) container regular or reduced-fat ricotta cheese
½ cup pesto
¾ pound tomatoes (2 regular tomatoes) sliced
1 (2.25-ounce) can sliced black olives, drained (optional)
1 to 2 cups grated regular or reduced-fat mozzarella

SPOON THE RICOTTA onto the pizza, spreading outward from the center, but leaving a rim of plain dough around the edges. Add the pesto, spreading with the back of a spoon. Distribute the tomatoes, olives and cheese on top.

◆ Grilled Focaccia ◆

That's Italian for "flatbread." Think of it as a nearly-naked pizza.

OIL THE DOUGH as directed and grill one side. Turn over and brush the uncooked side with oil. Sprinkle with coarse salt, such as kosher salt or sea salt, coarsely ground pepper, and fresh or dried rosemary, thyme, or other herbs

---

OVEN-BAKED PIZZA

If you want to use the oven, preheat it to 450°F. Sprinkle cornmeal on a cookie sheet or pizza stone, and place the uncooked crust on top. Brush with oil, sprinkle with toppings, and bake until the crust is brown and the cheese is melted, 15 to 20 minutes.

GRILLED VEGETABLES

THE BASIC METHOD for grilling vegetables is to coat them with olive oil (3 to 4 tablespoons per pound of veggies) and sprinkle them with salt (preferably coarse salt, such as kosher salt or sea salt) and coarsely ground black pepper. Grill them over direct medium heat. Preparation and grilling times for various vegetables as follows:

NOTE: If are making kebobs, ignore the slicing instructions and cut the vegetables into chunks and thread them on skewers. Since cooking times vary between meats and vegetables, it's smart to make all-meat skewers and all-vegetable skewers.

Asparagus:
Snap off tough ends before cooking.
GRILLING TIME: 6 to 8 minutes; turn as needed.

Bell Peppers:
Stem, seed, and cut into chunks. Lay them on the grill or thread them on skewers.
GRILLING TIME: about 8 minutes; turn as needed. Edges will begin to char.

Eggplant:
Use baby eggplant. (Larger ones have to be sliced, salted and allowed to sit for 30 minutes to get the bitterness out.) Stem and slice in half lengthwise.
GRILLING TIME: 12 to 15 minutes; turn once, halfway through.

Fennel:
Cut off tops and trim root end. Slice fennel bulb in half.
GRILLING TIME: 15 to 20 minutes; turn halfway through.

Mushrooms, Portobello:
Stem and clean, removing the dark gills only if you don't like the way they look (they add flavor).
GRILLING TIME: 12 to 15 minutes; turn once and baste with additional oil.

Mushrooms, button:
Stem and clean. Thread on skewers.
GRILLING TIME: 7 to 10 minutes; turn skewer once, and baste with additional oil if needed.

Zucchini and summer squash:
Slice on the diagonal into long pieces, ½-inch thick.
GRILLING TIME: 8 to 10 minutes, turning once.

Barbarians at the Plate

Potatoes:

Scrub but don't peel. If using tiny, golf-ball-sized new potatoes, leave them whole. If using larger potatoes, cut them into chunks. Boil until you can *just* pierce them with a sharp knife (a little less cooked than if you were eating them out of the pot) and drain. Add chopped rosemary, garlic, or other seasonings to the oil, season with salt and pepper, and grill, turning.

Grilling time: will vary depending on the size of the potatoes, but you want them to look crispy.

KATHY SCHULZ of Escondido, California, says her family's favorite recipe for "BBQ Potatoes" is as follows: Slice 4 large potatoes into thin (G-inch) rounds. Place them on a sheet of aluminum foil, scatter with chopped garlic, dot with butter, and sprinkle with salt and pepper. Wrap well in foil and grill for 20 minutes, gently turning the packet once.

GRILLED FRUIT

LIKE VEGETABLES, FRUITS on the grill are easy to make and delicious; the sugars caramelize, making the fruits even sweeter. Fruits should be brushed with butter to keep them from sticking; you may want to combine melted butter with a bit of rum, orange or pineapple juice, or honey and make a glaze. For some fruits, like bananas and peaches, you may want to sprinkle them with a bit of cinnamon, after glazing but before grilling. Grill fruits over direct medium heat. You can also cut fruits into large chunks and thread them on skewers, or use a grill basket for thinner slices. If you want to indulge in a little lily-gilding, top the fruits with ice cream, whipped cream, or toasted coconut.

Bananas:
Slice a whole, unpeeled banana in half crosswise. Peel and slice each half in half again, lengthwise (you will have four pieces).
GRILLING TIME: 6 to 8 minutes, turn once, halfway through.

Peaches, Nectarines, Plums:
Halve the fruit and remove the pits.
GRILLING TIME: about 10 minutes; turn once halfway through.

Pineapple:
Cut off the stem and the peel. Slice into ¾-inch-thick rounds.
GRILLING TIME: about 12 minutes; turn once halfway through.

Fire Up the Grill 153

THE COOKBOOK SHELF:

Purviance, Jamie and McRae, Sandra. *Weber's Big Book of Grilling.* Chronicle Books, 2001.

Raichlen, Steven. *How to Grill: The Complete Illustrated Book of Barbecue Techniques Featuring Easy-To-Make Recipes.* Workman, 2001.

Roker, Al. *Al Roker's Big Bad Book of Barbecue.* Scribner, 2002. Full disclosure: I worked on this book.

GRACE NOTES

SIMPLE SIDES

❖

DESSERTS AND BAKED GOODS

Simple Sides

COMPLEMENTS GALORE

IF YOU PLAY your cards right and make a one-pot meal, side dishes are unnecessary. But sometimes you will want to round out a meal with a starch or extra vegetables to complement the main course. Here are some quick ideas.

For starches:

- ❖ Couscous: available in most supermarkets; cooks in about 5 minutes (follow package directions).
- ❖ Rice: white and brown (page 199). White rice cooks in about 20 minutes, "instant" brown rice in 10, and regular brown rice in 45 (page 199). Also: basmati, jasmine, and wild rice.
- ❖ Pasta and egg noodles cook in about 10 minutes.
- ❖ Tabbouleh: a salad of bulgur wheat, available in most supermarkets and prepared in about 5 minutes (although the tabbouleh usually has to stand for 30 minutes before serving).
- ❖ Potatoes: Sweet potatoes and white potatoes can be cooked in the microwave (read the manufacturer's instructions) and can also be quickly done on the stovetop. (See Almost-Instant Mashed Potatoes, page 163.)

- Polenta: Making it from scratch (cornmeal and water) takes at least 45 minutes; you can buy tubes of prepared polenta in the supermarket; slice and heat it according to package directions.
- Grits: Being a northerner, I don't know beans about grits. I buy it at the supermarket and follow the package directions, and add grated cheddar and chopped chili peppers, and everybody in my family is happy. Southerners tell me I should buy stone-ground grits; Arrowhead Mills is a brand that is widely available.
- Corn on the cob: I'm not going to get in a fight about how to cook it. My method is: Plunge into boiling water for 3 to 5 minutes.
- Breads: Italian and French, focaccia, pita bread, biscuits (page 190), rolls (page 193), soda bread (page 191), lavash, Indian bread (pappadums, parathas), bagels, corn bread (page 192), tortillas.

Salads and other quick veggie dishes:

- Chickpea salad: Drain canned chickpeas and mix with chopped red onion or scallions. Toss with Italian dressing or, for a sinus-clearing treat, mustard oil (available in Indian specialty shops).
- Fennel salad: Trim fresh fennel bulbs (discard the feathery fronds) and chop the bulbs. Toss with Italian dressing and chopped red onions.
- Sugar snap, snow peas, or other edible-pod peas.
- Sliced tomatoes and . . . (see page 166).
- Mixed raw vegetables: carrots, bell peppers, celery, broccoli or cauliflower florets, cucumbers, zucchini or summer squash, asparagus. (The Jackowskis, of Brighton, Michigan, introduced me to the concept of eating asparagus raw . . . and they're good! Who knew?)

Dinner with the Gallaghers
CALAIS, VERMONT

IT'S JUST AFTER 5:30 on a Wednesday night, and Sarah Gallagher has been home from work approximately seven minutes. She has already changed from her work clothes into jeans and a T-shirt, cleared a space on the kitchen table while making a phone call, and checked on the progress of dinner in the slow cooker.

The kitchen is warmly lit, a massive wood-burning cook stove dominates the room, and on this fall day the unlit stove is piled with squash from the garden, mail, school papers, and boxes of odds and ends. (The Gallaghers use it as an auxiliary heat source during the cooler months; cooking is done on a standard gas range.) Various appliances—a food processor, a bread machine, a popcorn popper, a blender—crowd the countertops. One wall is occupied by a built-in china cabinet through which the Gallagher's extensive but not-necessarily-matching collection of crockery is visible. The heavy wooden table is covered with a blue woven tablecloth with a see-through plastic sheet over the top.

The phone rings. Dixie, the aging golden retriever, thumps her tail. The sound of Homer Simpson's thoroughly imitable "Doh!" wafts in from the other room where Sarah's husband, Steve—a lanky six-footer with a shock of unruly hair—and ten-year-old Isaac are watching television.

The Gallagher house—parts of it built in the early 1800s, the rest added on over time—sits in the center of the village of Maple Corner in the town of Calais, Vermont, across from the country store and almost next door to the old one-room school. It has white clapboards, dark green shutters, and a wraparound porch cluttered with brown paper bags full of returnable bottles, as well as bicycles, a tripod, old boots, and sagging furniture, upon which Nightshade Nellie and Peppy Le Pew, the household cats, sometimes nest.

A neighbor arrives with one of Sarah's nieces in tow and settles at the kitchen table. Sarah pours her a glass of wine. Sarah's sister-in-law cruises through to pick up her child. Sarah continues the task at hand, chopping vegetables for a salad. She chats with the neighbor, who finishes the wine and leaves. She puts rice on to boil and sets some chicken sausage—a new "find" at the local natural foods co-op—into a skillet to cook. She gets a stack of dishes out of the china cupboard. Isaac wanders in, and she reads aloud his spelling words as she works. "H-I-P-P-O-P-O-T-A-M-U-S," he intones. "S-O-C-I-E-T-Y. M-I-S-C-H-I-E-V-O-U-S."

Sarah's day began at 5:45 a.m. when she pulled on her sweatshirt, sweat-pants, and running shoes to jog three miles, a morning routine she shares with a neighbor. After making sure that her seventeen-year-old (by her first marriage), Cameron, was awake, she roused Isaac from bed and fed him breakfast (a bowl of cereal with milk), and packed his lunch (string cheese, a sourdough roll, peanut butter crackers, carrots, and an orange). She made some coffee, took a shower, and managed to throw ingredients for a veg-etable stew into her slow cooker. She left for work at 7 a.m.; it took her about 45 minutes to drive from her home to her office, where, sometime mid-morn-ing, she ate a carton of yogurt for breakfast. Sarah—a social worker with degrees from Harvard and the University of Vermont—works as a district manager for the state's department of social services. Her workdays are full of meetings, of crisis management, of ways to help solve problems with and for families described by the antiseptic phrase "at risk."

"Do you believe it? I cook almost every night," Sarah said when I called to ask her about how she feeds her family. She sounded just a tad embarrassed, as if she were confessing that her hobby was tatting, or that she preferred letter-writing to e-mail. It's nice, but . . . is it *necessary*?

Sarah thinks so. She learned that from her mother, who, through years of raising four kids solo while working (sometimes two jobs) outside of the home, managed to cook nearly every night. "She made a lot of casseroles," says Sarah. "But she was into natural foods, so there was never junk on the table." Sarah recalls that due to the family's low income level, she and her sib-lings qualified for free lunch at school. "But we never took it," she says. "It was not so much that Mom was too proud, it was that she didn't want us eating that stuff. She knew she could do better."

Sarah's job has also brought home to her the importance of family meals. She tells of an "at-risk" family that she says was "spiraling out of control."

160

Barbarians at the Plate

"The whole community was up in arms; it seemed like a disaster was imminent," Sarah says. "Their case worker came to me and said: 'They don't have a table.' So we bought them a table, and a chair for everyone to sit around it.

"The message was so strong," she says. "We were saying 'this is how to be a family' and we were saying it in a concrete way." The family is, predictably, still troubled, but, adds Sarah, "I really believe the table helped enormously."

There are things that Sarah sacrifices by cooking every night. She did not, for example, seek a second term on the local school board because it claimed too many evenings. She has put off the idea of getting a Ph.D. until Isaac is older.

She does her shopping on weekends, roughly planning out menus for the coming week and sometimes hitting as many as three stores—the regular supermarket, a cooperative market that specializes in natural foods and bulk grains, and the local bagel bakery. In the past, she also made monthly trips to a large warehouse-type store about an hour north, but she has discontinued the process: "I found I just spent way too much on 'bargains' we didn't really need." On weeks "when I'm sick of my own cooking," she says, she drags out a bunch of cookbooks and looks for new ideas. It's not unusual at the Gallaghers' house to find, say, Sloppy Joes on the menu one night, and Coconut-Thai Shrimp and Basmati Rice on the menu the next. Sometimes—like on Thai Shrimp Night—Isaac will eat only the rice, and maybe some of the mini-cut carrots. Sarah doesn't sweat it.

She relies heavily on her freezer—the big chest type—that stands near the door of the connecting barn. The family purchases meat from local farmers and, depending on the year, freezes a good bit of garden produce. Canned beans, canned tomatoes, canned broth, and frozen vegetables—especially peas and corn—are staples.

The meal is informal but ritualized. There is an identifiable place setting (dish, fork, knife, paper napkin, glass) and self-assigned seats (Sarah always sits closest to the sink, Steve with his back to the Glenwood, and Isaac by the china cupboard. Cam is at work as a cook at a restaurant and Sarah need not worry about his meal; Jamie, Cam's nineteen-year-old brother, is away at college). Isaac chatters away about an upcoming spelling bee; Steve, a carpenter, discusses a renovation project he is working on. The vegetable stew—from a Moosewood Cookbook recipe—and the chicken sausage disappear.

Isaac clears his plate. "Good dinner, Mom," he chirps. Steve steps up to the sink to do the dishes. Sarah sits at the kitchen table. She makes a phone call and opens mail. Later, after Isaac is in bed, she will pour herself a glass of wine and relax. She might take a mystery to bed. Or she might take a cookbook.

Barbarians at the Plate

◆ Almost-Instant Mashed Potatoes ◆

YIELD: 4 servings.

I once read that the secret to making "perfect" mashed potatoes was boiling the potatoes whole and unpeeled, to prevent them from absorbing water and getting soggy. So—this was before I had kids—I would boil whole potatoes until tender (this takes approximately forever), then peel them gingerly (they were hot!), and then put them through a ricer, adding hot milk and butter right before serving. I have to admit, this method makes killer mashed potatoes.

Then I had kids, and a mere nanosecond or two to get dinner on the table. Boiling, peeling, and ricing whole potatoes seemed like way too much work. But steaming tiny chunks of potatoes cooks them quickly, while avoiding sogginess. Leaving the skins on saves time, as does using a potato masher instead of a ricer. I try to use organic potatoes when leaving the skins on. These mashed taters are not really smooth, but they sure are delicious.

> 2 pounds thin-skinned white or red potatoes, scrubbed but not peeled
> ¾ to 1 cup whole, low-fat, or no-fat milk
> 2 tablespoons unsalted butter
> salt and pepper

FIT A LARGE pot with a steamer basket and pour in water to a depth of 1 to 2 inches. Bring the water to a boil while you cut the potatoes into ½-to-1-inch cubes. (The smaller you cut them, the quicker they will cook.) Steam the potatoes for 10 to 15 minutes, until very tender when pierced with a fork. Drain.

Return the potatoes to the pot. Heat the milk in a small saucepan on the stove or in a microwave-safe container in the microwave (about 1 minute on HIGH). Mash the potatoes with a potato masher, gradually adding the hot milk. Add the butter and continue mashing. Season with salt and pepper and serve.

ADDITIONS: 4 to 6 garlic cloves, peeled (add to potatoes while they are steaming, then mash with the potatoes); grated Cheddar, Monterey Jack, cream cheese, or blue cheese; cooked, crumbled bacon (page 91);

chopped fresh chives or other fresh herbs; regular or low-fat sour cream or plain yogurt (reduce milk in recipe as needed).

FREEZE: Up to 2 months.

VARIATION: ALMOST-INSTANT MASHED SWEET POTATOES

Peel and cut the potatoes and steam as directed. Mash with a potato masher and add 2 to 4 tablespoons unsalted butter, and season with salt and pepper. For a sweeter side dish, add a tablespoon or so of pure maple syrup or brown sugar and a dash or two of cinnamon.

◆ Oven Fries ◆

YIELD: 4 to 6 servings.

Okay, these are not quick, but they are delicious. Get these roasting right away and then start the rest of dinner. You can also "fry" carrots (see below).

> ¼ cup extra-virgin olive oil or canola oil
> 2 pounds potatoes (preferably large baking potatoes, such as russets), scrubbed
> salt, preferably a coarse salt like kosher or sea salt
> 1 tablespoon finely chopped fresh rosemary or 1½ teaspoons dried rosemary (optional)

CENTER A RACK in the oven and preheat the oven to 450°F.

Pour the oil into a 9-by-13-inch baking pan. Put the pan in the oven for 5 minutes, or until the oil gets very hot. The surface of the oil should look wavy.

While the oil is heating, slice the potatoes into strips about ¼-inch wide and ½-inch thick. Carefully place the potatoes into the hot oil and season them with salt and rosemary (if using).

Bake 40 to 50 minutes, turning halfway through. Serve immediately.

◆ Oven-Fried Carrots ◆

YIELD: 4 to 6 servings.

> 10 carrots
> 2 tablespoons olive oil or canola oil
> 1 teaspoon brown sugar
> salt and pepper

Barbarians at the Plate

PREHEAT THE OVEN to 425°F. Line a jelly-roll pan (a large shallow baking pan with sides) with aluminum foil and spray with cooking spray.

Peel the carrots, trim the ends, and slice each carrot lengthwise into 6 to 8 long thin pieces. Place them on the prepared baking sheet. Drizzle with the oil, and sprinkle with the sugar, salt and pepper, tossing the carrots gently so they are well coated. Bake until tender and well browned, about 20 minutes.

Serve hot or at room temperature.

VARIATION: Substitute parsnips for all or a portion of the carrots.

◆ Parsley Potatoes ◆

YIELD: 4 to 6 servings.

My friend Maya Kennedy, co-author (with me, and her husband, Jimmy) of The River Run Cookbook *(HarperCollins, 2001), calls these "Shaken Potatoes." This is her recipe.*

2 pounds potatoes, preferably red potatoes, scrubbed (peeling is optional)
3 to 4 tablespoons unsalted butter, cut into a few chunks
¼ cup chopped fresh parsley
salt and pepper

FIT A LARGE pot with a steamer basket and pour in water to a depth of 1 to 2 inches. Bring the water to a boil while you cut the potatoes into medium chunks (about 1½-inches). Steam the potatoes for about 15 minutes, until very tender when pierced with a fork. Drain. Remove the steamer and the water from the pot, and put the potatoes back in. Quickly add the butter, parsley, salt and pepper. Cover the pot and, holding the lid closed, shake the pot, as Maya says, "up and down and all around" to distribute the butter and seasonings. Serve immediately.

◆ Funji ◆

YIELD: about 4 servings.

Jacquie Wayans, mother of two in the Bronx, got this recipe from her mother, who is from British Tortola. Jacquie says that her mother spends hours cooking funji (which I've also seen referred to as "funchi," and which seems similar to a Barbados specialty called "cou-cou"), but Jacquie has figured out how to make it in about 15 minutes. Like grits or polenta—both creamy dishes of cooked, ground corn—funji

is "comfort food"; it's bland and filling, and goes especially well with dishes that have a spicy sauce, such as *Shrimp Creole* (page 104).

2 cups water
1 pound whole okra, stemmed
1 tablespoon salt
¾ cup cornmeal
2 tablespoons unsalted butter

Bring the water, okra, and salt to a boil over high heat. Adjust the heat so that the water simmers, and cook until the okra is tender, about 7 minutes. Add the cornmeal with one hand while stirring the water and okra continuously with the other. Keep stirring until the cornmeal thickens; this only takes a few minutes. Cook a little longer until the okra loses its form and blends into the meal. Adjust the heat to low, add the butter, and allow to melt for a few minutes. Stir again. Cover until ready to use; if it hardens—it shouldn't—just add a little water and/or some more butter.

Serve hot.

Make Ahead: Up to several hours.

◆ Tomatoes and . . . ◆

A platter of sliced ripe tomatoes, sprinkled with salt and coarsely ground pepper, makes an elegant side dish. Here are things to dress it up:

❖ Salad dressing: olive oil and vinegar, vinaigrette (page 167) or your favorite bottled dressing.

❖ Chopped, fresh herbs: basil, thyme, dill, parsley, cilantro, or chives.

❖ Cheese: Arrange sliced tomatoes with slices of good-quality mozzarella or tiny balls of mozzarella (bocconcini; pronounced "boh-kon-CHEE-nee"), available in the specialty cheese section of some supermarkets; or slices of ricotta salata—a sweet-tasting, solid form of ricotta cheese; or crumbled feta or blue cheese.

❖ Bread: cubes of stale or toasted bread, chopped tomatoes, basil, oil, vinegar, and sliced onions make "panzanella," a simple Italian bread salad.

SALAD BASICS

When I told a friend of mine that I was working on a family cookbook, she asked me if I had a recipe for a "quick" salad. At first I was dumbfounded; I think of *all* salads as quick. Then I realized that before I allowed myself the

166

luxury of buying prewashed, mixed lettuce, shredded vegetables, tiny grape tomatoes, and other "convenience produce," chopping all that stuff for salads seemed like a chore. Here are things you can put in salad:

- **PREWASHED GREENS:** mixed greens or "spring mix" (also called mesclun), romaine, iceberg, baby spinach.
- **GRAPE OR CHERRY TOMATOES:** I like to use these rather than slicing large tomatoes, because people who don't like tomatoes in their salads (e.g., my children) can avoid them easily, and there is no "tomato goo" (my daughter's words) on the lettuce.
- **OLIVES:** domestic and imported (if you don't buy pitted olives, and don't have the time to pit them, make sure you warn everyone at the table).
- **CHEESE:** the "usual suspects" (Cheddar, Jack) and also fresh goat cheese (chevre), feta cheese, blue cheese, shredded Parmesan or Asiago.
- **OTHER VEGETABLES:** bell peppers, red cabbage, cucumbers, broccoli or cauliflower florets, radishes, summer squash.
- **ONIONS:** scallions, shallots, red onions.
- **NUTS:** pecans, almonds, walnuts, pine nuts (pignoli), raw, hulled pumpkin seeds (pepitas), preferably toasted (see page 50).
- **DRIED FRUIT:** raisins, dried cranberries, dried cherries.
- **CHOPPED FRESH HERBS:** basil, cilantro, parsley, sage, oregano, chives, marjoram, dill.
- **SLICED AVOCADOS.**
- **CHOPPED APPLES OR PEARS, TANGERINE, CLEMENTINE OR GRAPEFRUIT SECTIONS.**

SALAD DRESSINGS

SALAD DRESSINGS ARE like pancakes and cakes: few people make them from scratch anymore. But nothing could be simpler. Here are three foolproof dressings.

OIL AND VINEGAR (OR LEMON JUICE): Sprinkle the salad with salt and pepper. Drizzle with good quality olive oil and vinegar, preferably balsamic vinegar, or squeeze a lemon over all. Toss.

VINAIGRETTE: This is essentially the vinaigrette that Rachel Samstat, the heroine of Nora Ephron's novel *Heartburn* (Pocket Books, 1984), teaches her unfaithful jerk of a husband how to make just before she leaves him: Mix together 2 tablespoons Dijon mustard, 2 tablespoons good red wine vinegar. Whisk in 6 tablespoons good-

Simple Sides 167

quality olive oil until the dressing is thick and creamy. That's it. You could also add a bit more oil (if you don't like your dressing too strong) and/or a clove of crushed garlic, some salt and pepper, and a pinch of sugar.

CREAMY BUTTERMILK DRESSING: Combine ¼ cup buttermilk, ⅓ cup mayonnaise, 1 clove of garlic (peeled and chopped), and a tablespoon of grated onion. Add pepper and a dash of hot sauce, if you like.

CIVILIZING TAKE-OUT

KAREN AND LOIS Gray, of Iowa City, Iowa, practice what Lois calls "tag-team parenting"; Lois is just about home from her job in the international programs office of the University of Iowa when Karen, an RN, has to leave for hers, in the neonatal intensive care unit of the university hospital. On the plus side of this arrangement, their daughters—Jesse, seven, and Lauren, five—always have a parent at home. On the minus side, the family rarely gets to eat a meal together. Neither woman considers herself a good cook, and without another adult around at suppertime, Lois says, she often succumbs to frozen foods, fast-food or take-out. "I feel tremendously guilty about it," she says.

But on a rare night at home together, Karen, Lois, and the girls do a pretty fair imitation of a family eating together. The centerpiece of the meal is a "gourmet" pizza from a nearby market, and Karen has dressed up the meal with a fresh spinach salad and apple slices. The girls set the table in the dining room of the couple's large new home. Everyone sits together and talks.

Take-out meals can, indeed, be civilized. The trick is to not let them take on that "rushed fast-food quality," as Chris Vineis, a mother of two in Columbus, Ohio, puts it. The reason you're buying take-out is that you're too tired or busy to cook, but a tiny little effort can go a long way. Think about ways you can increase the nutritional content and add a home-made touch when you are bringing prepared food in.

FOR PIZZA: Assemble an antipasto plate of canned and jarred items: marinated artichoke hearts, olives, roasted red peppers, eggplant caponata, dilly beans, pickled garlic, and anchovies. Make Fennel Salad (page 158) or an "Italian" salad (lettuce, spinach, arugula and/or radicchio, garnished with toasted pine nuts, tomatoes, oil-cured olives, and shaved Parmesan or Asiago cheese).

For dessert, offer a bowl of fresh seasonal fruit and nuts, or store-bought Italian ice.

CHINESE TAKE-OUT: Accompany with home-made Fried Rice (page 107), or Broccoli Slaw (page 171). Or thaw a package of

Barbarians at the Plate

frozen spinach and sauté with chopped garlic and soy sauce. For dessert, serve slices of fresh oranges, as some Chinese restaurants do. Brew some decaf tea to go with the meal. Don't forget the chopsticks, and plenty of napkins. You may want to leave the take-out in the containers, but open the sauce packets and squirt them into small bowls for dipping.

MEXICAN FOOD: To a meal of take-out burritos or tamales, think about adding: homemade salsa (page 174), or a "Mexican" salad (romaine, toasted pumpkin seeds, black pitted olives, tomatoes, sliced avocado, and shredded Monterey Jack). For dessert, serve sliced mango, papaya, pineapple, and melons or the "Strawberry Margarita Sorbet" (page 182). Offer several varieties of hot sauce, and a cooling drink (beer, lemon or limeade, iced tea, or water with a slice of lime).

❖ ❖ ❖

FOUR SLAWS

By all means, buy the cabbage already shredded. But for heaven's sake, throw out those packets of nasty-tasting dressing that come with it. These four slaws can be thrown together in a matter of minutes and make colorful, crunchy sides. All of the dressings here can be made up to two days ahead. Cover and refrigerate until needed.

◆ Classic Cole Slaw ◆

YIELD: 6 to 8 servings.

FOR THE DRESSING:
½ cup regular or reduced-fat mayonnaise
3 tablespoons canola oil or other vegetable oil
2 tablespoons cider vinegar
1 tablespoon sugar
salt and pepper
pinch of cayenne or several dashes hot sauce (optional)

FOR THE SALAD:
1 (16-ounce) bag shredded cabbage (6 cups) or shredded cabbage mixed
   with shredded carrots
⅓ cup chopped red or sweet onion

Simple Sides   169

Make the dressing: In a bowl or a jar with a lid, combine the mayonnaise, oil, vinegar, sugar, salt and pepper, and cayenne (if using). Whisk or shake to mix well. Taste and adjust seasonings if needed.

Place the cabbage and onion in a bowl. No more than 30 minutes before serving, pour the dressing over the cabbage and toss to coat.

Additions: Shredded carrots, finely chopped bell pepper (any color), chopped tart apple, slivers of zucchini or yellow squash, chopped fresh parsley, cilantro, or chives. Add to the dressing any or all of the following: celery salt, fresh or dried dill weed, prepared mustard or mustard powder, grated onion, finely minced garlic.

◆ Red Cabbage Slaw ◆

Yield: 4 to 6 servings.

FOR THE DRESSING:
- 3 tablespoons canola or other vegetable oil
- 2 tablespoons cider vinegar or red wine vinegar
- 1 tablespoon pure maple syrup
- salt and pepper

FOR THE SLAW:
- 1 (10-ounce) bag red cabbage (4 cups)
- 1 tart baking apple (such as Granny Smith), stemmed, cored, and chopped
- 2 strips bacon, cooked (page 91) and crumbled
- ½ cup chopped pecans, toasted (page 50)

Make the dressing: In a bowl or a jar with a lid, combine the oil, vinegar, maple syrup, salt and pepper. Whisk or shake to mix well. Taste and adjust seasonings if needed.

In a serving bowl, combine the cabbage and apple.

No more than 1 hour before serving, pour the dressing over the cabbage and toss. Just before serving, add the crisp bacon and toasted pecans and toss to combine.

◆ Carrot Slaw ◆

YIELD: 4 servings.

FOR THE DRESSING:
⅓ cup regular or reduced-fat mayonnaise
1 to 2 tablespoons lemon juice
1 teaspoon sugar
½ teaspoon cinnamon
dash of ground ginger
salt and pepper

FOR THE SLAW:
1 (10-ounce) bag shredded carrots (4 cups)
½ cup dried cranberries, golden raisins, or regular raisins
¼ cup dried, shredded coconut (optional)

MAKE THE DRESSING: In a bowl or a jar with a lid, combine the mayonnaise, lemon juice, sugar, cinnamon, ginger, salt, and pepper. Whisk or shake to mix well. Taste and adjust seasonings if needed.

Put the carrots into a bowl and add the dried cranberries (or raisins), and the coconut (if using).

No more than 1 hour before serving, pour the dressing over the carrots and toss to coat.

ADDITIONS: Toasted, chopped walnuts, almonds, or pecans (see page 50); chopped, tart apple; chopped crystallized ginger.

◆ Broccoli Slaw ◆

YIELD: 6 to 8 servings.

FOR THE DRESSING:
¼ cup rice wine vinegar or cider vinegar
¼ cup canola or other vegetable oil
4 teaspoons soy sauce
4 teaspoons Asian sesame oil (made with toasted sesame seeds)

FOR THE SLAW:
1 (16-ounce) bag shredded broccoli (6 cups)
1 (8-ounce) can sliced water chestnuts, drained
chopped fresh cilantro (optional)

MAKE THE DRESSING: Combine the vinegar, oil, soy sauce, and sesame oil in a small bowl or jar with a lid, whisking or shaking to mix well. Taste and adjust seasonings if needed.

Put the shredded broccoli in a serving bowl. Add the water chestnuts and cilantro (if using) and toss.

No more than 30 minutes before serving, pour the dressing over the slaw, and toss.

❖ ❖ ❖

◆ Cooked Greens ◆

YIELD: 4 to 6 servings.

I love the slightly bitter flavor of these greens, but, alas, my children do not. My husband and I make these for ourselves, and eat them all up. If your kids won't eat chard or kale, try this with spinach; 1½ pounds will do.

> 2 bunches Swiss chard (red or rainbow chard is pretty), kale, collards, or
>   turnip greens, well rinsed and drained
> olive oil
> juice of ½ lemon
> salt and pepper
> several tablespoons toasted pine nuts (pignoli) (optional; see page 50)

CHOP THE GREENS, stems and all, and put them in a deep skillet or a large pot and add enough cold water so that it almost, but does not quite, covers the greens. Place over high heat, bring to a boil, and adjust the heat so that the water simmers. Cook until tender; this can take anywhere from 5 to 20 minutes, depending on how old and tough the greens are. Transfer the greens with a slotted spoon to a serving bowl or platter, drizzle with lemon juice and olive oil, and season with salt and pepper. Scatter the pine nuts on top, if using. Serve hot or at room temperature.

Barbarians at the Plate

◆ Blackirican Hoppin' John ◆

YIELD: 4 to 6 servings.

*This recipe is from Yvonne Ortiz, a fabulous Puerto Rican cook and cookbook author (*A Taste of Puerto Rico, *Dutton, 1994) who lives with her husband and youngest son in Jersey City, New Jersey.*

> 2–2½ cups canned chicken broth or water
> 2 tablespoons olive oil
> ¼ cup recaíto (see note)
> 1 cup canned black-eyed peas, drained
> 1 cup long grain rice
> ½ to 1 teaspoon salt
> pepper

IN A POT set over medium-high heat, bring the chicken broth or water to a boil, adjust the heat so that the liquid simmers, and keep at a simmer until needed.

Heat the oil in a large pot. Add the recaíto and the black-eyed peas. Cook, stirring, over medium heat for 2-3 minutes. Add the rice and the hot liquid and stir. Bring the mixture to a boil. Adjust the heat so that the mixture simmers, add the salt and season with pepper, and cover and cook for 20 minutes, or until the rice is tender.

NOTE: Recaíto is a mixture of peppers, onions, cilantro, and other seasonings and is available in jars in many supermarkets (look for the Goya brand in the Hispanic, international, or "gourmet" aisle).
MAKE AHEAD: Up to 1 day. Cool, cover and refrigerate.
FREEZE: Up to 3 months.

Two Salsas

Both are best served the day they are made. Use them as a dip, with tortilla chips, or as a topping for your favorite Mexican dinners.

◆ Simplest Salsa ◆

YIELD: 1½ cups.
Recipe from Karen Branco, Bellevue, Ohio

4 plum tomatoes (also called Roma tomatoes)
1 onion, peeled
1 green bell pepper, stemmed and seeded
1 teaspoon lemon or lime juice
salt
chopped fresh cilantro (optional)

IF USING A food processor, roughly chop the tomatoes, onion, and bell pepper and pulse until the mixture reaches the consistency you like. Pour into a bowl and stir in the lemon or lime juice, salt, and cilantro (if using). If making by hand, finely chop the tomatoes, onion, and bell pepper, and combine with remaining ingredients. Serve immediately or cover and refrigerate.

◆ Not-Quite-as-Simple Salsa ◆

YIELD: 3 cups.

1 pound tomatoes (3 regular tomatoes), or 1 28-ounce can whole tomatoes, drained
1 green bell pepper, stemmed and seeded
½ onion, peeled
3 garlic cloves, peeled
1 fresh or canned jalapeño pepper (optional)
1 tablespoon lemon or lime juice
2 teaspoons canola or other vegetable oil
2 teaspoons ground cumin
½ teaspoon salt
¼ to ½ teaspoon cayenne (optional)

IF USING A food processor, roughly chop the tomatoes, bell pepper, and onion and pulse with the remaining ingredients until the mixture reaches the consistency you like. If making by hand, finely chop the tomatoes, bell pepper, onion, garlic, and jalapeños (if using) and combine with remaining ingredients. Serve immediately or cover and refrigerate.

The Cookbook Shelf:

MOST GENERAL COOKBOOKS contain plenty of recipes for delicious side dishes. Here are two that specialize in vegetables.

Bishop, Jack. *Vegetables Every Day: The Definitive Guide to Buying and Cooking Today's Produce With over 350 Recipes.* HarperCollins, 2001.
Waters, Alice. *Chez Panisse Vegetables.* HarperCollins, 1996.

Desserts
and Baked Goods

THE FINISHING TOUCH

MAKING DESSERTS OR baking breads is not an everyday task for most working parents. But sometimes, you just feel like doing something special. Perhaps your child has invited a friend for dinner, or some neighbors are coming for supper. Or maybe you've been invited to a school function and asked to bring dessert. The recipes in this chapter will fit the bill.

In addition, here are some ideas that take almost no preparation at all:

❖ Layer graham crackers and applesauce. Refrigerate, uncovered, for at least an hour; or while you're making and eating dinner. (This was my favorite weeknight dessert when I was a child.)
❖ Make a fruit salad and drizzle with a bit of orange or pineapple juice. Other possible additions: dried cranberries or cherries, chopped crystallized ginger, fresh mint. Top with yogurt, if desired.
❖ Melt 1½ cups chocolate chips in the microwave (page 218) or in a pan on the stove, stirring in ½ cup of cream, half-and-half, or evaporated milk and about 1 teaspoon pure vanilla or almond extract. Use for dipping pieces of banana, sections of oranges or tangerines, or fresh strawberries.

Barbarians at the Plate

❖ Grill fruits (page 153) and top with sorbet, ice cream, or yogurt.
❖ Roast a pineapple: Cut off the top, set the pineapple upright in a baking pan, and bake in a 350°F oven for one hour. When cool enough to handle, slice and serve. You can drizzle the slices with rum, and/or serve them with ice cream or whipped cream, if you like.

Dinner with the Jackowskis
BRIGHTON, MICHIGAN

MARY AND JEFF Jackowski make it all look easy. She plans the menus, he shops. She cooks, he preps and cleans up. They set the table every night with flowers and candles. The pantry in their spacious kitchen is stocked with tomatoes, herbs, and other vegetables that they grow in their well-tended garden each summer and preserve by canning or drying. Their older child, twelve-year-old Aaron, is a certified Junior Master Gardener and likes to grill. They compost and recycle and, in spring, have rows of plants thriving happily under grow lights in the living room. At the dinner table both Aaron and his nine-year-old sister, Amy, avidly munch on raw vegetables: asparagus, cucumbers, green peppers, and carrots.

Healthy food has always been a priority for Mary, a petite strawberry-blonde who grew up on a farm about two hours to the north of Brighton. It became a priority for Jeff—a tall, trim man who sports a mustache and a tiny earring in one earlobe—when, with Mary pregnant with Aaron, he made the decision that "no matter what it cost, she was going to have fresh fruits and vegetables."

"He made a pregnant woman very happy," she says. They decided early on to set a good example for the kids; no TV in the kitchen, everyone sits at the table. If the phone rings, the answering machine picks it up.

"This is sacred time," says Mary.

Mary typically awakes before 5:30 a.m. and is out the door by 6:20, driving the half hour to Ann Arbor, where she works as a medical technologist in an agency that handles organ donations. "If we don't sit down together in the evening, there is not one single moment in the day when we will be together as a family," she says.

Just before supper, Amy, a delicate blonde with a hint of freckles, is in the basement hopping on her pogo stick. Aaron, whose broad smile showcases his newly acquired orthodonture, is watching TV. When it's time to eat, the children light the floating candles in a bowl on the table. They say grace.

"I used to ask them, 'What happened at school?' and got a big 'nothing.' Now I say, 'Tell me one good thing that happened today.' And that often turns into ten things," says Mary.

Occasionally the kids' schedules are such that family dinners don't work out; Aaron might have a soccer game, or Amy a Brownie meeting or swim meet. Once a month, perhaps, the family buys a pizza to eat at home.

"We're not big on eating out," says Mary. "Frankly, I think we can cook much better things at home. And we can control the portion sizes."

With Mary off at a full-time job, Jeff, who works part-time as a carpenter and part-time as a magician (his professional name is "The Magic Dude") takes over a big portion of the work related to getting food on the table. "She clips the coupons, and I use them," he says. He does the weekly grocery shopping, but only after scouring the newspaper for sales. Occasionally Jeff does a "mega shop" to replenish staples, a list of which he keeps alphabetized on his computer. He makes the children's breakfasts and packs the family's lunches. (He is fond of doing something a little special for Mary's lunch; making tuna salad and forming it into the shape of a fish, for example, or creating a tic-tac-toe grid on her salad using strips of cheese and carrot rounds). He is an able sous chef, chopping and cleaning as he works alongside his wife.

"We have our best conversations while we're cooking," says Mary.

"It's when we do our heart-to-heart talking," adds Jeff. They work at a counter he designed and modified to swing out of the way when they need to accommodate large family gatherings during the holidays.

Somewhere along the line, Jeff grew interested in the barbecue grill. "When I married Mary, I couldn't grill a hot dog," he says. "For the life of me, I couldn't figure out how forest fires got started. I mean, I couldn't get my hibachi going with a can of kerosene and a hand grenade!" Now he's known in the family as "The Grill King" and is passing on his hard-earned knowledge to Aaron, who says that his favorite food to grill is "meat." The father-and-son team have grilled ribs and salmon and smoked whole turkeys.

On the night I visited, Mary and Jeff put together a dish of pasta shells stuffed with a taco filling (page 127), making two pans so that they could put one in the freezer for a later date. Mary got the recipe from a friend at work, who adapted it from a magazine.

Desserts and Baked Goods

"The kids love it," says Mary. "I find that almost any kind of Mexican food goes over well." She also experiments with Italian and Polish dishes, and has a repertoire of casseroles. Her family is always willing to try something new, she says. So far, sauerkraut is one of the few foods that hasn't made the grade with the kids.

After supper, an aura of calm prevails. The kids, who cleared their plates and the table, are doing their homework, Amy proudly reading a "chapter book" and Aaron attacking his math. The family's dog, a Boston terrier named Merlin (when he was a puppy "yellow puddles appeared as if by magic," says Jeff) plays with his ball.

The phone rings, and Mary answers.

Desserts and
Baked Goods Recipes

❖

◆ Almost-Instant Chocolate Pudding ◆

YIELD: 8 servings.

A truly last-minute dessert, this chocolatey pudding can be served warm or chilled. (We like it chilled).

6 tablespoons cornstarch
⅛ teaspoon salt
3 cups chocolate milk (store-bought or homemade, low-fat, or regular)
1 cup (6 ounces) semi-sweet chocolate chips or chopped semi-sweet
    baking chocolate
1 teaspoon pure vanilla extract
whipped cream, for serving (optional)

STIR THE CORNSTARCH and salt together in a saucepan and set the pan over medium–low heat. Pour in about ½ cup of the chocolate milk and whisk until the mixture is smooth. Increase the heat to medium and add the rest of the milk, stirring. When hot, add the chocolate and stir until melted. Adjust the heat so that large bubbles break on the surface of the pudding and keep whisking until thick, 3 to 5 minutes.

Remove from the heat and stir in the vanilla. Serve warm, or spoon into dessert bowls, ramekins, or small coffee cups. Allow to cool, cover with plastic wrap, and refrigerate until chilled, at least 1 hour. The pudding will get thicker as it cools. Serve with whipped cream if desired.

VARIATION: Mix 2 teaspoons instant espresso powder with the cornstarch and salt. OR: Substitute pure almond extract or orange extract for the vanilla extract.

MAKE AHEAD: Up to 2 days. Cool, cover and refrigerate.

These are truly quick, but you do need a food processor. An ice-cream maker makes them even quicker.

◆ Strawberry "Margarita" Sorbet ◆

YIELD: 1 quart, or 6 to 8 servings.

1 (10-ounce can) strawberry margarita concentrate, slightly thawed
½ cup water
4 cups frozen, unsweetened strawberries

PUT ALL INGREDIENTS in a food processor and pulse until pureed. Freeze in an ice-cream maker according to manufacturer's instructions. Alternatively, pour into a shallow pan and freeze several hours or overnight. About three hours before serving, remove from freezer, break into chunks, and puree in the food processor. Return to the container and freeze until ready to serve.

Remove from the freezer about 10 minutes before serving.

ADDITIONS: 2 tablespoons crème de cassis or chambord (raspberry-flavored liqueur).

◆ Cider Slush ◆

YIELD: 4 servings.

4 cups apple cider (not apple juice)
1 tablespoon lemon juice

PUT THE CIDER and lemon juice in an ice cream maker, stir to mix, and freeze according to manufacturer's instructions. Alternatively, pour into a shallow pan and freeze several hours or overnight. About three hours before serving, remove from freezer, break into chunks, and puree in the food processor. Return to the container and freeze until ready to serve.

Remove from the freezer about 10 minutes before serving.

ADDITION: 2 tablespoons calvados or apple jack brandy.

Barbarians at the Plate

◆ Banana "Ice Cream" ◆

YIELD: 4 servings.

4 frozen bananas, peeled (page 68)
orange or pineapple juice, as needed

BREAK THE BANANAS into chunks and put them into a food processor. Add a tablespoon of juice and puree until blended, adding juice—1 tablespoon at a time—until the mixture reaches a creamy consistency. Serve immediately.

◆ Brown Sugar Chews ◆

YIELD: 16 squares.

Of all the types of cookies, bar cookies are the quickest; this recipe is from my mom, and they don't require butter or other shortening. The nuts, however, are essential; if your family can't or won't eat nuts, don't bother making these.

1 packed cup light brown sugar
1 egg
1 teaspoon pure vanilla extract
¼ teaspoon salt
¼ teaspoon baking soda
½ cup all-purpose flour
1 cup chopped nuts, such as walnuts or pecans

PREHEAT THE OVEN to 350°F. Generously butter an 8-inch square pan.

Mix the brown sugar, egg, and vanilla together in a bowl. Add the remaining ingredients in order, stirring after each addition. Spoon the mixture into the prepared pan. It will make a thin layer.

Bake for 18 minutes—the cookies should still be soft (don't overbake!) Cool the cookies in the pan, on a wire rack. Cut into 2-inch squares and serve from the pan.

IF YOU HAVE TIME: Toast the nuts (page 50) before adding them to the batter.

No rolling pins required!

◆ Traditional Pastry Crust ◆

YIELD: 1 8- or 9-inch crust.

1⅓ cups all-purpose flour
2 tablespoons sugar
½ teaspoon salt
⅓ cup canola oil or other vegetable oil
1 tablespoon lemon juice
2 tablespoons ice water, or more, as needed

IN A FOOD PROCESSOR, combine the flour, sugar, and salt and pulse to mix. With the motor running, add the oil and lemon juice. Add 2 tablespoons of ice water and pulse to blend. If too dry, add more water, a teaspoon at a time, until the mixture forms a ball. (You can also mix this by hand in a bowl.) Press into an 8- or 9-inch pie plate with your fingers and chill before proceeding with your recipe. If you want to roll the dough out, wrap it in plastic wrap and chill it for at least 30 minutes. For a two-crust pie, double the recipe.

If the recipe calls for a partially prebaked shell, prick the pastry with the tines of a fork. Line with foil and weight the foil down with dried beans or pie weights (from a fancy cooking store). Cook in a 425°F oven for 10 to 12 minutes, remove the foil and weights, and bake an additional 3 to 5 minutes, until the dough no longer looks raw but is not yet golden brown. This shell can be filled and baked again. (It can also be frozen.) If the recipe calls for a fully baked shell, follow the same procedure for partial baking. After you remove the foil and weights, bake an additional 10 to 15 minutes, until the pastry looks golden brown. Cool on a wire rack.

FREEZE: Roll out the pastry into a circle larger than your pie plate. Wrap it in plastic and then in foil, and place it on a piece of cardboard or a cookie sheet so that it freezes flat. To use, thaw in the refrigerator for about 20 minutes, then fit into the pie plate and proceed with your recipe. You can also freeze the crust in a freezer-to-oven pie plate, but that takes up valuable freezer space.

◆ Graham Cracker Crust ◆

YIELD: 1 8- or 9-inch pie crust.

1¼ cups graham cracker crumbs (sold, boxed, in the supermarket;
   check the baking aisle; or make them by crushing graham crackers
   in the food processor)
3 to 4 tablespoons sugar
5 tablespoons unsalted butter, melted

MIX ALL OF the ingredients together and press into an 8- or 9-inch pie plate. Proceed with your recipe. (If it says to bake the crust, bake it for 8 minutes at 350°F. If it says not to bake the crust, simply chill it.)

◆ Chocolate Cookie Crust ◆

YIELD: 1 8- or 9-inch pie crust.

1½ cups chocolate wafer crumbs (made by crushing 25 - 30 chocolate
   wafers, such as Nabisco Famous Wafers)
2 tablespoons sugar
6 tablespoons unsalted butter, melted

MIX ALL OF the ingredients together and press into an 8- or 9-inch pie plate. Proceed with your recipe. (If it says to bake the crust, bake it for 8 minutes at 350°F. If it says not to bake the crust, simply chill it.)

ICE CREAM PIE

Make your own ice cream pie by filling a cookie crust (graham cracker or chocolate) with your favorite ice cream. Allow 3 cups of ice cream to soften slightly and spoon into the crust. Smooth the top with a spatula. Freeze until ice cream hardens. Serve plain, or topped with fudge or butterscotch sauce, pureed berries and/or whipped cream.

◆ Apple Tart ◆

YIELD: 8 servings.

Puff pastry from the freezer section of the supermarket makes this a true last-minute wonder.

  1 (10-by-10-inch) sheet frozen puff pastry, thawed according to package
     directions (half of a 17.3-ounce package)
  2 tablespoons unsalted butter, melted
  2 tablespoons sugar
  2 tart apples (such as Granny Smith) stemmed, halved, and cored
  ¼ cup dried cranberries, dried cherries, dried blueberries or golden raisins
  ground cinnamon
  ¼ cup sliced almonds or chopped pecans
  whipped cream or vanilla ice cream, for serving (optional)

CENTER A RACK in the oven and preheat the oven to 425°F.

Place the puff pastry on a cookie sheet. Brush with one tablespoon of the butter and sprinkle with 1 tablespoon of the sugar.

Slice the apples into ⅛-inch-thick slices. Place the slices in neat, slightly overlapping rows on the pastry, leaving a ¾-inch border of exposed dough all around. Brush with the remaining 1 tablespoon butter. Scatter the dried fruit and nuts over the apples and press them in gently with your hands. Sprinkle with cinnamon and the remaining tablespoon of sugar.

Bake until the apples are soft and the dough is golden, 18 to 22 minutes. Serve warm, with whipped cream or vanilla ice cream, if desired.

VARIATION: Substitute pears for the apples.

◆ Free-Form Berry Tart ◆

YIELD: 8 servings.

You can make this with any kind of berries. Pick a fruit preserve that will match or complement your choice of berries. (For example, peach preserves go well with fresh blueberries). When forming the tart, you really are going for a "free-form" look; think of the clay ashtrays you made in kindergarten.

  4 cups rinsed berries, stemmed, hulled, or sliced if necessary
  ¼ cup sugar

Barbarians at the Plate

2 tablespoons tapioca

pastry crust (page 184) or 1 9-inch pre-made, unbaked pie crust

1 (10-ounce) jar jam (your choice of flavor)

2 tablespoons unsalted butter, cut into tiny pieces

vanilla ice cream or whipped cream, for serving (optional)

CENTER A RACK in the oven. Preheat the oven to 400°F.

In a bowl, toss the berries with the sugar and tapioca and let sit at least 15 minutes.

While the berries are sitting, roll out the crust (homemade or store-bought) on a floured work surface to form a 13- or 14-inch circle.

Spoon the jam onto the crust, spreading to cover almost all of the crust except for a two-to-three-inch border around the edge. Spoon the berries on top of the jam. Turn up the border of the dough around the fruit. Scatter the butter on the fruit.

Bake for 30 to 35 minutes, or until the fruit is bubbling and the crust is golden. Serve warm, or at room temperature, plain or with ice cream or whipped cream, if desired.

◆ A Lovely Yellow Cake ◆

YIELD: 1 (single-layer) 8-inch cake, or about 6 servings.

My daughter recently made a yellow cake from a mix. She had to dump the mix into a bowl, add butter and eggs, and stir. This from-scratch recipe calls for butter and eggs, too, and takes about 2 more minutes to make. Either way, you've still dirtied a bowl and a baking pan. And this way you've got a lovely, homemade cake.

¾ cup (1½ sticks) unsalted butter, softened

¾ cup sugar

1½ teaspoons pure vanilla extract

3 eggs

¾ teaspoon baking powder

½ teaspoon salt

1½ cups all-purpose flour

PREHEAT THE OVEN to 350°F. Butter an 8-inch round cake pan.

In a mixing bowl, using an electric mixer or a spoon, cream the butter and sugar together. Add the vanilla and the eggs, beating well after each addition. Add the remaining ingredients, in order, and mix thoroughly.

Using a spatula, scrape the batter into the prepared pan and bake for 25 minutes, or until a tester inserted in the center comes out clean.

Set on a cake rack to cool for 15 minutes. Run a knife around the edges and remove from the pan.

VARIATION: Add ¼ teaspoon lemon extract and the finely chopped zest of one lemon.

FREEZE: Up to 1 month.

SERVING SUGGESTION: You can frost this cake, or you can serve it with a dusting of confectioners' sugar or sweetened shredded coconut, whipped cream, marmalade or jam, or with lemon curd (sold in the jam-and-jelly aisle of the grocery store).

◆ Brownies ◆

YIELD: 24 2-inch square brownies.

I know, I know . . . everyone uses a mix. But this recipe only dirties one pot and—wow!—what brownies! When I made these for my daughter's soccer team, I received thank-you notes*! Don't make them if you don't like really fudgy brownies. And don't even* think *about adding nuts.*

    12 tablespoons (1½ sticks) unsalted butter
    8 ounces unsweetened baking chocolate, cut into chunks
    2½ cups sugar
    ½ cup light corn syrup
    4 large eggs
    2 teaspoons pure vanilla extract
    ½ teaspoon salt
    ¼ teaspoon baking soda
    1¾ cups all-purpose flour

CENTER A RACK in the oven. Preheat the oven to 350°F. Grease and flour a 9-by-13-inch baking pan.

In large pot set over medium-low heat, melt the butter and chocolate, stirring occasionally. Remove the pot from the heat, and stir in the remaining ingredients, in order, mixing well.

Spoon into the prepared pan and bake 25 to 30 minutes, or until a tester inserted in the middle comes out with just a few crumbs. (They will be slightly underbaked.)

Allow to cool on a rack. Cut into 2-inch squares and serve from the pan.

FREEZE: Up to 1 month. (These are delicious right out of the freezer.)

Barbarians at the Plate

"PEOPLE ALWAYS THINK that etiquette is all about which fork to use," says Cindy Post Senning, sighing. "But what it's really about is respect, consideration, kindness, and honesty."

"Manners may change," she adds. "But the fundamental principles don't."

Senning should know. She is the granddaughter-in-law of Emily Post—yes, *the* Emily Post, the manners maven—and the codirector of the Emily Post Institute in Burlington, Vermont.

Dr. Senning is also a parent, the mother of two boys (now in their twenties), a former school principal (she has a Ph.D. in education) and the coauthor of several books, including *Emily Post's The Gift of Good Manners: A Parent's Guide to Raising Respectful, Kind, Considerate Children* (HarperCollins, 2002).

Yes, even an infant is learning at the table, says Senning: A bib introduces the concept of neatness; feeding your child with a spoon introduces the idea of utensils. A toddler can be taught not to interrupt. A preteen can master the art of winding spaghetti on a fork.

"It may be a simple family meal," she says, "but look at it as preparation for life outside the home."

There are two basic threads that run through Senning's approach to manners. First, know what you should expect—what's developmentally appropriate for your child—and then expect it.

Second, always behave in a way you want your children to behave. Senning calls this the "Golden Rule of Parenting." It may seem like the ultimate in common sense, but anyone who has dined with other people's children may feel that common sense is in desperately short supply.

"There are folks who let their kids run around at dinnertime, throw food, whatever—and after five years of this they put the kids into school, and the teacher has twenty of these children, and it's chaos," says my neighbor Matt Shippee, the father of three children. "They're not doing themselves, their children, or the rest of us any favors."

Shippee reflects on the dinner hour when his children were young: "Sometimes I just had to look at my kids and say *'Sit up straight and eat.'*"

Carol McD. Wallace, author of *Elbows Off the Table, Napkin in the Lap, No Video Games During Dinner: The Modern Guide to Teaching Children Good Manners* (St. Martin's Griffin, 1996) lists no less than eighteen behaviors that children between the ages of three and five can master in order to avoid the experience that she and her husband used to call "Dining Hell." Two rules are devoted to sitting at the table: "Stay Seated" and "Sitting Means Sitting" (not kneeling, perching, or slouching). She considers this—sitting—the most important lesson, along with "Don't Eat with Your Fingers." Both, she writes, are "crucial to pleasant meals."

It may be just coincidence—and my sampling of families was certainly not scientific—but the kids I met on my visits all seemed to have terrific manners for their respective ages. Ben Branco, age fifteen, met me at the door with a firm handshake, as did Mason Church, age nine. Six-year-old Sonali Durham set an elegant table. Four-year-old Caroline Hill asked to "please be excoosed," after sitting (relatively) quietly through dinner. Aaron Jackowski, twelve, actually *initiated conversation* with me at the table, listened attentively, and responded articulately to questions. Sure, I witnessed a few minor lapses: arguments about who got the best or biggest plate/piece of chicken/glass of juice, a dramatic burp or two, an overenthusiastic eater spraying corn kernels while talking; but these breaches were small potatoes compared to the pleasure of sitting at a table with families who were clearly happy to break bread together.

You don't have to be an etiquette expert to have your children behave at the table. Cindy Post Senning taught me that, strictly speaking, you don't even have to have a table. Though you might think that the granddaughter of Emily Post dines nightly at a setting of Baccarat and Limoges, it turns out that, when her boys were at home, she ate with them and her husband using tray tables in the living room. "The kitchen table is piled with too much junk, and we don't have a dining room," Senning says. So they ate together using the trays, with what she calls "casual but proper" place settings. The TV was turned off.

"The point is that we were having dinner together, looking at each other, and talking," she says. As Senning and all working parents know, it really isn't about the forks.

◆ Biscuits ◆

YIELD: 9 biscuits.

Homemade biscuits or soda bread (page 191), rolls (page 193) or corn bread (page 192) can turn a meal of canned soup into a feast. You can bake them or keep them in your freezer.

    2 cups all-purpose flour
    1 tablespoon baking powder
    1 tablespoon sugar

Barbarians at the Plate

½ teaspoon salt
5 tablespoons unsalted butter, well chilled
⅓ to ½ cup milk

CENTER A RACK in the oven and preheat the oven to 425°F. Grease a cookie sheet or line it with baking parchment.

In a large bowl, stir together the flour, baking powder, sugar, and salt. Cut the butter into small pieces and distribute throughout the flour. Then, using a pastry blender, or your fingers, mash the butter into the flour until the mixture is the consistency of coarse cornmeal. (You can also do this with a food processor.)

Add ⅓ cup of the milk and mix briefly, just until all dry ingredients are incorporated into the dough. Add the remaining milk (about 3 tablespoons), a bit at a time, if needed. Overmixing will make the biscuits tough.

Turn the dough out onto a well-floured surface and knead it about 5 times. Pat it out into a rough 6- or 7-inch square, and cut it into 9 equal pieces. (If you want round biscuits, you can cut them with a cookie cutter or the floured rim of a juice glass, but this takes longer.)

Transfer the biscuits to the prepared cookie sheet, and place them about 1½ inches apart. Bake about 12 to 15 minutes, or until golden brown.

FREEZE: Up to 2 months.

◆ Irish Soda Bread ◆

YIELD: 1 loaf, about 4 servings.

This is the easiest bread I know how to make. The recipe was given to me many years ago by the late Bob McCreanor of Narragansett, Rhode Island, who was a family man, a dog-lover, and a dear colleague.

    4 cups all-purpose flour, plus a little more for kneading
    1 tablespoon salt
    ¾ teaspoon baking soda
    ¾ teaspoon baking powder
    1½ to 2 cups buttermilk

PREHEAT THE OVEN to 375°F. Generously butter and 8-inch cake pan.

In a large bowl, mix together the flour, salt, baking soda, and baking powder. Add 1½ cups buttermilk and stir. If the mixture is too dry and will not form a ball, add more buttermilk until it does. Place the dough on a well-floured work surface and knead about 5 minutes. Form into a

round loaf and place in the prepared pan (the loaf will be smaller than the pan). Make an X on top with a sharp knife.

Bake for 35 to 40 minutes until light brown. The loaf will sound hollow when lightly tapped.

Serve warm or at room temperature. Leftovers make great toast.

FREEZE: Up to 2 months.

◆ Corn Bread ◆

YIELD: 8 2-by-4-inch squares.

Okay. You forgot to buy the mix. . . . think of it as an opportunity to treat your family to the real thing.

4 tablespoons (½ stick) unsalted butter, melted and slightly cooled
1¼ cups regular or low-fat milk
1 large egg
2 teaspoons baking powder
1 teaspoon salt
2 tablespoons sugar
½ cup all-purpose flour
1½ cups cornmeal

PREHEAT THE OVEN to 375°F. Butter an 8-inch square pan.

Mix all of the ingredients in order, stirring until just combined. Pour into the prepared pan.

Bake 30 minutes, or until golden and a tester inserted in the center comes out clean. Let cool five minutes and serve warm, from the pan.

FREEZE: Up to 2 months.

Barbarians at the Plate

♦ Sixty-Minute Dinner Rolls ♦

YIELD: 12 rolls.

I *call these "Elaine's Famous Rolls" because my neighbor, Elaine Fitch, should be famous for the recipe. They take exactly an hour, from start to finish, but there's very little actual work involved; most of it is just letting the yeast do its thing. Instead of making 12 dinner rolls, I sometimes make 6 larger rolls and use them for hamburgers. The larger rolls take a few minutes longer to bake.*

1¼ cups regular or reduced-fat milk

4 tablespoons (½ stick) unsalted butter

¼ cup lukewarm water (run the tap until the water feels just slightly warm)

2 (.25-ounce) packages regular (not rapid-rise) yeast (about 1½ tablespoons)

4 cups all purpose flour, or 3 cups all-purpose flour and 1 cup whole-wheat flour

1 teaspoon salt

3 tablespoons sugar

PLACE THE MILK and the butter in a pot set over medium-high heat and cook just until the butter is melted and bubbles appear around the edges of the milk. Set aside to cool.

Put the water in a large bowl and sprinkle the yeast on top. Let it sit ("proof") for 5 to 10 minutes; the yeast should begin to bubble. (If it doesn't, the yeast is too old to use, and you have to start over with fresher yeast.)

After the yeast has bubbled, add the flour, the milk mixture, salt, and sugar, and mix well. Turn onto a floured work surface and knead for a couple of minutes. Cover with a clean dish towel and let it rise for 15 minutes.

Line a cookie sheet with parchment paper. Preheat the oven to 375°F. Divide the dough into 12 equal portions, shaping them into rounds with your hands. Place on the prepared cookie sheet and set aside for 15 minutes.

Bake 12 to 15 minutes, until golden and hollow-sounding when tapped.

FREEZE: Up to 2 months.

Desserts and Baked Goods

193

◆ Yogurt Pancakes ◆

YIELD: about 6 pancakes.
Recipe from Lois and Karen Gray of Iowa City, Iowa.

These pancakes go well with yogurt or cottage cheese and fruit. They're so good you could serve them for dinner. If you make them in the blender, they are very quick, and you can pour the batter easily.

- 1½ cups all-purpose flour (or 1 cup all-purpose flour and ½ cup whole-wheat pastry flour)
- 3 tablespoons sugar
- 1½ teaspoons baking soda
- ⅛ teaspoon salt
- 3 eggs
- 1 (6-ounce) container of raspberry yogurt or other flavor of your choice
- ¾ cup water
- 3 tablespoons vegetable oil, plus more for oiling the pan

PREHEAT THE OVEN to warm.

Combine all of the ingredients in a bowl or the container of a blender. Mix or blend until smooth.

Pour about a teaspoon of oil into a skillet and use a paper towel to spread the oil and coat the pan. Set the skillet over medium–high heat and heat until a drop of water dropped on the surface sputters.

Pour a scant ½ cup of batter onto the skillet and reduce heat to medium. Cook until one side is brown, about 3 minutes, then, using a spatula, flip over and cook on the other side. Place on a platter in the oven and keep warm while you cook the remaining pancakes, lightly oiling the skillet with an oiled paper towel as needed.

NOTE: This recipe can easily be doubled.

MAKE AHEAD: Make the batter up to 12 hours ahead and store, covered, in the blender container in the fridge. Blend briefly to remix before using.

FREEZE: Stack cooked, cooled pancakes, separating each pancake with a square of waxed paper. Wrap well and freeze. Pop in toaster or toaster oven to reheat.

SERVING SUGGESTION: These pancakes are fairly sweet; if you plan on serving them with maple syrup, consider reducing the sugar to 2 tablespoons.

Barbarians at the Plate

THE COOKBOOK SHELF:

Bodger, Lorraine. *The Four-Sided Cookie: 55 Recipes for Delicious Squares and Bars.* St. Martin's Griffin, 2000.

Chattman, Lauren. *Instant Gratification: No-Hassle Desserts in Just About No Time.* Morrow Books, 2000. Also *Mom's Big Book of Baking.* Harvard Common Press, 2001.

Schloss, Andrew with Bookman, Ken. *One-Pot Cakes: 60 Recipes for Cakes from Scratch Using a Pot, a Spoon, and a Pan.* William Morrow, 1995. Out of print, but worth looking for.

Appendices

APPENDIX 1:
Making Meals Healthier

HERE ARE TEN simple things to keep in mind to help create more nutritious meals (that kids will still eat).

1. **READ LABELS:** Did you know that alleged "wheat" bread may be made to look "whole wheat-y" with food coloring? Or that reduced-fat products (like reduced-fat peanut butter) may have replaced "healthy" (unsaturated) fats with unhealthy trans-fats (and added sugar)? If you read labels, you do.

2. **VEG OUT DAILY:** Up the servings of vegetables and fruits: raw, cooked, canned, or frozen. A "rainbow" of colors—purple, green, yellow-orange, red, white—will help you get a "rainbow" of vitamins, minerals, and disease-fighting phytochemicals as well as fiber. Plus, these veggies are pretty, and nearly everyone—adults and well as children—responds to pretty.

   Think Pie: If you think of the plate as a pie chart, aim for filling half with fruits and vegetables, and one-quarter each with protein and high-fiber starch.

3. **GO WITH THE (WHOLE) GRAIN:** If your family balks, try gradually introducing them. Mix brown and white rice together after they are cooked (you can make big batches ahead of time, and mix and freeze them in family-sized portions). Make sandwiches with one slice of whole-grain bread and one slice of white. Combine a favorite breakfast cereal with one that has at least 3 grams of fiber per serving. Likewise, serving whole-wheat pasta is a good idea . . . in theory, at least. I keep trying.

   RICE IN A TRICE: Brown rice has twice as much fiber as white rice, but also takes twice as long to cook. I've always hated the texture of "instant" rice but was surprised to read (on the label of a box of Kraft Minute Instant-Whole Grain Brown

Rice) that it has the same nutritional profile of regular brown rice. I'm still not crazy about the texture, but faced with fiber-rich rice that cooks in 10 minutes (the "instant" type) versus rice that cooks in 45 (regular) . . . there's often no contest.

4. **AVOID THE GLOP ON TOP:** It's a travesty that individual portions of mini-cut carrots are now often packaged with fatty, salty dips; that caramel sauce is marketed as a coating for apple slices; that processed cheese food is touted as a microwaveable sauce for broccoli; and that yogurt is tarted up with sprinkles and candy. These foods taste great virtually unadorned. Bonus: Plain is often faster, easier, and cheaper.

5. **PUT WATER, WATER EVERYWHERE . . .** Especially on your table, in place of soda (or "pop," depending on where you live) or sugar water (those drinks that have only 10 percent juice). Don't practice "juice abuse," either. Doctors recommend that kids ages seven to eighteen should drink no more than 12 ounces of (100-percent) juice a day. That's 1½ juice boxes. Younger kids should drink no more than 6 ounces (1 juice box) per day. Otherwise, the juice is just adding sugar to the diet. Try feeding kids the whole fruit instead, so they'll get the fiber and vitamins, and make water everyone's beverage of choice.

     WATER SAFETY: Be aware that some brands of bottled water—even the kind marketed for children with cartoon animals on the bottles—contain sugar, caffeine, or artificial sweeteners. If you're worried about the taste or quality of your tap water, try using a filter pitcher or install a filter on your tap.

6. **KEEP YOUR EYE ON THE SIZE:** Too much of even healthy food is unhealthy. A USDA-recommended serving of bread is 1 slice; of rice, ½ cup. This doesn't mean you have to limit yourself to a half cup of rice, but it does mean that you should realize when you've eaten a 1-cup serving you've consumed two of the 6 to 11 daily recommended servings of grain.

     SERVING SENSE: Plating portions before serving may help keep everyone in the family from stuffing themselves to the extent they might if the pot is plopped on the table. Carole Naquin, a mother of two in Montpelier, Vermont, switched from using large dinner plates to smaller "luncheon" plates to keep portion sizes under control.

7. **DON'T LEAVE FAT TO CHANCE:** Fats, if you use the right kind (unsaturated), not only add flavor to food but are rich in health-enhancing properties. (See "The Skinny on Fats," page 201). But it makes sense to switch to reduced-fat (1 percent or

skim) milk, reduced-fat cheeses, sour cream, mayonnaise, and yogurt when practical. For taste and texture, most low-fat versions trump the no-fat versions, which often separate in cooking and have a grainy texture.

Sauté vegetables in a bit of chicken broth or white wine, or switch from sautéing in butter (saturated fat) or margarine (trans fat) to a healthier fat like olive or canola oil.

8. **REINTRODUCE FOOD:** As any parent knows, kids have mercurial tastes in foods. One week they love sweet potatoes, the next week they hate them. So keep introducing new foods, or going back to once-favorites. Some day, I just know it, my kids will be begging for fish.

9. **TAKE THE LONG VIEW:** Terri Brandmueller, a mother of two in New York City, takes "the long view" of her family's dinners, judging them over a week's time rather than day-by-day. "If we have pancakes for dinner one night—and, by the way, the eggs in the pancakes count as protein—then the next night I'll make something heavy on the vegetables," she says.

10. **PAT YOURSELF ON THE BACK:** You're not going to eat healthy 100 percent of the time. Probably not even 90 percent of the time. Don't sweat it. Do what you can, when you can, and be proud of yourself.

THE SKINNY ON FATS

OKAY, THERE'S "GOOD" cholesterol and "bad" cholesterol, but who can ever remember what they're called? Your aim is to increase the "good" stuff, called HDL (think: H is for "Healthy") and lower the "bad," or LDL ("L" is for "Loser," naturally).

- ❖ Good fats: Monounsaturated fats (olive, canola, sesame oil) and polyunsaturated fats (corn, vegetable, walnut oil).
- ❖ Bad fats: Saturated fats, found in meat, full-fat dairy products (including butter), lard, and tropical oils.
- ❖ *Really* bad fats: Trans fats, short for trans-fatty acids, are found in margarine (unless it is labeled "trans free") and solid vegetable shortening. Trans fats are also major players in most junk foods from chips and crackers to cookies and cakes. If the ingredients include the words *hydrogenated fats,* you know the product contains trans fats. Beginning January 1, 2006, food manufacturers will be required to list trans-fat content on the Nutrition Facts panel on food labels. Until then, we have to read the fine print.

ORGANICALLY SPEAKING

FOR SOME FOLKS, budget constraints put organic foods out of reach. Others are just plain confused. For one thing, there is so much contradictory information floating around—much of it put forward by "experts"—about organic foods, genetically modified foods, "natural" foods, artificial sweeteners, additives, and preservatives that the path to nutritional enlightenment is far from clear. But it makes sense to me that organic foods are desirable—they are a lot kinder to the environment, for one thing. And while I can't swear to you that I can taste the difference between an organically fed chicken and one grown on whatever it is they feed nonorganic chickens, I *can* tell you that the organic chicken looks better; and I feel better about feeding it to my family. I met some parents who buy organic everything; most pick and choose. Gigi Durham in Iowa City, for example, buys organic milk but regular (nonorganic) produce. I buy organic root vegetables (potatoes, onions, carrots) but regular milk. When I am feeling "healthy" and "concerned" (and flush with dough), I buy organic. When I'm feeling strapped for cash, I don't. I take comfort in the words of Ralph Waldo Emerson: "A foolish consistency is the hobgoblin of little minds." Of course, one could argue that buying organic is probably a "wise consistency."

A VEGETARIAN IN YOUR MIDST: DEALING WITH SPECIAL DIETS

"ONE OF THE BIGGEST disruptions in a family unit is when one person changes food habits," a psychologist once told me. "Food gives people a sense of community."

So I guess I can admit that, when my then-sixteen-year-old announced that she would no longer eat meat, poultry, or fish, I was a little peeved. We had been, up to that time, a family of happy omnivores, with a heavy list toward the carnivorous. Suddenly our mealtime routine—practically our very way of life—was being threatened. *From within.*

Well, after a few weeks of telling Hannah that she could jolly well nuke a veggie burger if she didn't want the lamb chops, I realized I wasn't acting much like a person with a "sense of community." I decided to take the high road: I began looking at her change in eating habits as a culinary challenge, and developed a repertoire of vegetarian meals that the whole family likes. I also learned that it's not too hard to leave meat out of some dishes and add it after my vegetarian daughter has been served. We probably eat healthier now because of my daughter's food choices. To her credit, she never makes us feel uncomfortable about our flesh-eating ways. Of

Barbarians at the Plate

course, when she's gone (which is often, now that she's in college), we eat plenty of meat. And sometimes I still tell her to nuke a veggie burger.

In some cases, of course, there's even more at stake. A medical diagnosis—diabetes, heart disease, food allergies and intolerances—can require a whole new approach to food. My advice is to read as much as you can, and to talk with a nutritionist who is experienced with the particular health issue in question. Come together as a family to figure it out. Remember that the emphasis in the phrase *family meal* should be on *family.* If you have strong relationships with each other, the food part will be a piece of (gluten-free, dairy-free, low-sodium, fat-free, meat-free, nut-free) cake.

THE COOKBOOK SHELF:

FOR DIABETES AND allergies: (I have no direct experience with these books, so I'm just passing on a few recommendations from others):

American Heart Association Kids' Cookbook: All Recipes Made by Real Kids in Real Kitchens! Clarkson Potter, 1993. Out of print, but highly recommended. Also: *The New American Heart Association Cookbook: Sixth Edition,* 1998.

Barber, Marianne S. *The Parent's Guide to Food Allergies: Clear and Complete Advice from the Experts on Raising Your Food Allergic Child.* Owl Books, 2001.

Betty Crocker's Diabetes Cookbook: Everyday Meals, Easy as 1-2-3. Betty Crocker Books, 2003.

Glick, Ruth and Baggett, Nancy. *One Pot Meals For People With Diabetes.* McGraw-Hill, 2002.

VEGETARIAN COOKBOOKS:

Lemlin, Jeanne. *Quick Vegetarian Pleasures.* HarperPerennial, 1992. Also: *Simple Vegetarian Pleasures,* 2002.

Moosewood Collective. *Moosewood Restaurant Cooks at Home: Fast and Easy Recipes for Any Day.* Fireside, 1993.

Raab, Evelyn. *The Clueless Vegetarian: A Cookbook for the Aspiring Vegetarian.* Firefly Books, 2000.

APPENDIX 2:
Supermarket Strategies

THE MOST IMPORTANT tool you have for cooking is, um . . . food. It has to get from the store into your house. It has to be there when you need it.

Wouldn't it be nice if, like those civilized Europeans we're always reading about, we had the time to stop at the market each day (here I envision a profusion of beautiful fruits, vegetables, and cut flowers) and take home fresh produce in our string bags for the evening?

Reality, for most of us, is that adding a stop at the store on our way home from work is just one more hassle that will delay getting dinner on the table. Some folks, like Diann Neal of Cromwell, Oklahoma, shop only once a month. Diann sticks everything she can in the freezer and relies on a nearby (okay, next door) convenience store for milk and eggs.

Most parents I found who manage to cook family meals shop once a week. Some go to only one store. Others, like Gigi Durham of Iowa City, hits an Indian store for special ingredients, a natural foods store, and her local supermarket, shopping at a "box store" once a month for paper and cleaning goods. (My neighbor Sarah Gallagher says that she used to go to box stores, but found she was spending a fortune on "bargain" impulse buys.)

If you can shop at off-times (i.e., not Saturday morning), you'll save a ton of time. Jeff Jackowski, of Brighton, Michigan, a carpenter and magician with a flexible schedule, does the weekly shopping on Monday mornings, when "there's no one there."

SHOP WITH A LIST

MOST SUPERMARKETS ARE large, warehouse-like, badly lit places with awful Muzak and screaming toddlers (possibly your own). Who wants to spend more time in them than absolutely necessary?

The only surefire way to save time shopping is to have a list and stick to it. Here's how to create an efficient one:

Barbarians at the Plate

First, **keep a running list**—on your fridge, your computer, wherever—of pantry items that need replenishing: (See "The Civilized Pantry," page 205). I add items to the big family calendar that hangs near the phone, because it's the handiest spot and I always look at it. Mary Kay Knox of Sturbridge, Massachusetts, hangs a bulletin board known as "Command Central" in her kitchen: It holds a shopping list along with a list of odd chores (not the daily stuff, but items like "change lightbulb in garage").

Second, **check the family calendar**. Factoring in lacrosse schedules, pottery class, and parent-teacher meetings, figure out which nights you will be able to sit down together as a family.

Third, **make a menu**. Many moms, like Karen Branco of Bellevue, Ohio, sit down with her kids once a week to plan. Make sure to include ideas for the nights one or more of you will be missing from the table—a slow cooker stew that a late-comer can dip into? Quesadillas that everyone can make as they come home?

Fourth, **meld the two lists**—the list of needed staples, and the list of specific foods for the week's menu. Following Karen Branco's lead, I now keep my shopping list on my computer, organized in the same way my favorite supermarket (okay, that's an oxymoron) is set up. Every week I open my Master List file, copy it to a new document, and start plugging in the stuff we need. I type the menu at the top; if Monday says "chili," it helps me to remember that I need to buy fresh cilantro, which my family likes on chili and which is not a weekly purchase. The notes I have written on my calendar will tell me that I'm out of canned kidney beans. It takes maybe fifteen minutes to come up with the list, and that's fifteen minutes I got to spend at home, sipping coffee at my computer, and not listening to a canned version of "Eleanor Rigby" on the sound system of the grocery store. My lists have saved me untold hours of wandering from aisle to aisle, backtracking from dairy (at one end of the store) to produce (at the other) because I forgot to put lemons in the cart.

SHOPPING WITH KIDS

THE GOOD NEWS is that supermarkets now cater to kids in all sorts of ways: child-sized carts that little ones can easily push, and big carts shaped like cars that kids can sit in and "drive" while you push. The bad news is that the stores still put all the most colorful, junky food at the kids' eye level. (Those candy-free checkout aisles are great, but the real challenge is getting the kids through the *cereal* aisle.)

Shopping is a good time for a little tough love. Head the kids off at the pass by setting ground rules about supermarket behavior and setting limits on treats (zero treats is fine, if you can enforce it). Deal with tantrums quietly

Supermarket Strategies

and immediately—leave your cart at the courtesy desk and remove your child/children to your car, where her/his/their screaming will cause a minimum of disruption for other shoppers. (I used to strap my daughters in their car seats and wait it out). Kids need to learn how to behave in public, and a supermarket is as good a place to start as any. (This "parking lot" method also works in many other venues, including restaurants.)

Also, consider this: Grocery shopping does not actually *have* to be horrible. If you have the time, a trip to an actual farmer's market, farm stand, natural foods store, or bakery can be an aesthetically pleasing, educational, and—dare I say it?—fun experience. If you start talking to the farmer or the baker, your children may begin to understand that food comes from somewhere other than a box or plastic tray. Encourage them to ask questions. You may even be able to introduce your children (and yourself) to a wonderful variety of "boutique" foods—striped beets, squash flowers, farmstead cheeses—and get them excited about cooking and eating. Even at the regular supermarket, you can "treat" yourselves to an exotic array of fruits and vegetables—star fruit, jicama, yucca, plantains—unusual fish (squid anyone?) and specialty meats (andouille sausage, short ribs, game hens). Your kids will get the message that experimenting is worthwhile. Yes, it can be expensive, but think of all the money you are saving on pizza delivery.

On the other hand, you and the kids might be happier if you shop without them. Gigi Durham shops on Saturday mornings while her husband, Frank, stays home with the kids and cleans the house. (Yes, real men do vacuum.) Diann Neal leaves teenagers in charge of the younger ones when she does her once-a-month, fill-the-van shop. You may even decide that money spent on a baby-sitter will be saved in time and the items you didn't buy when your children were whining.

COUPONS

I HATE COUPONS. I have always considered them a waste of time. Why don't they just make the stuff cheaper to begin with? Why should I have to spend hours searching, clipping, and filing?

But zillions of people use coupons, including my own mother and many families interviewed for this book. If you are going to use them, here are some tips:

❖ Clip the coupons only for things you actually use. You are not saving money if you get 75-cents off an item that no one likes. Don't be tempted to "treat" the kids to more junk food just because you have a coupon.

❖ Organize the coupons in a file or wallet.
❖ If the coupon is for an item that requires you to go to another store, consider chucking it. What you save in discounts may be minimal compared to what you spend in time and gas.

KATHY SCHULZ of San Diego recommends the online coupon site: *www.grocerygame.com*.

APPENDIX 3:
Stocking the Civilized Pantry

I**T'S A TRUISM** the bears repeating: Your meals will be only as good as the ingredients that go in them. Buy the very best you can afford. Fresh produce (local, when possible) will always beat the flavor of canned and almost always of frozen. Think seasonally: If it's winter, consider using frozen strawberries rather than those blah-tasting steroidal monsters you'll find in the produce aisle; at some times of the year, canned tomatoes are preferable to fresh. If you are worried about additives, pesticides, and genetically modified foods, think about buying organic; even regular supermarkets now carry a wide array (see page 202).

For this book I've tried to use only ingredients found in a decent-sized supermarket, and have noted some that might only be available, depending on where you live, in natural foods or specialty stores. I've offered substitutions when possible and can promise you will not have to mail-order any ingredients.

Whether your pantry is a single shelf, a cupboard, or a separate room, you need to stock it—and the fridge and freezer—intelligently. Consider these as possible basics:

OILS AND NONSTICK COOKING SPRAY: (See "The Skinny on Fats," page 201.) Oils not used within three months might get rancid; store them in the fridge. They may turn cloudy, but the flavor will be unaffected. Also, some oils—like organic oils and nut oils—come with instructions to refrigerate after opening. Check the bottle.

❖ A note on olive oil: Extra-virgin olive oil has low acidity and is mechanically, not chemically, produced. Virgin olive oil has a higher acidity, and the stuff sold as plain "olive oil" has been chemically refined. For taste and health, Deborah Krasner, author of *The Flavors of Olive Oil* (Simon and Schuster, 2002) says extra-virgin is the way to go. Among supermarket varieties, she gives the nod to Colavita Extra Virgin, Bertolli Extra Virgin, Filippo Berio Organic Extra Virgin, and the Lucini brand.

Barbarians at the Plate

CONDIMENTS: Mayonnaise, salad dressings, mustard, ketchup, salsa, barbecue sauce, Worcestershire sauce, soy and teriyaki sauce, capers, hot sauce, vinegar, pickles, relish, chutneys.

CANNED FOODS: Beans, soups (including canned chicken broth, vegetable broth, and beef broth), tomatoes (whole, crushed, sauce, and paste); and fish (tuna, salmon, clams, sardines . . . anchovies anyone?).

PASTA: We should all be eating whole-wheat pastas for more fiber. Some of us are not. Small shapes (orzo, pastina, ditalini) work well in soups; larger shapes (spaghetti, linguine, fettuccine, fusilli, etc.) hold up under sauce. Egg noodles make a nice side dish.

RICE AND GRAINS: Brown (quick-cooking or regular) and white rice, couscous (takes 5 minutes to make) and other grains such as bulgur, which can be used as a meat substitute (see Meatless Veggie Chili, page 88).

BREAD: Bread, rolls, etc., get tough in the fridge; keep them in a bread box (or drawer) or in the freezer. (Do not microwave bread or other baked goods because nuking them will also make them tough; reheat them in a toaster oven or regular oven.)

BREAKFAST CEREAL: I won't lecture you on the evils of cereal shaped like chocolate chip cookies if you don't lecture me on the non-nutritive values of Rice Krispie Treats. I always keep some Rice Krispies on hand to make them. For eating, not baking, look for cereals with at least 3 grams of fiber per serving.

BAKING SUPPLIES: Flour, cake, corn bread, and brownie mixes (health food stores carry brands made without hydrogenated oils), pure vanilla and almond extracts (the extra flavor kick is worth the extra dough), chocolate chips, baking chocolate, molasses, sugar (brown, white, and confectioners') and pure maple syrup.

DRIED HERBS AND SPICES: Most recipes in this book call for dried herbs (except for parsley, cilantro, and, occasionally, basil). If you want to substitute fresh herbs, use twice as much. Store all dried herbs and spices away from heat (i.e., not over the stove).

A note on salt and pepper: Kosher salt has less sodium than regular table salt (but no iodine). In a few cases where it's important, recipes call for "coarsely ground pepper," which you can buy in the spice section if you don't own a peppermill.

Stocking the Civilized Pantry

209

NUTS: Freeze them for long-term storage. In addition to the usual suspects (walnuts, pecans, almonds) think about stocking pine nuts (pignoli) and shelled pumpkin seeds (pepitas): toasted, they make a great addition to salads.

DAIRY PRODUCTS: See page 67 for information on freezing cheese, milk, butter, and eggs.

❖ A note on butter: I prefer unsalted butter because it is said to be fresher (salt, a preservative, is added to prolong shelf life) and because I like to control the amount of salt in recipes. I don't use margarine because I never liked the taste. Also, most brands are high in trans-fatty acids (page 201).

PRODUCE: If you are planning a long hiatus between shopping trips, use up the delicate fruits and vegetables (lettuces, pears) first, and save the longer-lasting ones (broccoli, root vegetables, apples) for later on. Pre-chopped or shredded items cost more but save lots of time.

MEATS, POULTRY, AND SEAFOOD: Buy in bulk and freeze individual or family-sized portions. Remember that shrimp, though expensive, can make an incredibly quick and tasty meal (see page 59).

FROZEN VEGETABLES: Especially handy are frozen chopped onions and chopped green peppers.

FROZEN FRUITS: Stock a variety for pie fillings, ice-cream toppings, or smoothies. Frozen lemon juice tastes almost like fresh-squeezed, and not like the bottled concentrate (which tastes like Mr. Clean).

PREPARED PIZZA DOUGH, PIE DOUGH, AND PUFF PASTRY: Look in the deli or bakery aisle of your supermarket for bags of pizza dough—just like they used to sell at old Italian bakeries. This stuff is cheap (about $1 per bag), resilient (no holes when stretched), and darn good. You can keep it in the fridge for a day or so, or freeze it for several months. Pre-made pie shells, available in the dairy case, are quick and freeze beautifully. Frozen puff pastry can be topped with fruit and turned into dessert quickly see page 186. It also makes a good crust for pot pie; see page 48.

MISCELLANEOUS: Spaghetti sauce, olives, marinated artichoke hearts, jars of roasted red peppers, juice, bread crumbs, Asian chili paste,

Barbarians at the Plate

corn meal, peanut butter, sun-dried tomatoes, marshmallows (for last-minute campfires and those Rice Krispie Treats—see "Breakfast Cereal," above), hoisin sauce. Evaporated skim milk can stand in for milk during a "baking emergency"; I sometimes use it in coffee. Frozen ravioli, tortellini, and gnocchi (potato dumplings) make quick meals.

WINES AND SPIRITS: I hate to open a bottle of wine just to add a few tablespoons to a dish. For cooking, I keep dry white vermouth on hand. Vermouth is a fortified wine that can hang around on the shelf indefinitely after being opened. Red vermouth, which is quite sweet, can be used in place of cooking sherry (but not in place of dry red wine). If you do not like to cook with spirits, substitutions are usually given; try broth or fruit juice.

FOODS SOMETIMES SOLD UNDER OTHER NAMES:

- ❖ Cilantro = fresh coriander (or Chinese parsley).
- ❖ Flat-leaf parsley = Italian parsley
- ❖ Scallions = green onions
- ❖ Fennel = anise
- ❖ Chickpeas = garbanzo or ceci ("cheh-chee") beans
- ❖ Cannellini beans = white kidney beans
- ❖ Yams = sweet potatoes (true yams are almost never available in the U.S., although various kinds of sweet potatoes, especially canned sweet potatoes, are often erroneously labeled "yams").
- ❖ Fish names change from region to region, if not store to store. Rockfish, for example, may be sold as Ocean Perch, Pacific Red Snapper, or Rock Cod. For help with this—along with great recipes—consult Mark Bittman's book *Fish: The Complete Guide to Buying and Cooking* (Macmillan Publishing, 1994).

CONVENIENCE FOODS

THIS IS A highly subjective list, reflecting my own preferences with additions made by the families I interviewed for this book.

BAGGED, PRECUT, PRESHREDDED EVERYTHING: "Spring mix" salad (also called "mesclun"), baby spinach, shredded cabbage, shredded broccoli, shredded carrots, mini-cut carrots, grated or shredded cheese (Monterey Jack, Cheddar, Parmesan, Asiago, mozzarella).

CANNED TOMATOES: Whole, pureed, diced, sauce, and paste.

CANNED BROTH AND BOUILLON CUBES: What? You're not making your own stock from scratch? Just kidding. . . . If you have the extra dough, try the "natural" beef, chicken (free-range), fish stock, and organic vegetable broth in aseptic packaging (boxes) sold in many supermarkets. The taste really is better than canned, but canned is fine, too. When you need broth and don't have any, use bouillon cubes or granules, or soup base, dissolved in hot water.

CANNED BEANS: Black beans, chickpeas (garbanzo beans) red kidney beans, white kidney beans (cannellini beans), black-eyed peas, refried beans.

PIZZA DOUGH: See "Stocking the Civilized Pantry," page 208.

PREPARED POLENTA: In my supermarket, it is sold in the deli section in plastic tubes; it resembles a yellow sausage. It can be sliced and grilled, sautéed, or baked; just follow the package directions.

PREPARED PIE CRUSTS: For best taste, look for ones with only flour, water, and butter (and maybe salt) as ingredients. These are found in upscale markets and natural foods stores. Otherwise, the kind sold in the dairy section of the supermarket (like the Pillsbury brand) do just fine. Freeze them and defrost according to package directions. Use for quiche, as a topping for chicken pot pie (page 48), or for desserts like a free-form tart (page 186). For homemade crust, see page 184.

BOTTLED BARBECUE SAUCE: Barbecue mavens will get violent about their choice of "boutique" brands. I buy what's on sale.

SALSA: Too much choice! When I'm using it in cooking or as a topping for burritos or other foods, I buy what's cheap. If I'm serving it plain, with chips, I like to buy one of the fresh salsas sold at the natural foods store or make my own (see page 174).

SALAD DRESSING: Good Season Italian, Ken's Steakhouse Caesar Dressing, Newman's Own Oil and Vinegar, and Annie's Naturals Goddess Dressing and Shiitake & Sesame Vinaigrette. For homemade dressing, see page 167.

FROZEN PIZZA: American Flatbread is hands-down the best frozen pizza I've ever tasted; I've never met a kid who didn't love it. It's a bit pricey, and is more like a crispy flatbread-with-herbs-and-a-bit-of cheese than a traditional, cheesey pizza. It is sold in supermarkets and specialty stores east of the Rocky Mountains and in California. Also, Amy's brand frozen pizzas—I'm partial to the Roasted Vegetable—are excellent, and available in most supermarkets.

FROZEN VEGGIE BURGERS: With a vegetarian in the family, I have to keep these on hand.

FROZEN ONIONS AND GREEN PEPPERS: They are terrific in anything cooked, but tend to disappear in slow cooker dishes. If serving as a topping (say, in a salad, or on tacos) or using the slow cooker, you have to buy and chop the fresh stuff.

ROASTED RED PEPPERS: In jars, in the condiment aisle. Use them whenever a recipe calls for you to char a pepper over an open flame. (No recipe in this book will suggest such a thing).

MAC AND CHEESE: Annie's Homegrown Shells & White Cheddar. Several mothers told me their children would have starved without this. For homemade mac and cheese, see page 110.

SPRAY-CAN WHIPPED CREAM: Cabot is the only brand I've found that tastes like real whipped cream. And it comes in a can with a cute black-and-white-cow pattern.

FROZEN PUFF PASTRY: Great for making last-minute desserts (see page 186) or for use as a topping for Chicken Pot Pie (page 48).

FROZEN FRUITS: Strawberries, raspberries, blueberries, peaches. Puree in a blender with a bit of fruit juice to make a sauce for ice cream, sorbet, pancakes or waffles, or add yogurt and make a smoothie. Extend a fresh fruit salad (and add color, too). Add to pancakes and baked goods. Cranberries keep very well in the freezer; since they are usually only available during the fall-winter holiday season, I like to freeze a package or two for use at other times of the year.

FROZEN FRENCH FRIES: It's hard to avoid those "really bad" trans fats and salt in buying French fries, and I usually say the heck with it and go for Ore-Ida Shoestrings. If I'm being virtuous (but still not making my own), I buy Cascadian Farm French Fries at the natural foods store. They make great home fries, too. For homemade Oven Fries, see page 164.

Stocking the Civilized Pantry 213

FROZEN BURRITOS: Amy's brand burritos are terrific, and make your house smell like a really good Mexican restaurant.

REAL BACON BITS: Emphasis on *real*. Great for sprinkling on baked potatoes and salads or in eggs.

FROZEN CHICKEN NUGGETS: Bell & Evans Breaded Chicken Breast Nuggets. For homemade chicken nuggets, see page 124.

CAKE, BROWNIE, CORN BREAD MIXES: They sure are quick, but I'm still convinced that I make better ones from scratch.

FROZEN FISH STICKS: The excellent book, *The Mom's Guide to Meal Makeovers,* by Janice Newell Bissex, M.S., R.D, and Liz Weiss, M.S., R.D. (Broadway Books, 2004) recommends Natural Sea Fish Sticks, Trader Joe's Cod Sticks, and Ian's Lightly Breaded Fish Sticks.

HOT DOGS: My line on hot dogs is the same as my line on soda (or "pop," depending on where you live) and marshmallow fluff. That is, we all have enough opportunities outside of the house—birthday parties, ball games, barbecues, other people's homes—to enjoy these items without me buying them and keeping them at home. Again, the "Mom's Guide" (above) recommends nitrite-free brands, including Coleman All Natural Uncured Beef Hot Dogs, Hans' All Natural Uncured Beef Hot Dogs, and Applegate Farms Beef (or Chicken) Hot Dogs. Nitrite-free hot dogs are more perishable; it's easiest to freeze them once you've opened the package.

THE COOKBOOK SHELF:

Eckhardt, Linda West and DeFoyd, Katherine West. *Half-Scratch Magic: 200 Ways to Pull Dinner Out of a Hat Using a Can of Soup or Other Tasty Shortcuts.* Clarkson Potter, 2003.

Schwartz, Arthur. *What to Cook When You Think There's Nothing in the House to Eat.* HarperPerennial, 2000.

Schloss, Andrew. *Almost From Scratch: 600 Recipes for the New Convenience Cuisine.* Simon & Schuster, 2003.

APPENDIX 4:
Equipping the Civilized Kitchen

IN FEBRUARY 2004, *Newsweek* ran an article which described a Cleveland couple who, despite owning a home with not one but *two* fully equipped kitchens, dine nightly on take-home food from the deli counter of the supermarket. I thought of this couple when I met Jacquie Wayans, a single mother of three who is employed part-time and attends college part-time; whose Bronx, New York, apartment lacks a dishwasher; and who still manages to produce homemade meals on a daily basis. (She was also one of the most nutritionally savvy folks I met, and, perhaps not coincidentally, one of the trimmest.) Clearly, you don't need what *Newsweek* termed a "Versaille-quality kitchen" to cook. And no recipe in this book requires anything fancy. Here's a paired-down list:

- ❖ Mixing bowls of various sizes. These can double as serving bowls.
- ❖ Knives, etc: one good paring knife, one good chopping knife (chef's knife or cleaver), and a cutting board or two. A grater is essential (friends are raving about the new Microplane grater/zesters); and a serrated bread knife is nice, as is a vegetable peeler. Before I owned a food processor, I relied heavily on a mezzaluna, a device with two wooden handles and a blade shaped like a half (*mezza* in Italian) moon (*luna*), used for chopping nuts, garlic, onions, herbs, etc. You can buy one for under $20; I still use mine.
- ❖ Scissors: for everything from opening those impenetrable plastic packets of meat, to snipping bacon and fresh herbs and cutting pizza and flowers. (If I owned a good pair of real kitchen shears, which I don't, they would also be handy for cutting poultry.)
- ❖ Spatulas: the rubber kind (for scraping bowls) and the metal kind (for flipping burgers).
- ❖ Spoons: a couple of wooden spoons and a slotted metal spoon. Also a whisk.
- ❖ Pots and pans: a Dutch oven, some saucepans with lids, and a couple of good skillets (cast iron ones are usually available at yard sales

and flea markets). Have at least one pot that will hold 4 to 6 quarts of water, for boiling pasta.

❖ Baking pans: a pie plate or two, cake pans (make sure you have two of the same size, for layer cakes), at least one baking pan (13-by-9-inch), two cookie sheets, and a muffin tin. I recently read the pronouncement that "no one owns a rolling pin anymore." I do, and I use it.

❖ Colander and hand-held sieve—for rinsing vegetables and fruits, draining pasta. A salad spinner is an awfully nice tool; after destroying three or four cheap ones through heavy use, I broke down and bought a really sturdy Oxo brand spinner. Money well spent.

❖ Thermometer: Instant-read thermometers cost under $10 and will help you know when the meat is cooked well enough that you won't kill everyone by serving it. Enough said. (See Appendix 6: Food Safety.)

❖ Electric gadgets: A blender is nice, a food processor even nicer. A microwave is not strictly necessary, as most folks who actually cook (as opposed to nuking frozen entrées) seem to use it only for reheating coffee, making popcorn, and defrosting meat. Hand-held mixers (KitchenAid and Black & Decker make good ones) are usually all that you need; I recently bought a fancy stand mixer and find the best thing about it is that I can leave it to do its thing while I roam around the kitchen doing other chores (like finding ingredients). The appliances that seemed to find favor with the families I interviewed included: slow cookers, George Forman grills, rice cookers, bread makers, food dehydrators, juicers, and ice-cream makers. Of course, there are a zillion gadgets out there. Think about your counter space before you buy; I find that if I can't keep an appliance on the counter, it never gets used.

A note on a device that I can't live without: Being a popcorn addict, I treasure my Presto PowerPop microwave popper, which cost about $15 and allows me to air- (or oil-) pop regular popcorn in the microwave and has thereby liberated me from the time-consuming and messy process of popping corn in a pot, and from those fake-tasting, greasy, preseasoned, expensive microwave popcorn packets.

Barbarians at the Plate

MICROWAVE COOKING SHORTCUTS

ALMOST NO ONE I met on my travels used the microwave for cooking anything; but it does come in handy for many tasks, including defrosting and cooking frozen foods, reheating coffee, and popping corn. Here are some other things you can do with the microwave. Time will vary according to the age and power of your microwave; experiment with small quantities first. Make sure you follow the manufacturer's directions and use the proper plates, containers, and utensils.

SOFTEN BUTTER: 1 stick (½ cup) at 40 percent power for 10 seconds. Check at 5-second intervals thereafter. (If the butter is frozen, it will take about 30 seconds to soften.)

MELT BUTTER: Place 1 stick (½ cup) in a large bowl and microwave on HIGH for about 80 seconds.

MELT CHOCOLATE: Place 1 cup chocolate chips or 6 ounces chopped baking chocolate in a bowl and cook on HIGH for 1½ minutes. Stir. Continue cooking, checking at 30-second intervals.

PLUMP DRIED FRUITS AND TOMATOES: Place in a bowl, cover with water, and cook on HIGH for 20 seconds.

TOAST SHREDDED COCONUT: Spread 1 cup coconut in a single layer; cook on HIGH for 2 minutes.

TOAST NUTS (see page 50).

DRY FRESH HERBS: Make sure herbs are very dry, otherwise they will soften and cook, not dry. Arrange a small amount of herbs in a single layer between two paper towels. Cook on HIGH for 2 to 3 minutes. Check. If not dry and brittle, continue cooking, checking at 30-second intervals. Place on a rack to cool. Store in an airtight container.

SQUEEZE MORE OUT OF LEMONS: To get more juice out of citrus fruits when squeezing them, first zap on HIGH for 20 seconds.

SOFTEN ICE CREAM: Soften 1 pint ice cream by nuking on HIGH for 15 seconds.

SOFTEN BROWN SUGAR: Loosen hard-packed sugar by placing an apple slice in the bag and cooking on HIGH for 5 seconds.

THAW FROZEN JUICES: Remove the top metal lid and cook on HIGH for 30 seconds for a 6-ounce can.

FRESHEN STALE BAKED GOODS AND CHIPS: Zap on HIGH for 10 seconds.

APPENDIX 5:
Filling the Civilized Cookbook Shelf

Y**OU DON'T NEED** a lot of cookbooks; you just need the right ones. How to choose? Start at your local library and check some out, or borrow from a friend; the ones you actually cook from and keep returning to are the ones that are worth buying. If you are intimidated about cooking, or unsure of your skills, borrow or buy a good children's cookbook (see page 131); you want one with recipes for real food, not just pancakes shaped like teddy bears.

Throughout this book, I have listed cookbooks that I have found to be helpful and family friendly. Here are some general cookbooks that were not previously mentioned.

As for basic cookbooks, Betty Crocker is alive and well in America's kitchens, if the families I visited are any measure. Two of "her" most recent are *Betty Crocker's Quick and Easy Cookbook* (Betty Crocker Books, 2003), and *Betty Crocker's Cookbook: Everything You Need to Know to Cook Today,* 2000.

For all-around, comprehensive information, I'm still a fan of the *Joy of Cooking* by Irma S. Rombauer and Marion Rombauer Becker first published in 1936 which runs the gamut of culinary instruction from boiling water to skinning squirrels. This book was rewritten by the Rombauer/Beckers and a team of food authorities, and published by Scribner in 1997. The "new" *Joy* is excellent, but I still have a soft spot in my heart for the older editions.

Books by TV cooking personalities Nigella Lawson, Rachael Ray, and Alton Brown are also popular. Here are some other useful cookbooks:

Bittman, Mark. *The Minimalist Cooks Dinner.* Broadway Books, 2001.
Family Circle Quick & Easy Recipes. Broadway Books, 2001.
Glass, Peggy K. *Home-Cooking Sampler: Family Favorites From A to Z.* Prentice Hall Press, 1989. Out of print but worth finding.
Gold, Rozanne. *Cooking 1-2-3: 500 Fabulous Three-Ingredient Recipes.*

Stuart, Tabori and Chang, 2003. Some recipes, despite having only three major ingredients, are elaborate; others are simple.

Gunst, Kathy. *The Parenting Cookbook: A Comprehensive Guide to Cooking, Eating and Entertaining For Today's Families.* Castle Books, 1996. Out of print but worth finding.

Hodgman, Ann. *One Bite Won't Kill You: More than 200 Recipes to Tempt Even the Pickiest Kids on Earth.* Houghton Mifflin, 1999.

Pepin, Jacques. *Fast Food My Way.* Houghton Mifflin, 2004. Yes, he's a big-deal French chef, but these recipes are simple and delicious.

Recipe Web sites:

More and more, people are turning to the Internet for recipes. Sites recommended, and those I have used, include: www.epicurious.com, www.allrecipes.com, and www.foodtv.com.

Barbarians at the Plate

APPENDIX 6:
Food Safety

I*T'S A BIG*, complicated, science-y subject, but fortunately for us home cooks, common sense and a minimum of knowledge will get us safely through our three meals a day. Here are the basics:

1. Clean cooking and cutting surfaces, utensils and food storage containers, and wash your hands frequently. Keep the fridge clean, and don't pack it too densely; for food to keep cool, air must circulate.
2. Refrigerate or freeze perishable food, prepared food and leftovers within two hours. Never leave any perishable foods—raw or cooked— at room temperature longer than two hours, or one hour on a hot day (90°F or above).
3. Keep hot foods hot (above 140°) and cold foods cold (below 40°F).
4. Use the refrigerator or microwave, or a cold water bath to defrost frozen foods. (For notes on defrosting a frozen turkey or chicken, see page 45.)
5. Separate raw meat, poultry, and seafood and keep them wrapped, separated from other foods in the refrigerator. Remove stuffing from poultry, and meats and refrigerate it in a separate container. Never place cooked food on a plate which previously held raw meat, poultry, or seafood.
6. Eggs should be cooked until the yolk and white are firm, not runny. Eating raw meat (e.g., steak tartare), raw fish (seviche, sashimi), raw eggs (mousse, eggnog), and raw shellfish (oysters, clams) is a food safety no-no; proceed at your own risk.
7. Use a meat thermometer (see page 217) to insure that the internal temperature of foods has reached a safe level (page 223). If you frequently cook foods in the microwave, buy a microwave-safe thermometer.

GROUND BEEF OR PORK: 160°F

ROASTS AND STEAKS: 145°F (medium rare) to 170°F (well done)

GROUND POULTRY: 165°F

POULTRY PARTS: 180°F to 185°F

PORK: 160°F (medium) to 170°F (well done)

WHOLE CHICKEN, TURKEY OR OTHER POULTRY: 180°F

STUFFING (ALONG OR INSIDE A BIRD): 165°F

FISH: 145°F

EGG DISHES (CASSEROLE): 160°F

LEFTOVERS (REHEATED): 165°F

For further information, consult *www.foodsafety.gov*

The USDA Meat & Poultry Hotline is: (888) 674–8854

The FDA Food Safety Hotline is: (888) 723–3366

Barbarians at the Plate

Index

Barbarians at the Plate

Barbarians at the Plate

Barbarians at the Plate

Index 231

About the Author

Marialisa Calta is a syndicated food writer whose weekly column, "Food," appears in more than one hundred newspapers across the country. Her articles on food, travel, and lifestyles have appeared in *The New York Times, Gourmet,* and elsewhere. She is the coauthor of *The River Run Cookbook* (with Jimmy and Maya Kennedy), and she helped create the recipes for *Al Roker's Big Bad Book of BBQ.* She lives in Calais, Vermont, with her husband and her two mostly civilized daughters.